Creu

A Divider Not a Uniter

George W. Bush
and the American People

SECOND EDITION

GARY C. JACOBSON
UNIVERSITY OF CALIFORNIA, SAN DIEGO

Longman

Boston   Columbus   Indianapolis   New York   San Francisco   Upper Saddle River
Amsterdam   Cape Town   Dubai   London   Madrid   Milan   Munich   Paris
Montreal   Toronto   Delhi   Mexico City   Sao Paulo   Sydney
Hong Kong   Seoul   Singapore   Taipei   Tokyo

Editor-in-Chief:	Eric Stano
Senior Marketing Manager:	Lindsey Prudhomme
Editorial Assistant:	Elizabeth Alimena
Production Manager:	Wanda Rockwell
Project Coordination, Text Design and Electronic Page Makeup:	Aptara®, Inc.
Creative Director:	Jayne Conte
Cover Designer:	Bruce Kenselaar
Cover Illustration/Photo:	Shutterstock
Printer and Binder:	Edwards Brothers
Cover Printer:	Lehigh-Phoenix Color/Hagerstown

Library of Congress Cataloging-in-Publication Data

Jacobson, Gary C.

A divider, not a uniter: George W. Bush and the American people / Gary C. Jacobson. — 2nd ed.

p. cm.

ISBN-13: 978-0-205-77603-0

ISBN-10: 0-205-77603-5

1. United States—Politics and government—2001–2009. 2. United States—Foreign relations— 2001–2009. 3. Iraq War, 2003– 4. Bush, George W. (George Walker), 1946—Influence. 5. Bush, George W. (George Walker), 1946—Public opinion. 6. Bush, George W. (George Walker), 1946—Political and social views. 7. Polarization (Social sciences)—United States. 8. Political participation—United States. 9. Political parties—United States. 10. Public opinion—United States. I. Title.

E902.J33 2011

973.931092—dc22   2010018234

1 2 3 4 5 6 7 8 9 10— EB —13 12 11 10

Longman
is an imprint of

www.pearsonhighered.com

ISBN-13: 978-0-205-77603-0
ISBN-10:   0-205-77603-5

For Lynne and Wendy

Contents

Preface

This book aims to explain why George W. Bush's presidency provoked the widest partisan divisions ever recorded in the more than fifty years that surveys have regularly gauged the public's assessment of presidential performance. The idea of writing the book occurred after I had already done a good deal of the research in the course of other projects on party polarization in Congress and the electorate, electoral politics, and mass opinion. I had initially been investigating the political consequences of polarized views of the president, but that naturally raised the question of why partisans reacted to the president as they did. I began to address this question in a series of talks and seminars I gave around the country during the 2004–2005 academic year, most of them as part of my service as a Phi Beta Kappa Visiting Scholar. At the end of the year, I realized that the question deserved a more thorough treatment than I could give it in a lecture or journal article, and the result was the first edition of this book.

I updated the analysis following the 2006 election by tacking on a new chapter covering the Bush administration's eventful sixth year, but I did not revise the other chapters for that edition. In this edition, I examine the entire Bush presidency, revising earlier chapters as necessary to incorporate new data, research findings, and accounts of what went on in the Bush White House. A number of the figures showing key trends in public opinion now cover the administration's full eight years, so I make many references in later chapters to evidence displayed in charts appearing earlier in the book. Dedicated readers might find bookmarks or sticky flags handy.

I incurred more than the usual number of obligations in completing this project. Jim Caraley, David Brady, Fred Greenstein, George W. Edwards III, Susan Webb Hammond, Mat McCubbins, and Michael Nelson were all instrumental in stimulating and helping to publish research studies from which some of the evidence and arguments in this

book are drawn.[1] I greatly appreciate their encouragement and suggestions. As will be immediately apparent, I rely heavily on the major media
polls for essential data, and I am grateful to Richard Benedetto, Adam
Clymer, Jon Cohen, Claudia Deane, Michael Dimock, Kathleen Fran-
covic, John Harwood, Richard Morin, Jill E. Darling Richardson, Brian
Scanlon, and Maura Strausberg for patiently answering requests for
detailed information on the results of their surveys and often for the surveys themselves; Ms. Deane deserves special thanks in this regard. I also
owe special thanks to Steve Ansolabehere for his help in producing the
Cooperative Congressional Election Studies data. I leave a more complete
account of data sources for the Appendix; here I wish only to acknowledge the enormously valuable contribution made by the producers of
high-quality media-sponsored surveys to the research reported in these
chapters.

I am obliged also to the many people who helped arrange the various
talks and seminars at which I was able to explore and debate the ideas
and analyses woven into the book. Kathy Navascues heads the list for
arranging my itinerary as Phi Beta Kappa Visiting Scholar; there are too
many deserving people at the nine campuses I visited in that guise for me
to thank them all here, but I can at least acknowledge the institutions and

---

[1] These works include "Congress: Elections and Stalemate," in Michael Nelson, ed., *The Elections of
2000* (Washington, DC: Congressional Quarterly Press, 2001), 185–209; "A House and Senate Divided:
The Clinton Legacy and the Congressional Elections of 2000," *Political Science Quarterly* 116 (Spring
2001): 5–27; "Terror, Terrain, and Turnout: The 2002 Midterm Election," *Political Science Quarterly*
118 (Spring 2003): 1–22; "Partisan Polarization in Presidential Support: The Electoral Connection,"
Congress and the Presidency 30 (Spring 2003): 1–36, also updated and reprinted in George W. Edwards
III, ed., *Readings in Presidential Politics* (Belmont, CA: Wadsworth, 2006), 69–108; "The Bush Presidency and the American Electorate," in Fred Greenstein, ed., *The George W. Bush Presidency: An Early
Assessment* (Baltimore: Johns Hopkins University Press, 2003), 197–227, and also in *Presidential Studies
Quarterly* 32 (December 2003): 701–729; "The Congress: The Structural Basis of Republican Success,"
in Michael Nelson, ed., *The Elections of 2004* (Washington, DC: Congressional Quarterly Press, 2005),
163–186; "Polarized Politics and the 2004 Congressional and Presidential Elections," *Political Science
Quarterly* 120 (Summer 2005): 199–218, and reprinted in Robert Y. Shapiro, ed., *The Meaning of
American Democracy* (New York: Academy of Political Science, 2005), 185–204; "Explaining the Ideological Polarization of the Congressional Parties Since the 1970s," in David Brady and Mathew McCubbins,
eds., *Process, Party and Policy Making: Further New Perspectives on the History of Congress* (Stanford,
CA: Stanford University Press, 2007), 91–101; "The President, the War, and Voting Behavior in the
2006 House Elections," in Jeffrey J. Mondak and Donna-Gene Mitchell, eds., *Fault Lines: Why the
Republicans Lost Congress* (New York: Routledge, 2008), 128–147; "The 2008 Presidential and Congressional Elections: Anti-Bush Referendum and Prospects for the Democratic Majority," *Political Science
Quarterly* 124 (Spring 2009): 1–30; "The Effects of the George W. Bush Presidency on Partisan
Attitudes," *Presidential Studies Quarterly* 39 (June 2009): 172–209; "George W. Bush, the Iraq War,
and the Election of Barack Obama," *Presidential Studies Quarterly* 40 (June 2010): 207–224; "Perception, Memory, and Partisan Polarization on the Iraq War," *Political Science Quarterly* 125 (Spring
2010): 1–26.

their uniformly hospitable Phi Beta Kappa chapters and political science faculty: Rockford College, George Washington University, Rhodes College, Wayne State University, University of North Carolina–Greensboro, Virginia Tech, Furman University, the University of North Dakota–Grand Forks, and the University of Missouri–Columbia. I am also grateful to Denis Lacorne (Paris), Chris Wlezien (Oxford), Desmond King (Oxford), Stephan Bierling (Regensburg), and Charles-Philippe David (Montreal) for inviting me to present some of this work internationally, and to Elizabeth Garrett, John Geer, Bruce Oppenheimer, Andrea McAtee, Russell Renko, Bernie Grofman, Diana Evans, Jack Citrin, Lanethea Mathews-Gardner, Ted Carmines, Larry Jacobs, Rich Fleisher, Herb Weisberg, Shanto Iyengar, and Richard Almeida for arranging opportunities for presentations at their institutions. The interest these colleagues and the audiences showed in the research was a major stimulus to putting it all into a book in the first place and to completing the story with this edition.

I also appreciate the comments and suggestions I have received from Stephan Bierling, Tom Edsall, John E. Mueller, Sam Popkin, Paul Abramson, and Adam Berinsky; the data supplied by my colleague Keith T. Poole; and the support and enthusiasm that George Edwards III and Eric Stano, in their capacities as Longman editors, have given the project. My thanks also to Mary Benis and Jogender Taneja for their valuable editorial and production work on this new edition.

Finally, I've dedicated this book to my sisters, Lynne H. Rosenthal and Wendy M. Reilly. It was not until a family reunion in Idaho with them and our extended families in July of 2004 that I fully realized how intensely even people without particularly strong partisan or ideological views had come to feel about George W. Bush.

CHAPTER I

Introduction

In his convention speech accepting the Republican presidential nomination in August 2000, George W. Bush pledged to be "a uniter, not a divider," offering himself as an outsider with "no stake in the bitter arguments of the last few years" who could "change the tone of Washington to one of civility and respect."[1] It was a message well gauged to appeal to a public weary of the fierce partisanship characteristic of the previous administration, epitomized by the congressional Republicans' attempt to impeach and remove Democratic president Bill Clinton less than two years earlier. Moreover, coming from a candidate who, as governor of Texas, had worked effectively with a Democratic legislature, the message was credible. And indeed, for a time during his first term, in the aftermath of the attacks on New York City and Washington, DC, by al Qaeda terrorists, Bush did rally virtually the entire nation, politicians and public alike, behind his leadership. But in the months before the events of September 11, 2001, had radically altered the political context, Bush had inspired the widest partisan differences in evaluations of a newly elected president ever recorded. And by the time he sought reelection in 2004, he had become by a wide margin the most divisive and polarizing president in the more than seventy years that public opinion polls had regularly measured citizens' assessments of presidents, and he remained so through the end of his presidency.

---

[1] Speech to Republican National Convention, August 3, 2000, accepting the nomination.

I

FIGURE 1.1
Approval of George W. Bush's Job Performance, 2001–2009

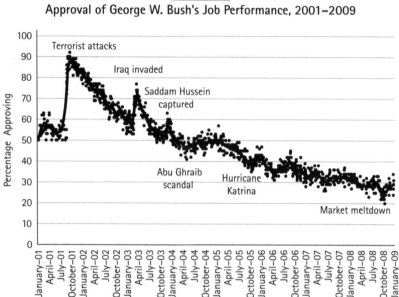

Source: 1,021 national polls taken by fourteen major media polling organizations, reported at http://www.pollingreport.com.

The overall trends in public evaluations of George Bush are displayed in Figure 1.1 (in this and many subsequent figures, the trends are highlighted by lowess smoothing).[2] Summarized briefly—I will have much more to say about these patterns later—Bush's overall approval ratings drifted in the mid-50 percent range until the September 11 terrorist attacks, and the president's resolute response to them provoked the greatest "rally"[3] in presidential approval ever observed. Over the following

---

[2] Each point in the figure represents the proportion of respondents in a poll who responded "approve" when asked, "Do you approve or disapprove of the way George W. Bush is handling his job as president?" or some close variant. The lowess-smoothed trend is shown by the solid line. Data are from the CBS/*New York Times,* Gallup, NBC News/*Wall Street Journal,* Pew Research Center for the People and the Press, *Newsweek,* ABC News/*Washington Post, Los Angeles Times, Time,* CNN/*Time,* and Associated Press/IPSOS polls reported at http://pollingreport.com/iraq.htm (accessed September 13, 2005). Only surveys that sample the entire adult population are included.

[3] The term entered the literature with John E. Mueller's *War, Presidents, and Public Opinion* (New York: John Wiley and Sons, 1973), 53.

fifteen months, Bush's ratings returned gradually to where they had been before 9/11. The effects of another, more modest rally following the invasion of Iraq in March 2003 eroded more quickly, as did the even smaller spike in approval inspired by the capture of Saddam Hussein in December. Bush's low point for 2004 coincided with the Abu Ghraib prison scandal in the spring; his ratings recovered a bit around his reelection but continued on a downward trajectory thereafter, reaching a new low in September 2005 in the face of rising gas prices and criticism of the administration's response to the devastation wrought by Hurricane Katrina. After rebounding briefly, the trend turned downward, reflecting continuing difficulties in Iraq. By the time the "surge" (discussed in Chapter 9) succeeded in cutting United States casualties sharply and restoring some optimism about the war, the national economy had sunk into recession; Bush's low point in September 2008 coincided with a financial crisis that heralded the sharpest economic downturn since the Great Depression. By the end of his presidency, his approval ratings were lower than those of any previous exiting president except Richard Nixon's.[4]

These trends reflect the signal events of Bush's presidency more or less as the standard literature on presidential approval would predict.[5] Far less standard is their partisan composition. When the data are disaggregated by the respondent's party identification (Figure 1.2),[6] it is apparent that independents and Democrats accounted for nearly all of the temporal variance in the president's job approval during his first term but virtually none of it in the second. Bush received relatively low marks from Democrats until the terrorist attacks, after which the Democrats rallied to deliver the highest approval ratings ever given to a president by rival-party identifiers, reaching a record 84 percent in one October 2001 Gallup poll. Thereafter, the steady downward trend in approval among Democrats was interrupted only temporarily by the onset of the Iraq War and later capture of Saddam Hussein and, by the beginning of 2004, had dipped below 20 percent. Democrats' approval fell further during the campaign, revived slightly at the beginning of Bush's second administration,

---

[4] Harry Truman's average approval in the Gallup series for his final quarter as president was 32 percent; Jimmy Carter's was 33 percent; Nixon's was 25 percent; and Bush's was 29 percent.
[5] Cf. Richard A. Brody, *Assessing the President* (Stanford, CA: Stanford University Press, 1991) and Mueller, *Wars, Presidents, and Public Opinion*.
[6] Unless otherwise specified, I do not include leaners in the partisan categories; I do so not on theoretical grounds (although some, notably Warren E. Miller and J. Merrill Shanks in *The New American Voter* [Cambridge, MA: Harvard University Press, 1996], ch. 6, would argue that I should) but because most of the polls I examine here treat leaners as independents.

FIGURE 1.2
Approval of George W. Bush's Job Performance, 2001–2009, by Party Identification

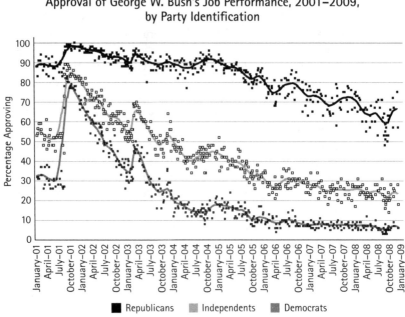

■ Republicans   ▨ Independents   ▨ Democrats

Source: 421 CBS News/*New York Times* and Gallup polls.

then dropped into single digits, where it stayed for the remainder of his presidency. The average during his last three years in office was 8 percent, hitting the all-time low of 3 percent in three Gallup surveys taken in September and October 2008. To put this figure in perspective, it is 8 percentage points lower than Richard Nixon's worst showing among Democrats just before he resigned in disgrace in 1974.

Among Republicans, in contrast, approval rates were very high from the start and remained so until 2005, when they began trending gradually downward, a pattern that accounts for most of Bush's overall decline in approval during his second term. The economic problems that emerged at the end of 2007 and became extraordinarily severe in the summer of 2008 clearly hurt, but Bush ended his presidency with solid majorities of ordinary Republicans behind him.

During his presidency, then, partisan differences in George W. Bush's approval ratings went from the widest for any newly elected president,

FIGURE 1.3

Presidential Approval, Eisenhower Through G. W. Bush (Quarterly Averages)

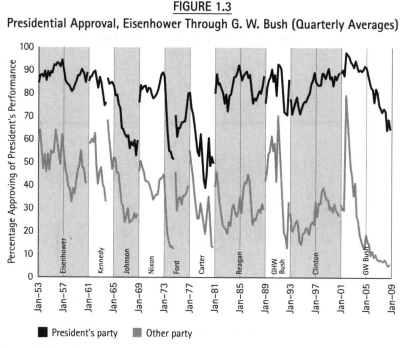

■ President's party ■ Other party

Source: Gallup polls.

to the narrowest ever recorded (after 9/11), and then to the widest for any president at any time by the end of his first term in office. Figures 1.3 and 1.4 confirm the historical singularity of partisan responses to Bush. Despite his late-term decline, Bush's career average rating among Republicans in the Gallup polls, at 85.6 percent, is only 2 points below that of Dwight D. Eisenhower, the all-time leader. Bush's average level of approval among Republicans during his first administration, 92.3 percent, exceeded the next highest for a single term, that of Dwight D. Eisenhower (89.5 percent in his first), by a statistically significant margin ($p<.001$). Among the opposing party's supporters, Bush's ratings have been both higher (immediately after 9/11) and lower than those for any of his predecessors. Before Bush and going back to Eisenhower, the partisan difference in approval ratings had never exceeded 70 percentage points in any Gallup poll and never averaged 66 points for any quarter (Figure 1.4). In the 166 Gallup polls taken between January 2004 and

FIGURE 1.4

Partisan Differences in Presidential Approval, Eisenhower Through G. W. Bush (Quarterly Averages)

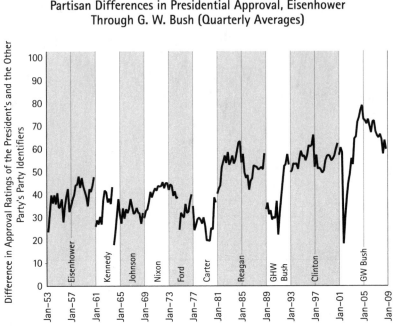

Source: Gallup polls.

January 2009, the gap exceeded 70 points more than half the time, reached a quarterly average as high as 77 points, and topped out at 83 points (94 to 11) in a couple of surveys taken near the 2004 election. The partisan divisions were deep as well as wide; in the thirty-three ABC News/*Washington Post* surveys taken when polarization was at its peak (from the beginning of 2004 through the end of 2006) that asked respondents how strongly they approved or disapproved of the president, an average of 60 percent of Republicans approved strongly (comprising 71 percent of all Republican approvers), while 67 percent of Democrats disapproved strongly (comprising 81 percent of all Democratic disapprovers).[7]

---

[7] On average in these polls, 67 percent of all respondents expressed strong approval or disapproval of the president, compared to 30 percent who said they approved or disapproved "somewhat." These surveys are accessible at http://www.washingtonpost.com/wp-dyn/politics/polls.

The data in Figure 1.4 also reveal that partisan differences in presidential approval have grown since the 1970s. From Eisenhower through Carter, the partisan gap averaged 34 percentage points. The average for Reagan rose to 52 points. For the senior Bush, the average gap was similar to that for pre-Reagan presidents, 36 points, but by the end of the G. H. W. Bush presidency it was as wide as it had been for Reagan. The average gap for Clinton was 55 points, and for G. W. Bush, 61 points, the widest recorded for any president despite the extraordinarily high level of approval the younger Bush received from Democrats in the year following 9/11. I will have more to say in the next chapter about the trend toward increasing partisan division.

Finally, returning to Figure 1.2, notice that Bush's approval level among self-identified independents was generally closer to that of Democrats than of Republicans. This is unusual. During Bill Clinton's last two years in office, for example, his average approval rating among independents was 30 points higher than among Republicans and 27 points lower than among Democrats. Independents were thus only about 3 points closer to one set of partisans than to the other, and the average ratings of independents were virtually identical to those of all respondents combined. Bush's rating among independents averaged 39 points lower than among Republicans, 20 points higher than among Democrats, and thus 19 points closer to the latter. If analysis is confined to polls taken since the beginning of 2004, the difference is even larger, 27 points, and Bush's rating among independents is 6 points lower than his average among all respondents. From this perspective, it was only Bush's unusual success in maintaining the backing of his own partisans that kept his overall support level from falling even lower than it ultimately did.

Questions on Bush's handling of specific policy domains also produce large partisan differences, with the distribution of responses from independents again generally tracking closer to that of Democrats than of Republicans. The trends in these evaluations differ to some extent, but all show steep increases in partisan polarization during Bush's first administration followed by modest declines during the second term. Figure 1.5 indicates that Bush's handling of the economy always drew rather widely divergent partisan evaluations, with the gap closing briefly after September 11 and again at the end of his presidency, when the economic crisis soured even many Republicans on his economic management. Prior to the terrorist attacks, the partisan difference averaged 52 percentage points; for the year after the attacks, the average was down to 43 points, but by

FIGURE 1.5
Approval of G. W. Bush's Handling of the Economy

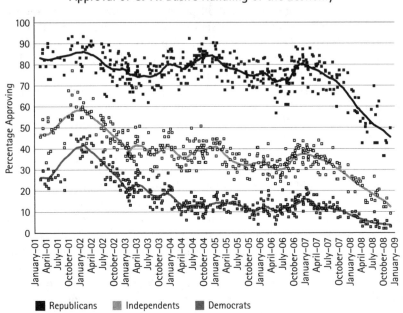

Republicans   Independents   Democrats

Sources: 387 ABC News/*Washington Post,* CBS News/*New York Times, Los Angeles Times,* NBC News/*Wall Street Journal, Time,* Quinnipiac, CNN, *Newsweek,* Pew Center for the People and the Press, AP-Ipsos, and Gallup polls.

2004 it had risen to more than 60 points and remained above that level until 2008, when it diminished to an average of 45 points.

Initial reaction to Bush's handling of terrorism was strongly positive regardless of party (Figure 1.6). Partisan differences increased slowly during the year after the attacks, but majorities of Democrats (and independents) continued to approve. The question was not asked between May and September 2003 in these polls, and when it reappeared, partisan differences had grown, reaching a peak around the November election (averaging 66 percentage points in October and November). Still, Democratic approval of Bush's performance in this domain was notably higher than in other domains. From July 2004 through the end of his presidency, an average of 24 percent of Democrats approved Bush's handling of terrorism, a figure more than twice as high as approval of his handling of the economy or Iraq.

FIGURE 1.6
Approval of G. W. Bush's Handling of Terrorism

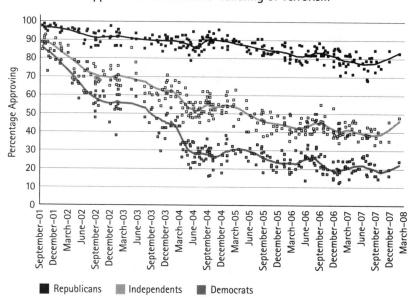

■ Republicans   ■ Independents   ■ Democrats

Sources: 254 ABC News/*Washington Post*, CBS News/*New York Times*, *Los Angeles Times*, *Time*, Pew Center for the People and the Press, Quinnipiac, *Newsweek*, and Gallup polls.

Evaluations of Bush's handling of the situation in Iraq follow yet another trend (Figure 1.7). Among Democrats (and independents), approval rose substantially during the administration's campaign of justification leading up to the war, peaking around the time Baghdad fell. Approval then fell off sharply until Saddam Hussein's capture in December 2003, after which it resumed its downward trajectory; for Bush's last two years in office, it remained in single digits. Republicans' ratings on this domain remained much higher and declined more gradually; near the end of 2007, they rose again after the dramatic decline in United States casualties that eventually followed the surge (Chapter 9 has the details). From 2004 through the end of Bush's presidency, the partisan approval gap on the war averaged 62 points.

Comparing trends in partisan polarization in presidential approval across domains and overall (Figure 1.8) makes it evident that each displayed its own unique dynamic but moved largely in parallel for the last

FIGURE 1.7
Approval of G. W. Bush's Handling of Iraq

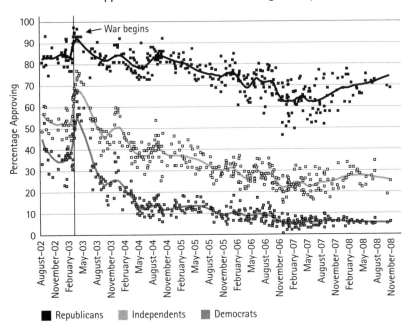

■ Republicans   ▨ Independents   ▨ Democrats

Sources: 362 ABC News/*Washington Post*, CBS News/*New York Times*, *Los Angeles Times*, *Time*, Pew Center for the People and the Press, NBC News/*Wall Street Journal*, Quinnipiac College, CNN, CCES, ANES, AP-Ipsos, and Gallup polls.

five years of Bush's presidency (the economy in 2008 is the exception). Polarization on every domain peaked around the 2004 election—not surprising and discussed further in Chapter 7—and shrank only modestly thereafter. The patterns of polarization established by the end of Bush's first term thus generally stabilized for the rest of his presidency.

In retrospect, George W. Bush's pledge in 2000 to be a "uniter, not a divider" turns out to be deeply ironic, as he became, by the measures examined here, the most divisive occupant of the White House on record. The irony was underlined by responses to a question posed by Gallup in October 2004, displayed in Figure 1.9. Asked if Bush had done more to unite or to divide the country, Americans as a whole divided precisely in half, 48 percent choosing each alternative; 87 percent of Republicans said that he had done more to unite the country, while

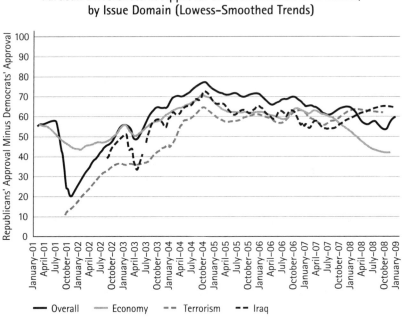

FIGURE 1.8

Partisan Differences in Approval of G. W. Bush's Performance, by Issue Domain (Lowess-Smoothed Trends)

Source: Figures 1.2, 1.5, 1.6, and 1.7.

81 percent of Democrats said he had done more to divide it. This is the rare survey question that, in the distribution of responses, effectively answered itself. By the end of the second term, however, the public was no longer divided on this question; asked in December 2008 if the statement "[He] has united the country and not divided it" applied to Bush, 82 percent said it did not, including 64 percent of Republicans, 85 percent of independents, and 88 percent of Democrats.[8]

This brings us to the central question I address in this book: Why did the public become so thoroughly divided along party lines about this president? There is, I shall argue, no single answer, but rather a complex set of converging political forces, events, and decisions that brought public

---

[8] Survey by Cable News Network and Opinion Research Corporation, December 19–21, 2008. Retrieved July 21, 2009, from the iPOLL Databank, The Roper Center for Public Opinion Research, University of Connecticut, http://www.ropercenter.uconn.edu/ipoll.html.

FIGURE 1.9
Was George W. Bush a Uniter or a Divider?

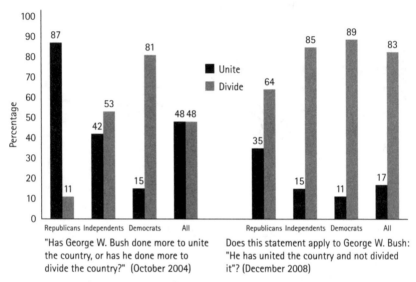

Source: Gallup poll (October 22–24, 2004) and CNN poll (December 17–21, 2008).

opinion on this president to its extraordinary state. Responses to Bush were shaped by both deep, enduring historical currents and random historical accidents; they were affected by the president's own character, policy choices, and strategies, as well as by conditions entirely beyond his (or anyone else's) control. In examining these diverse causal strands, I hope not only to explain why George W. Bush became such a polarizing figure, but to use this exploration to illuminate some central developments in American politics over the past several decades, to address questions of interest to political scientists about the sources of mass political opinion and behavior, and to assess Bush's legacy to the Republican Party, to his successor, Barack Obama, and to the American polity.

I begin by putting the Bush administration in its historical context, for one major obstacle to Bush's becoming "a uniter, not a divider" was taking office in the wake of more than three decades of growing partisan polarization in national politics. Chapter 2 describes and seeks to explain this pervasive, widely noted trend, arguing that it left political elites and ordinary citizens alike primed to respond in partisan terms with only the mildest provocation. Provocation, of course, came even before Bush took office, in the form of the fight over Florida's electoral votes. Chapter 3 focuses on the 2000 election and its denouement in the Supreme Court; it also analyzes the cultural and economic divisions created and exposed by that election, with particular attention to the strong cultural affinity Bush had forged with religious conservatives before and during the campaign.

Chapter 4 covers the first two years of the Bush administration. It begins with an examination of the president's agenda and political strategies for implementing it—both, I argue, contributing to partisan polarization. The September 11 terrorist attacks changed everything—including the meaning of the presidential approval question—for a time. The effects persisted long enough to serve Republicans well in the 2002 election, but their use of the terrorism issue in the campaign left a residue of partisan bitterness that shadowed the rest of Bush's presidency.

Chapters 5 and 6 begin to delve into what I shall argue is the principal reason Bush leaped ahead of Bill Clinton and Ronald Reagan to become the most divisive president on record: the Iraq War. Chapter 5 looks into the public's divergent views on the war, its necessity, and Bush's justifications for it prior to the invasion of Iraq in March 2003. Chapter 6 explores how views of the war and the president changed—or, in the case of most Republicans, did not change—as the war's basic premises, that Saddam Hussein possessed weapons of mass destruction and was in league with al Qaeda, became increasingly untenable. The chapter shows how the strikingly divergent responses of ordinary Republicans and Democrats to both factual and attitudinal questions about the war created by far the largest partisan difference in support of any war in the past half century.

The Iraq War was, not surprisingly, a central issue in the 2004 presidential campaign, which is the subject of Chapter 7. Partisan polarization in attitudes toward the war and the president, along with the Bush campaign's successful strategy of mobilizing core supporters rather than reaching out to swing voters, inspired the highest level of party-line voting yet observed in the fifty-two year history of the National Election Studies. Because of the Republicans' structural advantage in House and Senate elections (a more efficient distribution of voters), this highly partisan atmosphere not only produced a narrow Republican presidential victory, but also solidified the party's control of both houses of Congress.

Chapter 8 examines the 2004 election's aftermath and events leading up to the Democratic victories in the 2006 election. It reviews public responses to Bush's failed attempt to reform Social Security, the Terri

Schiavo incident, and the administration's response to Hurricane Katrina, and the chapter documents the polarizing effects of continuing troubles in Iraq. It also describes how the administration tried and failed to maintain Republican control of Congress by portraying Democratic opponents of the war as naïve appeasers. Instead, the 2006 election became a clear negative referendum on Bush and the war.

Chapter 9 covers the final two years of the Bush administration. It reviews Bush's decision to reject the Iraq Study Group's recommendation to wind down the United States involvement in Iraq in favor of a surge (additional troops and a new strategy) and explains the inability of the Democrats in Congress to place restraints on Bush's Iraq policies. The chapter shows how the surge eventually succeeded in reducing United States casualties and reviving optimism about the war without reviving either public support for it or approval of its architect. It also describes how the declining economy and September financial crisis and bank bailout pushed Bush's approval ratings to their lowest level of his presidency. I also digress a bit here to tie together several strands of evidence, some introduced in previous chapters, to develop a detailed account of how the psychological process posited by the theory of "motivated reasoning" reflected and contributed to polarization on the war.

Chapter 10 explores the contribution of the Bush presidency to the historic election of Barack Obama to the White House. The chapter documents the cumulative damage during Bush's second term to the Republican Party's image and attractiveness as an object of identification, particularly among younger voters. It examines the effects of public responses to the Bush presidency on the nominations, particularly Obama's, as well as on voting in the general elections for president and Congress. The chapter concludes that Obama's victory and the solid Democratic majorities elected to the House and Senate in 2008 were Bush's most immediate political legacies.

In the final chapter, I step back to take a wider view of the Bush administration's mindset and its contribution to partisan division and acrimony. I argue that Bush's desire to be a "uniter" was tactical rather than an end in itself, to be discarded if unhelpful for winning legislative and electoral victories. His actions left partisan divisions on a variety of public issues, not merely the Iraq War, wider at the end than at the beginning of his presidency. Bush also failed to achieve his other political objective, a durable Republican majority, leaving instead a diminished, more uniformly white, southern, and conservative party. I end by considering how this legacy was shaping national politics during the first year of Barack Obama's presidency.

CHAPTER 2

Primed for Partisanship

In December 1998 the House of Representatives voted to impeach President Bill Clinton. All but four Republicans voted for at least one of the four articles of impeachment. Only five Democrats voted for any of them. In what was billed as a "conscience" vote, 98 percent of Republican consciences dictated a vote to impeach the president, while 98 percent of Democratic consciences dictated the opposite. The Senate's verdict after the impeachment trial was only slightly less partisan. Every Democrat voted for acquittal, while 91 percent of the Republicans voted for conviction on at least one article.

Although Americans on the whole opposed impeachment, popular partisan divisions on the issue were also huge, with a large majority of Republican identifiers favoring impeachment and an even larger majority of Democratic identifiers opposing it (Table 2.1). In the end, 68 percent of Republicans wanted the Senate to convict and remove Clinton, with only 30 percent favoring acquittal; among Democrats, 89 percent favored acquittal, while only 10 percent favored conviction.[1] Indeed, it was ordinary Democrats' steadfast opposition to impeachment that kept nervous congressional Democrats from abandoning the president en masse. Partisan divisions among the congressional parties' respective electoral coalitions—the

---

[1] Gallup/CNN/*USA Today* Poll, February 12–13, 1999, reported at http://www.pollingreport.com/scandals.htm (accessed February 15, 1999).

TABLE 2.1

"Just from the way you feel right now, do you think President Clinton's actions are serious enough to warrant his being impeached and removed from the Presidency, or not?"
(Responses are percentages)

	ALL RESPONDENTS	REPUBLICANS	INDEPENDENTS	DEMOCRATS
Yes	33.1	61.9	27.6	12.8
No	63.5	34.7	65.2	84.5
Don't know	3.5	3.4	7.2	2.7
Number of cases	12,161	4,096	1,309	5,956

SOURCE: Thirteen CBS/*New York Times* polls taken between August 1998 and February 1999.

voters who supported the successful Republican or Democratic candidates—were even wider, and divisions among the parties' activists were wider still.[2]

An implicit premise behind George W. Bush's 2000 campaign promise to be a "uniter, not a divider" and to "change the tone in Washington to one of civility and respect" was that partisan polarization was an inside-the-beltway phenomenon with little popular resonance. But the public's highly partisan response to Clinton's impeachment was no more aberrant than the party-line voting on it in Congress; both reflected the extension of trends several decades in the making. The two trends are intimately entwined and are part of a larger sea change in American political life. Their origins are multiple, complex, and still in some dispute among scholars. But their consequences are clear: Anyone elected president in 2000 would have faced a Congress and public primed to respond in sharply partisan terms with even the gentlest provocation.

---

[2] Gary C. Jacobson, "Public Opinion and the Impeachment of Bill Clinton," in Philip Cowley, David Denver, Andrew Russell, and Lisa Harrison, eds., *British Elections and Parties Review*, vol. 10, (London: Frank Cass, 2000), 1–31.

SOURCES OF PARTISAN POLARIZATION

A variety of forces contributed to partisan polarization among politicians and citizens alike during the final third of the twentieth century. These included changes in the political attitudes of citizens, changes in the way citizens sort themselves into parties based on their attitudes, and changes in the way partisan voters are sorted into states and districts. The forces also included changes in the subset of citizens who become political activists, the motives of people who pursue public office, the policy issues addressed by government, and congressional rules and procedures. And they included specific events and political battles, deliberate political strategies, and the character and style of rival partisan leaders. Telling the full story would take a volume by itself.[3] A general outline and some basic evidence will be sufficient to my purpose here, which is to demarcate the polarized political context in which George W. Bush assumed his presidency.

PARTISAN POLARIZATION
IN CONGRESS

Widening partisan divisions in the United States were first observed by scholars examining roll-call voting patterns in Congress, and subsequent research has abundantly confirmed and extended their initial findings.[4] By every observed measure, the distance between the congressional parties has been growing steadily since the 1970s. The widening gap appears in party loyalty on roll-call votes,[5] adjusted ADA scores,[6] and presidential

---

[3] Fortunately, one has been published: Barbara Sinclair, *Party Wars: Polarization and the Politics of National Policy-Makings* (Norman: University of Oklahoma Press, 2006).

[4] Keith T. Poole and Howard Rosenthal, "The Polarization of American Politics," *Journal of Politics* 46 (1984): 1061–1079.

[5] David W. Rohde, *Parties and Leaders in the Postreform House* (Chicago: University of Chicago Press, 1991), 13–16; John H. Aldrich, *Why Parties? The Origin and Transformation of Party Politics in America* (Chicago: University of Chicago Press, 1995), 195–201; Barbara Sinclair, "Hostile Partners: The President, Congress, and Lawmaking in the Partisan 1990s," in Jon R. Bond and Richard Fleisher, eds., *Polarized Politics: Congress and the President in a Partisan Era* (Washington, DC: Congressional Quarterly Press, 2000), 137–140; Jason M. Roberts and Steven S. Smith, "Procedural Contexts, Party Strategy, and Conditional Party Voting in the United States House of Representatives, 1971–2000," *American Journal of Political Science* 47 (2003): 305–319.

[6] Americans for Democratic Action (ADA) rates members on a liberal-conservative index based on a series of key votes. See Tim Groseclose, Steven D. Levitt, and James M. Snyder, Jr., "Comparing Interest Group Scores Across Time and Chambers: Adjusted ADA Scores for the United States Congress," *American Political Science Review* 93 (1999): 33–50.

support scores,[7] as well as, most prominently, in Keith Poole and Howard Rosenthal's first dimension DW-Nominate scores.[8] The Poole–Rosenthal data show that the wide ideological distance between the congressional parties observed in recent Congresses is by no means unprecedented (Figures 2.1 and 2.2); the parties were as far apart in the latter half of the nineteenth century as they are now, and the recent increase in polarization followed a period in which the congressional parties were, by historical standards, unusually close to one another on the liberal-conservative dimension.[9] Nonetheless, the steep increase in polarization since the Nixon administration is unprecedented, and by the time George W. Bush took office in 2001, the parties in both chambers had moved further apart than they had been at any time since before World War I. As the parties pulled apart ideologically, they also became more homogeneous internally; the standard deviations of each party coalition's DW-Nominate scores and adjusted ADA scores have declined among both parties in both chambers since the early 1970s.[10] By the time Bush took office, these changes had left the House and Senate with the most divergent and internally homogeneous party coalitions since the early twentieth century.

POLARIZATION AND ELECTORAL CHANGE

Initially, congressional party polarization seemed anomalous, because at the time it first began to draw scholarly attention, many journalists and not a few political scientists viewed Americans as "dealigning," growing

---

[7] Richard Fleisher and Jon R. Bond, "Partisanship and the President's Quest for Votes on the Floor of Congress," in Bond and Fleisher, *Polarized Politics*, 168–173; Gary C. Jacobson, "Partisan Polarization in Presidential Support: The Electoral Connection," *Congress and the Presidency* 30 (Spring 2003): 4–8.

[8] The DW-Nominate scale is calculated from all nonunanimous roll-call votes cast across all Congresses; each member's pattern of roll-call votes locates him or her on a liberal-conservative dimension ranging from −1.0 (most liberal) to 1.0 (most conservative), allowing us to compare the distribution of positions along the dimension taken by Republicans and Democrats in different Congresses. See Keith T. Poole and Howard Rosenthal, *Congress: A Political-Economic History of Roll Call Voting* (New York: Oxford University Press, 1999), ch. 2, and Nolan M. McCarty, Keith T. Poole, and Howard Rosenthal, *Income Redistribution and the Realignment of American Politics* (Washington, DC: AEI Press, 1997). DW-Nominate is an updated version of their D-Nominate measure; I am obliged to Keith Poole for providing these data, which may be found at http://voteview.com/ (accessed July 21, 2009).

[9] Keith T. Poole, "Changing Minds? Not in Congress!" manuscript, University of Houston, at http://voteview.com (accessed October 14, 2003); Sean M. Theriault, "The Case of the Vanishing Moderates: Party Polarization in the Modern Congress," manuscript, University of Texas, Austin, 2003.

[10] McCarty, Poole, and Rosenthal provide alternative measures of dispersion within the parties that display the same trends for the period under examination here; see *Income Redistribution*.

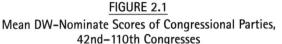

FIGURE 2.1
Mean DW-Nominate Scores of Congressional Parties, 42nd–110th Congresses

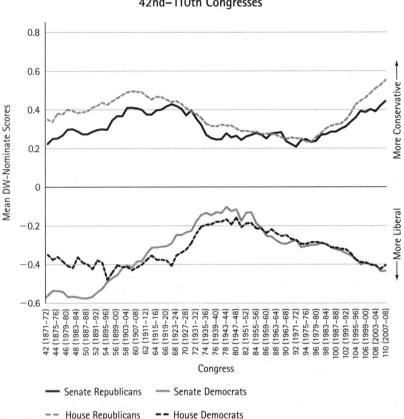

less partisan and less ideological in their politics.[11] Indeed, as late as 2000, an astute journalist could write that "the American electorate is far less ideological than it once was and . . . far less patient with sharply

[11] Martin P. Wattenberg, *The Decline of American Political Parties* (Cambridge, MA: Harvard University Press, 1994); Everett C. Ladd, "The 1994 Congressional Elections: The Realignment Continues," *Political Science Quarterly* 111 (Spring 1995): 1–23; Everett C. Ladd, "The 1996 Election: The 'No Majority' Realignment Continues," *Political Science Quarterly* 112 (Spring 1997): 1–28; Daniel M. Shea, "The Passing of Realignment and the 'Base-Less' Party System, *American Politics Quarterly* 27 (January 1999): 33–57; John Kenneth White and Daniel M. Shea, *New Party Politics: From Jefferson and Hamilton to the Information Age* (Boston: St. Martin's Press, 2000), ch. 6.

FIGURE 2.2

Party Differences in Mean 1st Dimension DW-Nominate Scores,
42nd–110th Congresses

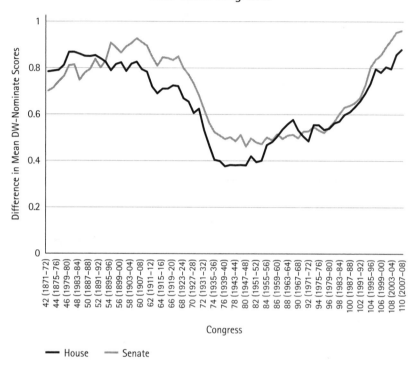

House   Senate

partisan appeals."[12] This view of the electorate raised a pointed scholarly question. Political scientists look reflexively to the "electoral connection"[13] for explanations of basic legislative behavior; how could legislators, supposedly so acutely sensitive to their constituents' sentiments, become increasingly divided by party and ideology as the people who elect them became less so? The answer turned out to be that ordinary voters, like the leaders they elected, were actually growing more rather

---

[12] Richard Berke, "A Race in Which Candidates Clung to the Center," http://www.nytimes.com/2000/11/07/us/the-2000-campaign-looking-back-a-race-in-which-candidates-clung-to-the-center.html?pagewanted=1 (accessed November 10, 2000).
[13] David R. Mayhew, *Congress: The Electoral Connection* (New Haven, CT: Yale University Press, 1974)

than less divided by party and ideology over these decades. Congressional partisans and their electoral constituencies were thus moving in the same, not opposite, directions.

Two major trends gave the congressional parties increasingly divergent electoral coalitions. First, the partisan, ideological, and policy views of voters grew more internally consistent, more distinctive between parties, and more predictive of voting in national elections.[14] Second, electoral units into which voters were sorted became more homogeneously partisan.[15] That is, changes in the preferences, behavior, and distribution of congressional voters gave the congressional parties more internally homogeneous, divergent, and polarized electoral bases.

A principal source of mass electoral change was of course the partisan realignment of the South.[16] The civil rights revolution, and particularly the Voting Rights Act of 1965, brought southern blacks into the electorate as Democrats, while moving conservative whites to abandon their ancestral allegiance to the Democratic Party in favor of the ideologically and racially more compatible Republicans. In-migration also contributed to an increasingly Republican electorate, which gradually replaced conservative Democrats with conservative Republicans in southern House and Senate seats. Figure 2.3 displays the growth of southern Republicanism. Fifty years ago, Republicans were rare in the South; by the time George W. Bush sought the presidency, they comprised a majority.[17]

---

[14] Gary C. Jacobson, "The Electoral Basis of Partisan Polarization in Congress," presented at the Annual Meeting of the American Political Science Association, Washington, DC, August 31–September 3, 2000; Larry M. Bartels, "Partisanship and Voting Behavior, 1952–1996," *American Journal of Political Science* 44 (January 2000): 35–50; Delia Baldassarri and Andrew Gelman, "Partisans Without Constraint: Political Polarization and Trends in American Public Opinion," *American Journal of Sociology* (September 2008): 408–486.
[15] Jeffrey M. Stonecash, Mark D. Brewer, and Mach D. Mariani, *Diverging Parties: Social Change, Realignment, and Party Polarization* (Boulder, CO: Westview Press, 2003); Gary C. Jacobson, *The Politics of Congressional Elections*, 6th ed. (New York: Longman, 2004), 236–243; Bill Bishop, *The Big Sort* (New York: Houghton Mifflin, 2008).
[16] Earle Black and Merle Black, *Politics and Society in the South* (Cambridge, MA: Harvard University Press, 1987); Paul Frymer, "The 1994 Aftershock: Dealignment or Realignment in the South," in Philip A. Klinkner, ed., *Midterm: The Elections of 1994 in Context* (Boulder, CO: Westview Press, 1995), 99–113; Richard Nadeau and Harold W. Stanley, "Class Polarization Among Native Southern Whites, 1952–90," *American Journal of Political Science* 37 (August 1993): 900–919; M. V Hood III, Quentin Kidd, and Irwin L. Morris, "Of Byrd[s] and Bumpers: Using Democratic Senators to Analyze Political Change in the South, 1960–1995," *American Journal of Political Science* 43 (April 1999): 465–487; Martin P. Wattenberg, "The Building of a Republican Regional Base in the South: The Elephant Crosses the Mason-Dixon Line," *Public Opinion Quarterly* 55 (1991): 424431.
[17] If analysis is confined to voters, the Republican rise is even steeper; Figure 2.3 treats independents who lean toward a party as partisans.

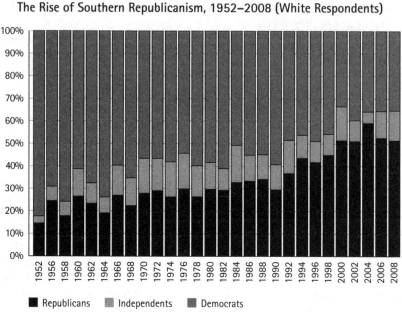

FIGURE 2.3

The Rise of Southern Republicanism, 1952–2008 (White Respondents)

■ Republicans ▦ Independents ▦ Democrats

Sources: American National Election Studies, 1952–2004 and 2008; and Cooperative Congressional Election Survey, 2006.

This change was primarily a result of the gradual movement of conservative whites into the Republican camp (Figure 2.4).[18] In the 1970s, white southern conservatives were about as likely to consider themselves Democrats as Republicans. By 2004, they had become overwhelmingly Republican. Conservative whites outside the South also increasingly sorted themselves into the ideologically appropriate party, though they did not have as far to go as southern conservatives. By the 1990s, regional differences between the two groups had virtually disappeared. The proportion of self-identified liberals calling themselves Democrats also grew during this period, from about 73 percent in the 1970s to about 84 percent since 1994, while the proportion identifying themselves as Republicans fell from 15 percent to 11 percent. Thus, the level of consistency

---

[18] Conservatives are those respondents who placed themselves at 5–7 on the ANES 7-point liberal-conservative scale; the liberal end of the scale is 1–3; 4 is the middle (moderate) category.

FIGURE 2.4

Party Identification of White Conservatives, 1972–2008

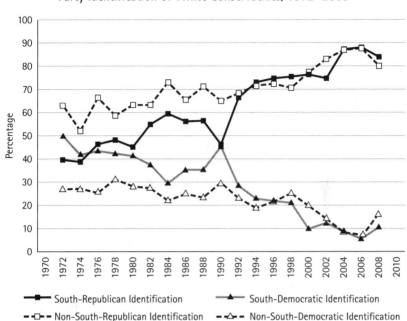

- ■ South-Republican Identification　　▲ South-Democratic Identification
- □ Non-South-Republican Identification　　△ Non-South-Democratic Identification

Sources: American National Election Studies, 1952–2004 and 2008; and Cooperative Congressional Election Survey, 2006.

between party identification and ideology grew across the board—and at a time when the proportion of voters who were willing to place themselves on the liberal–conservative scale, and the proportion doing so who chose other than the center category, also grew substantially.[19]

Party loyalty among congressional voters also increased over this period, so the relationship between ideology and voting became notably stronger.[20] Figure 2.5 displays the growing proportion of self-identified liberals, and diminishing proportion of self-identified conservatives, voting for Democratic candidates for the House and Senate since 1972. The shift among conservatives is particularly notable, as is the pivotal role of the 1994 election in solidifying support for Republican candidates among

---

[19] Jacobson, "Electoral Basis of Partisan Polarization."
[20] Jacobson, *Politics of Congressional Elections*, 119–120.

FIGURE 2.5
Ideology and Voting in Congressional Elections, 1972–2008

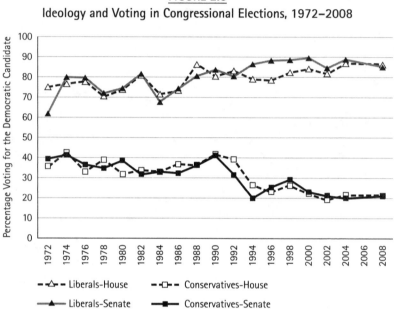

Note: Data are for contested elections only; liberals are those who place themselves at 1–3 on the ANES 7-point liberal-conservative scale; conservatives, those who place themselves at 5–7.
Source: American National Election Studies.

conservatives. In the most recent congressional elections, 84 percent of self-identified liberals voted for Democrats, while 80 percent of conservatives voted for Republicans. Among presidential voters in 2004, 82 percent of conservatives voted for Bush, while 92 percent of liberals voted for John Kerry; in 2008, 83 percent of conservatives voted for John McCain, while 89 percent of liberals voted for Barack Obama (these elections are analyzed in more detail in Chapters 7, 8, and 10).[21]

These changes in voting behavior gave the parties increasingly divergent electoral coalitions (Figure 2.6). The gap between the mean locations on the 7-point liberal-conservative scale of Democratic and Republican voters grew for all three types of federal elections. Although the changes may not seem large—totaling about a point for House and Senate voters

---

[21] Based on ANES surveys for the two elections.

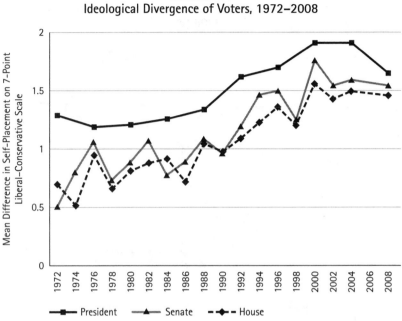

FIGURE 2.6
Ideological Divergence of Voters, 1972–2008

Source: American National Election Studies.

on a 7-point scale—the trends for both Republican and Democratic voters are statistically significant ($p < .001$). It is also worth noting that the scale is effectively only a 5-point scale, as only 5 or 6 percent of respondents choose the extreme points; the enlarged gap thus covers a larger proportion of the effective scale than appears at first glance.

The electorate's growing partisan coherence is also evident in correlations between voters' party identification and positions on several of the ANES's 7-point issue scales and the abortion question, displayed in Figure 2.7.[22] On every issue—ranging from the government's economic role, to race, to abortion policy—the overall trend is upward. Notice that although economic issue positions are normally most strongly related to

---

[22] I use the tau-b statistic to measure the relationship because the analysis is of ordinal variables; alternative measures of association, including the product-moment correlation, reveal precisely the same trends; all of these analyses are confined to respondents who reported voting for one of the major party candidates in the House election.

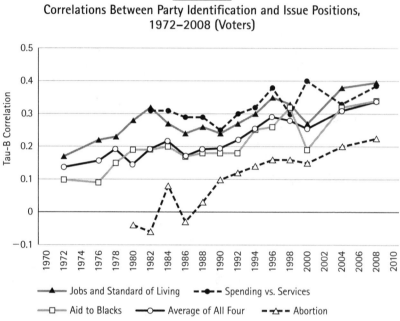

FIGURE 2.7
Correlations Between Party Identification and Issue Positions,
1972–2008 (Voters)

Source: American National Election Studies (ANES).

partisanship—reflecting the venerable New Deal cleavage—the steepest
increases have occurred on the social issue of abortion. For example,
twenty-five years ago, opinions on abortion were unrelated to party identification (indeed, Republicans tended to be a bit more pro-choice than
Democrats); now we observe a substantial correlation. In 1980, only
29 percent of voters who thought abortion should be illegal under all circumstances identified themselves as Republicans; by 2008, 69 percent
did so; the proportion of these voters calling themselves Democrats fell
from 61 percent to 31 percent.[23]

National politicians and ordinary voters, then, have not moved in
opposite directions since the 1970s; both have become increasingly

---

[23] For additional evidence regarding the partisan effects of the abortion issue, see Greg D. Adams,
"Abortion: Evidence of an Issue Evolution," *American Journal of Political Science* 41 (July 1997):
718–773. Much more evidence of the growing connection between partisanship, ideology, and issue
positions may be found in Joseph Bafumi and Robert Y. Shapiro, "A New Partisan Voter," *Journal of
Politics* 71 (January 2009): 1–24.

divided along party lines by political issues and ideology. But it is clear that political leaders were the first movers: Changes in the electorate were mainly a response to shifts in political fault lines initiated or furthered by national leaders and their policy choices. The passage of civil rights legislation during the Johnson administration, for example, contributed decisively to the gradual but cumulatively radical electoral change in the South. Political leaders' responses to the 1973 Supreme Court decision in *Roe v. Wade* helped turn abortion into an issue that redefined the two parties, altering their popular basis and mobilizing new cohorts of activists. Battles over taxes, spending, and budget deficits initiated during the Reagan administration and continuing (with a brief respite during the second Clinton administration) to this day repeatedly pitted the parties against one another in a high-stakes standoff that crystallized and expressed fundamental political differences.

Nor is there any doubt that elite partisanship was proactive and strategic as well as resonant of national policy disputes. Although the increasingly bitter partisan struggles observed in Washington over the past thirty years reflected sincere disagreements, strategic considerations were never far from the surface, with divisive issues and confrontational tactics selected as much to move activists and electorates as to prevail on the Hill.[24] The Republicans' devotion to slashing taxes, for instance, has always been as much an electoral ploy as an expression of ideological faith and has, since the Reagan administration, helped frame budget politics in starkly partisan terms. The action in Washington has shaped the electoral environment by redefining party images through the clash of personalities (Ronald Reagan, Tip O'Neill, Henry Hyde, Newt Gingrich, Bill Clinton, Tom DeLay, George W. Bush) as well as conflict over issues. These clashes have also had a strategic component; inflaming partisan conflict was part of Newt Gingrich's successful strategy for achieving Republican control of Congress.

Evidence that these struggles inspired changes in mass attitudes and behavior lies not only in the temporal sequence—for example, realignment in the South following the Democrats' decision to champion civil rights, partisan divisions on the abortion issue surfacing first in Congress, then in the electorate[25]—but also in variations in responses to

---

[24] John Gilmour, *Strategic Disagreement: Stalemate in American Politics* (Pittsburgh, PA: University of Pittsburgh Press, 1995).

[25] Adams, "Abortion," 720–735.

these issues. Their effects were calibrated by a citizen's level of political involvement and awareness: Activists and strong partisans were more inclined to adopt the ideological positions staked out on economic, social, and racial issues by their national leaders than were the less politically involved; and the more attentive and informed the involved citizens were, the more their views came to mirror those of their leaders.[26] Political independents, along with nonvoters and other politically uninvolved people, participated in the polarizing trends marginally if at all.[27]

IS POLARIZATION CONFINED TO ACTIVISTS?

Morris P. Fiorina takes this point further, arguing that the observed partisan polarization among citizens is almost entirely confined to a narrow political class—politicians, activists, commentators, journalists, bloggers, and other political junkies—with most ordinary Americans appearing to diverge only because extremists on both sides have reduced the choices to polar opposites, excluding middle options.[28] In Fiorina's view, popular polarization—or at least the aspect of it characterized as a "culture war"—is a myth. He reads the survey evidence to show that the distribution of Americans' opinions on cultural issues such as abortion, homosexuality, and gun control has not become measurably more polarized—except among the minority of citizens most active in politics as candidates, activists, and professional observers. Both out of sincere belief and for tactical reasons (raising money, mobilizing the faithful, keeping an audience), these zealots of the left and right bring a fiercely contentious agenda and tone to national politics that are alien to the real needs and sentiments of a large majority of Americans. Fiorina also shows how shifts in policy positions taken by the parties or the emergence of a new issue dimension can polarize the electorate even if its members' opinions

---

[26] Geoffrey C. Layman and Thomas M. Carsey, "Party Polarization and 'Conflict Extension' in the American Electorate," *American Journal of Political Science* 42 (October 2002): 786–802; John Zaller, *The Nature and Origins of Mass Opinion* (Cambridge: Cambridge University Press, 1992), 98–113; Jacobson, "Electoral Basis of Partisan Polarization," 25–28.

[27] Alan I. Abramowitz and Kyle L. Saunders, "Is Polarization a Myth?" *Journal of Politics* 70 (April 2008): 542–555.

[28] Morris P. Fiorina, *Culture War? The Myth of a Polarized America* (New York: Pearson, 2005); Morris P. Fiorina, Samuel A. Abrams, and Jeremy C. Pope, "Polarization in the American Public: Misconceptions and Misreadings," *Journal of Politics* 70 (April 2008): 556–560.

do not change at all. Ordinary Americans, by this argument, do not share the passion or extremism of the active stratum but are forced into what appear to be polar camps because the set of alternatives includes only polar options.

Fiorina's argument highlights the important distinction between polarization in general and *partisan* polarization. That voters have increasingly sorted themselves into parties consistent with their ideological and policy positions says nothing about how divided the public as a whole is on ideology or policy dimensions. But even with no change in the distribution of mass opinion, or even increasing signs of consensus on some formerly divisive issues,[29] if opinion cleavages fall increasingly along party lines, the political consequences can be and, as I show in subsequent chapters, have been profound.

Moreover, Fiorina's analysis implies that political leaders and operatives have been free to follow their own ideological fancies, leaving voters no choice but to line up accordingly. But as strategic vote-seekers, candidates and parties anticipate voters' potential responses to their political initiatives and so are constrained by them. The Republican "southern strategy" emerged because Republican strategists saw an opportunity to win converts among conservative white southerners hostile to civil rights legislation. Ambitious Republican candidates adopted conservative positions on social issues to attract voters alienated by the Democrats' tolerance of nontraditional lifestyles but indifferent at best to Republican economic policies. Democrats emphasized "choice" on abortion because they recognized its appeal to well-educated, affluent voters who might otherwise think of themselves as Republicans. In the budgetary wars of the past two decades, Democrats have vigorously defended middle-class entitlements such as Social Security and Medicare while Republicans have championed tax cuts, because each position has a large popular constituency. In adopting positions, politicians are guided by the opportunities and constraints presented by existing configurations of public opinion on political issues. Intensified partisan conflict in Washington on such issues depended on the expectation that voters would reward or at least not punish the politicians engaging in it.

If party polarization were alienating ordinary, more moderate citizens, we would expect to observe the distance between respondents'

---

[29] John R. Evans, "Have Americans' Attitudes Become More Polarized?—An Update," *Social Science Quarterly* 84 (2003): 71–90.

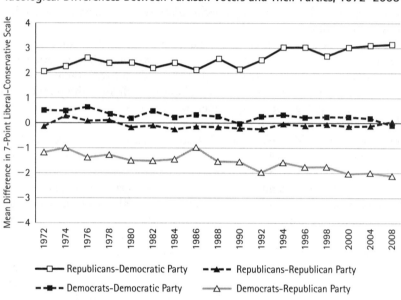

FIGURE 2.8

Ideological Differences Between Partisan Voters and Their Parties, 1972–2008

Source: American National Election Studies.

self-described ideological locations and those they estimate for both parties and their candidates to grow over time. This has not happened. Figure 2.8 displays the gap between the self-placement of partisan voters and their placement of the parties on the 7-point liberal-conservative scale in ANES surveys from 1972 through 2008. Democrats have tended to place themselves slightly to the right of their party, and Republicans, slightly to the left of theirs, but the distance between partisans and their own parties is small and, more important, did not increase at all over this period; among Democrats, it has actually narrowed a bit (with the trend significant at $p < .001$). What has changed is the gap between partisans' locations and the perceived locations of the rival party, which has grown by a full point on the scale for both Republican and Democratic voters (both trends significant at $p < .001$).[30]

---

[30] The same results hold if we include nonvoters in the analysis, although the degree of change in perceived distance from the rival party is slightly smaller.

Similarly, the mean distance between perceived ideological locations of partisans and their own party's House candidates has been modest all along and does not increase over time (Figure 2.9). Moreover, Republicans place themselves on average slightly to the right of their candidates, and Democrats place themselves slightly to the left of theirs. Again, the ideological gap widens only between partisan voters (especially Democrats) and the other party's candidate, although it is not as wide for candidates as for parties. Party leaders and candidates have not, by this evidence, drawn away from their followers, but they have come to be viewed as considerably more distant by those of the other side.

Nonetheless, Fiorina is certainly right in highlighting the crucial contribution of the activist stratum to partisan polarization over the past several decades. The most active participants in politics did display the steepest increase in partisan coherency, consistency, and loyalty; as theory predicts, they were more likely than other Americans to be aware of and respond more readily to intensified party and ideological conflict in

FIGURE 2.9
Ideological Difference Between Partisans and House Candidates, 1978–2008

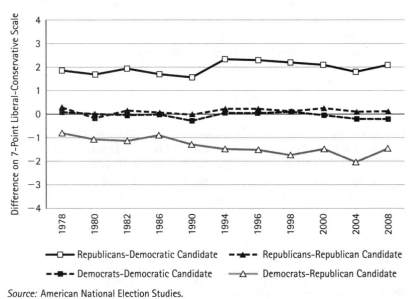

Source: American National Election Studies.

Congress and other national institutions.[31] And there is also little doubt that activists made their own independent contribution to partisan polarization. Devotion to ideological or policy goals is one reason citizens become activists. People attracted to electoral politics by the strategically calculated appeals of campaigners end up constraining the winning candidates, shaping the party's agenda and public image, and supplying the next generation of candidates, campaign professionals, and party leaders. Thus, for example, in many parts of the country, the social conservatives who found a home in the Republican Party in the 1970s and early 1980s have become its core constituency, main recruitment pool, and public face.

Fiorina is also surely right in pointing out that the character and style of Bill Clinton aggravated culturally based partisan divisions. Clinton came to exemplify (not least through the calculated efforts of his opponents) everything social conservatives detested about the post-1960s trends in American culture, while the religious right's attacks on Clinton provoked a backlash among social liberals alarmed by what they saw as a fundamentalist takeover of the Republican Party.[32] But the cultural divisions that came to a head during the Clinton administration began long before 1992 and did not end when Clinton left office in 2001. In particular, the religious dimension of partisan conflict had been growing for nearly two decades before Clinton sought the presidency and did not fade with his departure; quite the contrary, religious cleavages became a primary source of the public's highly polarized responses to George W. Bush.

RELIGION AND PARTISANSHIP

The relationship between religion and partisanship changed in several notable ways between the 1960s and 1990s. As Figure 2.10 shows, white, non-Latino Roman Catholics and evangelical Protestants became more Republican, while white mainline Protestants and seculars showed no sustained trend (neither did African Americans or Jews).[33] Note that

---

[31] Zaller, *Mass Opinion*, 100–113.

[32] Louis Bolce and Gerald De Maio, "Religious Outlook, Culture War Politics, and Antipathy Toward Christian Fundamentalists," *Public Opinion Quarterly* 63 (Spring 1999): 29–61.

[33] David C. Leege, Kenneth D. Wald, Brian S. Krueger, and Paul D. Mueller, *The Politics of Cultural Differences* (Princeton, NJ: Princeton University Press, 2002), 232–233.

FIGURE 2.10
Religion and Partisanship, 1960–1996 (Whites)

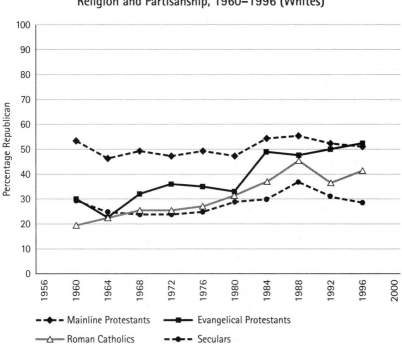

Source: ANES data reported in David C. Leege, Kenneth D. Wald, Brian S. Krueger, and Paul D. Mueller, *The Politics of Cultural Differences* (Princeton, NJ: Princeton University Press, 2002), 232–233.

most of the change among evangelicals occurred during the Reagan administration, well before Bill Clinton appeared on the scene. The abortion issue was of course a crucial source of these trends, but it was only the most salient of a congeries of social issues, including those involving race,[34] that contributed to partisan change. Research sensitive to distinctive currents within these broad categories suggests that trends have also varied widely depending on, among other things, the respondent's (or the respondent's denomination's) theological stance, level of

---

[34] Nicholas A. Valentino and David O. Sears, "Old Times There Are Not Forgotten: Race, Religion, and Sectional Conflict in Contemporary Partisanship," *American Journal of Political Science* 49 (July 2005): 672–688.

involvement in religious activities, and the nature of his or her religious faith.[35] The Republican Party has been most attractive to theological traditionalists, regular attendees, and, among Christians, those who consider themselves "born again," and least attractive to theological modernists or seculars, the nonobservant, and those for whom religion is not so important. The largest swing to the Republicans occurred among white evangelicals with strong religious commitments.[36] These aggregate changes are naturally related to, although by no means entirely explained by, the southern realignment, for the South is where evangelical Christianity and religious traditionalism are most widespread.

The multidimensional character of religious identity and behavior defies easy survey measurement, but Figure 2.11 illustrates some key patterns in the relationship that developed between religiosity and partisanship by the time Bush became president. Lyman Kellstedt and his colleagues developed a classification of religious affiliations that includes what they designate the *religious tradition* (the main categories in Figure 2.11) and further subdivisions within the three largest Christian traditions based on a combination of reported beliefs and behaviors.[37] Their analysis reveals that among white Christians, partisanship is more strongly related to the degree of religious traditionalism—theological orthodoxy and/or identification with sectarian movements (fundamentalist, Pentecostal, and charismatic)—than to membership in the broader groupings. Specifically, Republican identification is much more prevalent among religious traditionalists of all denominations.

These developments in the confessional basis of partisanship set the stage for Bill Clinton to become the nexus of sharp, culturally fueled partisan divisions. Reinforced by the Clinton years, the partisan cultural divide primed Americans to react in strongly partisan terms to any president whose rhetoric, positions, or behavior brought its symbols

---

[35] Lyman A. Kellstedt and Corwin E. Smidt, "Doctrinal Beliefs and Political Behavior: Views of the Bible," in David C. Leege and Lyman A. Kellstedt, eds., *Rediscovering the Religious Factor in American Politics* (New York: M. E. Sharp, 1993), 177–198; Kyle L. Saunders and Alan I. Abramowitz, "Ideological Realignment and Active Partisans in the American Electorate," *American Politics Research* 32 (2004.): 285–309.

[36] Warren E. Miller and J. Merrill Shanks, *The New American Voter* (Cambridge, MA: Harvard University Press, 1996), 540.

[37] Lyman A. Kellstedt, John C. Green, Corwin E. Smidt, and James L. Guth, "Faith and the Vote: The Role of Religion in Political Alignments," presented at the Annual Meeting of the American Political Science Association, Atlanta, September 20, 1999.

FIGURE 2.11
Religiosity and Party Identification, 1996

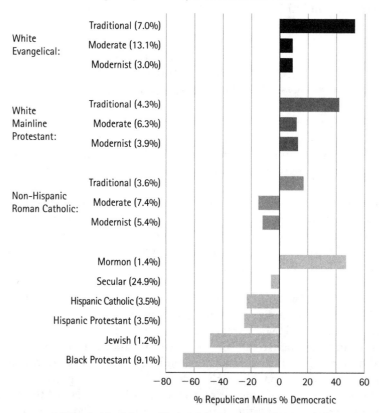

White Evangelical:
- Traditional (7.0%)
- Moderate (13.1%)
- Modernist (3.0%)

White Mainline Protestant:
- Traditional (4.3%)
- Moderate (6.3%)
- Modernist (3.9%)

Non-Hispanic Roman Catholic:
- Traditional (3.6%)
- Moderate (7.4%)
- Modernist (5.4%)

- Mormon (1.4%)
- Secular (24.9%)
- Hispanic Catholic (3.5%)
- Hispanic Protestant (3.5%)
- Jewish (1.2%)
- Black Protestant (9.1%)

−80   −60   −40   −20   0   20   40   60

% Republican Minus % Democratic

Source: Lyman A. Kellstedt, John C. Green, Corwin E. Schmidt, and James L. Guth, "Faith and the Vote: The Role of Religion in Political Alignments," presented at the 1999 Annual Meeting of the American Political Science Association, Atlanta, September 2–5.

to the forefront. George W. Bush and his campaign strategists were well aware of this and, as we shall see in the next chapter, worked effectively during the 2000 campaign to cultivate strong ties to religious conservatives but with sufficient subtlety to avoid provoking a backlash from more secular moderates. Later, when the president's policies, particularly regarding Iraq, did provoke increasing hostility from Democrats and independents, Bush's support among religious conservatives remained very high, contributing strongly to the record partisan gap approval of his job performance and the Iraq War (see Chapters 6 and 9).

ECONOMIC EQUALITY AND THE IDEOLOGICAL FRAGMENTATION OF THE NEWS MEDIA

Two other components of the political context inherited by the George W. Bush administration deserve mention. McCarty, Poole, and Rosenthal mark increasing economic inequality as both a cause and a consequence of increasing partisan polarization. They show that partisanship became increasingly stratified by income between 1952 and 2002, interpreting the change as a response to heightened partisan conflict in Washington over redistributive issues (taxes and social spending).[38] Again, the southern realignment contributed importantly to this change, as upscale whites moved into the Republican camp. Thus, cultural cleavages have not supplanted economic cleavages but have been added to them.[39]

In addition, the sources of information Americans rely on for political news have become increasingly fragmented, ideologically diverse, and openly biased. Mainstream news sources—the network news programs and the mainstream press—have lost audiences to tendentious radio talk shows, Internet bloggers, and Fox News. Most of the innovation has come from the right side of the political spectrum, often with the intention of countering the alleged liberal bias of the mainstream media. Fanning the flames of partisan and ideological conflict is central to the business model. Not only does this development make for a more polarized public sphere—if nothing else, it makes politics *seem* more nastily contentious—but it also enables people to adopt news sources that tend to confirm and reinforce rather than challenge their beliefs and opinions (I have more to say about the news media in Chapter 9).

---

[38] Nolan McCarty, Keith Poole, and Howard Rosenthal, *Polarized America: The Dance of Ideology and Unequal Riches* (Cambridge, MA: MIT Press, 2006), ch. 3.
[39] Fiorina, *Culture War?* 70–72.

CONCLUSION

George W. Bush assumed the presidency after three decades of increasing partisan and ideological polarization among political elites and ordinary voters alike. This situation did not foreordain his presidency to set new records for divisiveness; Bush's own strategies and political choices, unexpected events, his reactions to these events, and the partisan config-uration of Congress were necessary factors as well. But the American polity was thoroughly primed to respond to his presidency in highly partisan terms if offered any opportunity, and the first of these arose even before he took the oath of office.

CHAPTER 3

To the White House Through Florida

Although ordinary Americans took part in the trend toward greater partisan and ideological polarization in national politics during the final decades of the twentieth century, they did not like its manifestations. Partisan squabbling in Washington has never been popular,[1] and the spectacle presented by impeachment politics in 1998 and 1999 exemplified for many people its worst aspects. In a poll taken just after the Senate had voted to acquit Bill Clinton, 78 percent said they thought the whole process had been more about politics than about the investigation of possible crimes (58 percent of Republicans as well as 91 percent of Democrats took this view), 71 percent believed the Senators voted on the basis of partisan politics rather than the facts of the case, and 81 percent said they were sick of hearing about the whole thing.[2] Popular revulsion against the partisan fighting over impeachment and more broadly during the Clinton administration gave George W. Bush one of his central campaign themes for 2000: He was an outsider with no role or stake in the DC wars who could therefore bring the country together again.

As governor of Texas, Bush had worked effectively and cordially with Democrats in the legislature on an agenda aimed at reforming

---

[1] Alan Rosenthal, Burdett A. Loomis, John R. Hibbing, and Karl T. Kurtz, *Republic on Trial: The Case for Representative Democracy* (Washington, DC: CQ Press, 2003), 136–140.
[2] CBS/*New York Times* Poll, February 12, 1999, and ABC News Poll, February 12, 1999, at http://pollingreport.com/scandal1.htm (accessed June 3, 2005).

Texas's education, juvenile justice, tort, and welfare systems. He refrained from campaigning against Democrats who backed his initiatives, and many returned the favor, offering support or at least positive reviews of his performance in Texas when Bush sought the White House.[3] It helped that Democrats in Texas's amateur, part-time legislature were on the whole far more conservative than those he would find in Congress. Bush's record of consensus building helped make him the consensus choice among Republican leaders, particularly fellow governors, looking for a candidate who could reach beyond the party's conservative base to build a coalition broad enough to take back the White House.

"COMPASSIONATE CONSERVATISM"

Bush's stance as an outsider was also calculated to distinguish him from the hard-line Republicans in Congress who had been the party's national face since 1994. Bill Clinton and his allies had worked with some success to characterize Republican leaders as mean-spirited, partisan ideologues, hostile or insensitive to the interests of minorities, women, and the needy. Aware of this, Bush did not spare Republicans when denouncing partisan bickering in Washington. More important, by his choice of campaign issues and themes, Bush offered himself as a different kind of Republican. The focus on education ("Leave no child behind"), the promise to "strengthen" Social Security and to support a prescription drug benefit, the advocacy of a "compassionate conservatism" that both acknowledged and proposed to address social ills, were all aimed at attracting moderate swing voters, not only by poaching on issue turf Democrats claimed as their own, but by giving the party a softer, more inclusive and attractive image. The effort to make the party look inclusive verged on self-parody during the first day of the 2000 Republican national convention, which featured a parade of speeches delivered almost exclusively by women, children, and minorities expounding on themes of compassion and inclusion.[4] But its intent was clear: portraying a party and candidate

---

[3] John C. Fortier and Norman J. Ornstein, "President Bush: Legislative Strategist," in Fred I. Greenstein, ed., *The George W. Bush Presidency: An Early Assessment* (Baltimore: Johns Hopkins University Press, 2003), 141–145.
[4] In fact, no more than 10 percent of the delegates were African American, Latino, or Asian American.

that people who were not conservative white males could still feel comfortable supporting.

Congressional Republicans, eager to defeat Clinton's heir, went along with this strategy, keeping unusually quiet during the months leading up to the election and avoiding any confrontation with Clinton that might reinforce their party's negative image among moderate voters. Republican leaders and the rest of the party's conservative base could also see that Bush's new "compassionate conservatism" did not require any serious pruning of the old Republican agenda. To economic conservatives and the corporate and business sectors, Bush promised major tax cuts, partial privatization of Social Security, deregulation of business, tort reform, and priority for resource extraction over environmental protection. For social conservatives, his platform included support for a constitutional amendment banning abortion; opposition to gay rights, gun control, and affirmative action; and support for school vouchers. Bush's ability to appeal effectively to the party's two main constituencies—the business community and social conservatives of the religious right—was a major reason so much of the Republican establishment had rallied behind his nomination.

ONE OF US

The relationship George W. Bush forged before and during the campaign with religious conservatives, particularly Christian evangelicals, deserves special attention, as it is central to understanding the forces that have made him such a polarizing figure. Bush had served as his father's political ambassador to religious conservatives, and their doubts about the devotion of the father to their cause did not extend to the son. More important, evangelical Christians came to regard the son, quite rightly, as one of their own. His personal story of turning at age forty from alcohol to God with the help of evangelist Billy Graham, his naming Jesus Christ as his favorite philosopher because "he changed my heart," and his unaffected references to the role of prayer and Bible reading in his life allowed no doubt about his religious identity. Moreover, unlike Bill Clinton or Al Gore, also self-described born-again Christians, Bush shared religious conservatives' positions on social issues: opposition to abortion (Bush made exceptions for rape, incest, or protecting the life of the mother), opposition to gay rights (including gay marriage, gay adoptions, and coverage of gays by hate crimes legislation), promotion of "absti-nence only" sex education, and support for tuition vouchers usable in religious schools.

Bush's identification with the religious right was strengthened during the campaign with the unwitting help of Senator John McCain, Bush's last remaining rival for the nomination. McCain had attacked Bush for speaking during the South Carolina primary campaign at Bob Jones University, a fundamentalist stronghold, without condemning the anti-Catholicism of its founder or its policy banning interracial dating. Bush won that primary handily but, after losing the Michigan primary to McCain, felt compelled to apologize and disavow any anti-Catholicism or support for racial discrimination. McCain then went on to lump Jones together with religious conservative leaders Pat Robertson and Jerry Falwell as "agents of intolerance" akin to Al Sharpton and Louis Farrakhan, going so far as to call Falwell and Robertson "evil." McCain's intemperate outburst instantly alienated large blocs of Christian conserv-atives, delivering them en masse to Bush in subsequent primaries.[5]

Bush's standing among evangelical Christian conservatives as "one of us" gave him leeway to state his positions in language designed to avoid scaring off more moderate voters without running the risk that social conservatives would mistake his true beliefs. Rather than dwelling on his support for a constitutional ban on abortion, he could talk about fostering a "culture of life" that would eventually lead to broad public support for such a step. He could temper his opposition to gay rights by refusing to condemn gays wholesale and expressing his willingness to appoint gays to his administration. He could call for tolerance of all religions, even of atheists, without raising doubts about his own commitment to Jesus Christ as his personal savior. The leaders of the religious right, for their part, were sophisticated enough to keep a low profile during the campaign and to refrain from pushing Bush to make overly explicit commitments to their agenda. Knowing what he *was,* they worried less about what he *said.* The Bush campaign could thus pursue its strategy of presenting a more moderate, inclusive, and toler-ant candidate and party without much danger of a backlash from social conservatives.

---

[5] James W. Ceasar and Andrew E. Busch, *The Perfect Tie: The True Story of the 2000 Presidential Election* (Lanham, MD: Rowman & Littlefield, 2001), 92–93.

THE CAMPAIGNS

Bush's opponent, Al Gore, also presented himself as more moderate than his congressional party, although by the end of the campaign he was indulging in some old-fashioned liberal corporate bashing. His selection as his running mate of Joe Lieberman, among the most socially conservative Democratic senators, signaled his centrist intentions. On social and economic issues, Gore was a "New Democrat" in the Clinton mold, supporting the death penalty and welfare reform, advocating middle-class tax cuts, and proposing a prescription drug benefit and a few other modest new social programs. He was also a supporter of "charitable choice," a sort of compassionate conservatism lite, pioneered during the Clinton administration. Indeed, across a broad range of issues, the two candidates were not very far apart; they both offered more continuity than change, not surprising in the prevailing context of peace and prosperity.[6]

Running against peace and prosperity, George W. Bush's only hope was to make Clinton's moral legacy weigh more heavily than his economic legacy in voters' minds. The Bush campaign worked endlessly to keep the Clinton-Gore connection at the forefront. As Dick Cheney said in accepting the vice presidential nomination, "Mr. Gore tries to separate himself from his leader's shadow. But somehow we will never see one without thinking of the other."[7] At least not if the Bush campaign had anything to do with it. The idea was to exploit the public's unhappiness with the moral tone as well as the partisan acrimony of the Clinton years to offset contentment with the economy and its beneficial social fallout (reduced unemployment, crime, welfare dependency, and so forth). In both his acceptance speech and later regularly on the stump, Bush roused the Republican faithful with this peroration: "And so, when I put my hand on the Bible, I will swear to not only uphold the laws of our land, I will swear to uphold the honor and dignity of the office to which I have been elected, so help me God." It not only called attention to the supposed dishonor and indignity visited on the office by Bill Clinton (and by

---

[6] Ibid., 36–37; Kathleen Frankovic and Monica McDermott, "Public Opinion in the 2000 Election: The Ambivalent Electorate," in Gerald M. Pomper, ed., *The Election of 2000* (New York: Chatham House, 2001), 84.

[7] Reported at http://www.cbsnews.com/stories/2000/08/02/politics/main221310.shtml (accessed June 14, 2005).

association, Al Gore), but it also served to remind listeners of Bush's fealty to God and the Bible. Bush's references to Clinton's morals were almost always this indirect; Republicans had learned the hard way that frontal attacks on Clinton could backfire, doing as much damage to the attacker as to the target.

With disputes over policy issues somewhat muted, the contest (at least as portrayed by the news media) tended to center on character, ability, and personality. Gore was knowledgeable, but was he stiff and perhaps disingenuous? Republicans sought to hammer home the idea that Gore was a serial exaggerator who would say anything to win (and who thus shared Clinton's deviousness). Bush was pleasant and jovial, but inarticulate and vague; was he up to the job? Democrats portrayed him as intellectually shallow, uninformed, and dependent on family ties for whatever success he had achieved in business or politics.

To the degree that campaigns focused on the candidates' personal traits, they were not particularly polarizing, for the traits at issue did not themselves carry partisan overtones. Neither, according to various postelection analyses, were other salient aspects of the electoral environment in 2000. Gerald Pomper characterized the race as "sharply contested but reasonably civil. Attacks abounded, but they focused on real issue differences between Gore and Bush, as each contestant worried over the public's declared aversion to personal, negative campaigning."[8] In Wilson Carey McWilliams's view, "The campaign certainly didn't set off any skyrockets. Neither candidate aroused much enthusiasm, let alone suggested greatness, nor was either the object of much antipathy."[9] Kathleen Frankovic and Monica McDermott emphasized the candidates' similarities in background and agenda, voters' ambivalence on many policy issues, their complacency, and their generally positive if unenthusiastic evaluations of the candidates. The authors conclude: "Because voters could not resolve issue conflicts in their own minds, their candidate support was muddled. The candidates had similar strengths and weaknesses, and although the choice satisfied most voters, many of them ended up on election day with qualms about their vote."[10]

---

[8] Gerald M. Pomper, "The Presidential Election," in Pomper, *Elections of 2000,* 144.
[9] Wilson Carey McWilliams, "The Meaning of the Election," in Pomper, *Elections of 2000,* 179.
[10] Frankovic and McDermott, "Ambivalent Electorate," in Pomper, *Elections of 2000,* 90.

THE VOTE

The 2000 presidential campaigns were, then, not calculated to emphasize partisan divisions or polarize the electorate; if anything, the opposite. And there is little evidence that the candidates and their campaigns did arouse strong partisan feelings in most voters. All the more noteworthy, then, that party-line voting—Republicans for Bush, Democrats for Gore—equaled its highest recorded level to that date in the entire forty-eight-year history of the National Election Studies: 87 percent.[11] Party loyalty reported in the national exit poll was even higher, 89 percent, the highest since the beginning of exit polling in 1976.[12] Despite campaigns designed to broaden each candidate's appeal, neither attracted many voters from the opposite party; according to the NES, Bush won 11.1 percent of Democrats, Gore, 9.4 percent of Republicans; if partisan leaners—independents who say they lean toward one of the parties (and who tend to vote like weak partisans of that party)—are excluded, the defection rates become 7.7 percent and 7.6 percent, respectively.

The high level of party loyalty in 2000 reflected, in part, the absence of any detectable partisan tide that might have favored one party over the other.[13] But it also reflected the general rise in partisan coherence and consistency documented in Chapter 2; if many voters were ambivalent about their decisions—and in the exit polls, 55 percent reported having reservations about their vote—they were remarkably consistent in resolving the choice in their own party's favor. One consequence was that the vote in 2000 expressed the underlying distribution of party support with unusual accuracy, and exit poll results offered a clear snapshot of the sources of partisan division in the electorate as Bush was about to enter the White House.

Figure 3.1 displays some of the salient demographic characteristics that distinguished Bush voters from Gore voters. The bars on the graph show how far support for Bush fell above or below the 50 percent mark among people in each category. The percentage of the electorate comprising

---

[11] The party loyalty rate for 2000 was 86.5 percent, 0.1 percent below that of 1988 but at least 0.7 percent higher than that for any other previous election.

[12] The 2000 Voter News Service election poll data are available from the Roper Center, http://www.ropercenter.uconn.edu/. Results from earlier election polls are in *The Public Perspective* (December/January 1997), 8–10.

[13] Gary C. Jacobson, "A House and Senate Divided: The Clinton Legacy and the Congressional Elections of 2000," *Political Science Quarterly* 116 (Spring 2001), 7–8.

FIGURE 3.1
Demographic Characteristics and the Presidential Vote

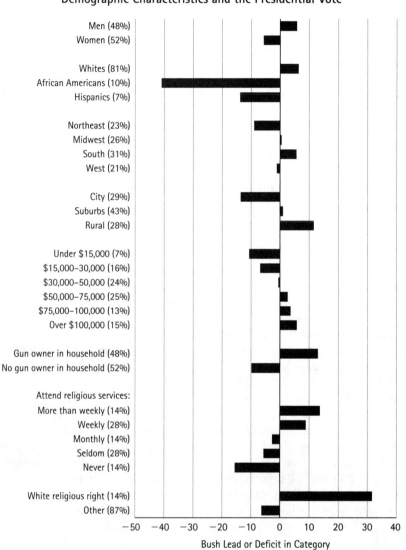

Bush Lead or Deficit in Category

Source: 2000 National Exit Polls.

each category appears in parentheses. Men favored Bush, women Gore, the difference amounting to 11 percentage points. Bush won decisively among whites, while Gore took more than 90 percent of the African American vote. Hispanic voters also went for Gore, but by smaller margins than in past exit polls, reflecting Bush's support among Latinos in his home state of Texas. Bush was a strong favorite in the South, while Gore was a strong favorite in the Northeast. The division in the Midwest was nearly even, as it was in the West, where Democratic majorities in the coastal states were balanced by the solidly Republican mountain states. Urban–rural differences were even sharper than regional differences.

Support for the candidates differed by income category in the expected direction: the higher a voter's income, the more likely a vote for Bush. But notice that differences in support for the candidates based on the two noneconomic factors, gun ownership and religiosity, are even larger than differences associated with income. The difference in support for Bush and Gore between the lowest and highest income categories is 17 percentage points, while the difference between people in households with and without guns is 23 percentage points, and between the most and least religiously active voters, 29 percentage points. Bush's greatest advantage was among whites who considered themselves part of the religious right; comprising 14 percent of the electorate, they gave Bush 80 percent of their votes, Gore, only 18 percent.

The idea that noneconomic considerations were at least as potent as economic issues in sorting voters into electoral coalitions is reinforced by examining the relationship between the presidential choice and voters' positions on selected issues (Figure 3.2). Support for the candidates varied most widely according to views on abortion, with support for Bush 51 percentage points higher among people who thought abortions should always be illegal than among people who thought they should always be legal. The third largest difference is associated with opinions on gun control (41 points), exceeded slightly by differences related to the tax question (42 points). On these and other matters—school vouchers, tax cuts, prescription drug programs for seniors, the partial privatization of Social Security, economy growth vs. environmental protection—Bush won the support of those who favored his approach but was opposed by those who did not. Not at all surprising, of course, but a sign that Bush's agenda, should he have the opportunity to pursue it, would be a divisive one.

FIGURE 3.2
Issue Positions and the Presidential Vote

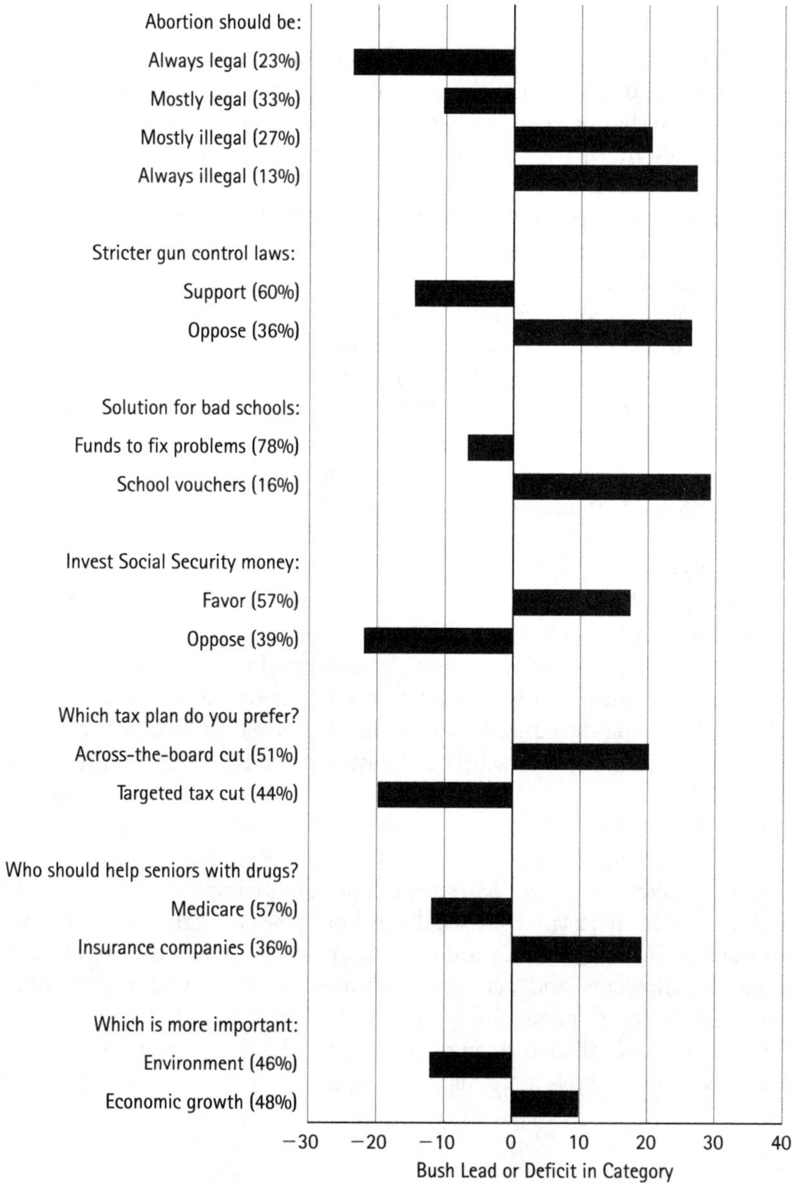

Source: 2000 National Exit Polls.

FLORIDA

Any illusion that the bitter partisanship of the Clinton years was a thing of the past, and any hope George W. Bush might have entertained for an inauguration that bridged the partisan divide, expired almost instantly in the election's aftermath. Gore won the popular vote by about 540,000 of the 105 million votes cast, but presidents are chosen by the Electoral College, and election night found George W. Bush with a tiny lead in Florida which, if sustained, would give him a majority of electoral votes and thus the White House. The close Florida tally triggered an automatic machine recount amid revelations of balloting irregularities sufficiently serious and widespread to leave the accuracy and legitimacy of any final count forever in question. On November 26, following the machine recount, Florida's Republican secretary of state certified Bush as the winner by a margin of 537 votes. Gore's lawyers contested the result the next day in state court, eventually persuading Florida's Supreme Court to order a recount of all ballots not included in the machine count and to include ballots from hand counts submitted after the certification deadline. Bush's lawyers appealed to the United States Supreme Court, which on December 4 issued an order halting the count of disputed ballots pending a hearing. On December 12, a day after that hearing, the Court, by a 5 to 4 majority, concluded there was not enough time for the state court to fashion a constitutionally valid process for counting disputed ballots, effectively ending the contest. Gore conceded defeat on December 13.

From election night onward, and ignoring the real uncertainties about what had occurred, partisan elites and activists rallied in lock-step to their party's presidential candidate. Both the heated rhetoric ("They're stealing it, they're stealing it, they're stealing it" is how Republican representative Charles W. Pickering, Jr. of Mississippi put it, unprompted, to a reporter[14]) and the clean partisan split loudly echoed the struggle over Clinton's impeachment. And as with impeachment, partisan divisions were not confined to politicians and activists. Although ordinary voters were more bemused by than passionately involved in the postelection events in Florida, they too divided strongly along party lines in responding to questions about them. Polls assessing public opinion on the election's aftermath

---

[14] Andrew Taylor, "First Test of Promised Comity Is Late Lame-Duck Session," *Congressional Quarterly Weekly Report*, November 18, 2000, 2723.

found immediate, sustained, and huge differences between Bush and Gore supporters (that is also to say, between Republicans and Democrats[15]) on relevant questions. Some examples appear in Table 3.1. Among Bush voters, 93 percent were satisfied with the election outcome, 92 percent thought Bush had won the election legitimately, and 95 percent approved of the Supreme Court's decision stopping the manual recount of ballots in Florida. Among Gore voters, 89 percent were dissatisfied with the outcome, 81 percent thought Bush was not the legitimate victor, and 80 percent disapproved of the Supreme Court's decision. Most Gore supporters (65 percent) thought the Court's decision was partisan, while most Bush supporters (84 percent) thought it was impartial. Gore voters were convinced that more Florida voters intended to vote for Gore than for Bush (83 percent), while most Bush voters believed the opposite (59 percent, with another 28 percent uncertain). The two sides were also sharply divided on whether the Court's decision to stop the vote count was fair.

The Florida controversy was, in fact, ideally suited to provoke polarized partisan responses of this sort. The balloting and vote count were such a mess that no one honestly knew for sure who had won the most votes (or whom more of Florida's voters had actually preferred). The appropriate procedure for settling the question was equally uncertain. Under such conditions, everything we have learned about the psychology of political opinion formation predicts that partisans would believe their side's leaders and arguments and reject (or ignore) those of the other side.[16] Ambiguity provides nothing to override the default option and thus gives partisan priors full sway.

Moreover, the public had good reason to view the conflict through partisan spectacles. Once the action began in Florida, the fight *was* nakedly partisan, which shifted the odds overwhelmingly in Bush's favor because his party controlled all the venues where the ultimate decision might be made. To be sure, Florida's attorney general and many local election officials were Democrats, and Democratic appointees dominated the Florida Supreme Court, where Gore won some initial skirmishes. But

---

[15] Polls that report responses broken down by party identification rather than presidential preference replicate the results reported in Table 3. For example, a Gallup poll taken December 15–17 found 85 percent of Republicans saying that Bush won "fair and square," while 49 percent of Democrats thought he had won on a technicality, and 37 percent said he stole the election; the survey data are available from the Roper Center, http://www.ropercenter.uconn.edu.

[16] Richard E. Petty and Duane T. Wegener, "Attitude Change: Multiple Roles for Persuasion Variables," in Daniel T. Gilbert, Susan T. Fiske, and Gardner Lindzey, *The Handbook of Social Psychology*, 4th ed., vol. 1 (Boston: McGraw-Hill, 1998), 331.

TABLE 3.1
Public Opinion on the Presidential Election Outcome (Percentages)

	ALL	GORE VOTERS	BUSH VOTERS
1. "In general, are you satisfied or dissatisfied with the outcome of the election?"			
Satisfied	50	9	93
Dissatisfied	45	89	6
Don't know	5	2	1
2. "Would you say George W. Bush legitimately won the election, or not?"			
Legitimately won	53	11	92
Did not	40	81	3
Don't know	7	8	5
3. "As you may know, on Tuesday the United States Supreme Court ruled in George W. Bush's favor and stopped the manual recounting of votes in Florida that had been ordered by the Florida Supreme Court. Do you approve or disapprove of the United States Supreme Court's ruling that stopped the manual recount?"			
Approve	54	16	95
Disapprove	42	80	4
Don't know	2	4	1
4. "Do you think the Supreme Court's decision was based more on partisan politics, or more on an objective interpretation of the law?"			
Partisan politics	37	65	10
Objective interpretation	54	29	84
Both (volunteered)	1	1	2
Neither (volunteered)	1	0	1
Don't know	7	5	3

	ALL	GORE VOTERS	BUSH VOTERS
5. "Regardless of what the current vote total is, who do you think more Florida voters intended to vote for: Al Gore or George W. Bush?"			
Gore	46	83	13
Bush	34	7	59
Don't know	20	10	28
6. "This week, by a margin of 5 to 4, the United States Supreme Court reversed the Florida court's decision and stopped hand recounts of presidential ballots in Florida. All in all, do you think the Supreme Court's decision to stop hand recounts in Florida was fair or unfair?"			
Fair	51	88	19
Unfair	44	9	78
Don't know	5	3	3

SOURCES: Questions 1–5, CBS News Poll, December 14–16, 2000; Question 6, *Newsweek* Poll conducted by Princeton Survey Research Associates, December 14–15, 2000; both reported at *http://www.pollingreport.com*, January 3, 2000.

Florida's secretary of state was a Republican activist, and Bush could count on his brother, Republican governor Jeb Bush, as well as Republican legislative majorities, if Florida's legislature chose the state's electors (which it threatened to do if the vote count was not completed in time to certify an official slate). Had the dispute moved to Congress for resolution, Republicans would have had the votes to award the election to Bush. And the United States Supreme Court had the authority to trump the Florida court, as it finally did when five Supreme Court justices, all conservative Republican appointees, preemptively terminated the recount, making certain that Bush received Florida's decisive electoral votes. Democrats were thus likely to think the process was rigged against their candidate no matter how the final decision was reached.

The denouement in Florida had two important effects on public attitudes toward the newly elected president. First, it divided the public along party lines over the legitimacy of his victory in a way that persisted throughout Bush's entire first term in the White House and beyond (Figure 3.3). If anything, partisan differences on this question were wider in October 2004 than they had been four years earlier, with more than 90 percent of Republicans saying he had been elected legitimately, and three-quarters of the Democrats saying he had not (a slim majority of independents agreed with the Republicans on this question). As late as 2007, only 15 percent of Democrats thought he'd won the election "fair and square." Even the post-9/11 rally barely softened their view on this question.

Second, the Florida resolution deprived Bush of any early-term "honeymoon" during which citizens who had opposed his election might have been willing to withhold judgment or give him the benefit of the doubt. As Figure 3.4 shows, Bush provoked the widest partisan differences in responses to the Gallup Poll's job approval question during the first quarter of an administration of any newly elected president going back to Eisenhower, surpassing the runner-up Bill Clinton by more than 7 percentage

FIGURE 3.3
Partisan Opinions on the Legitimacy of the 2000 Election

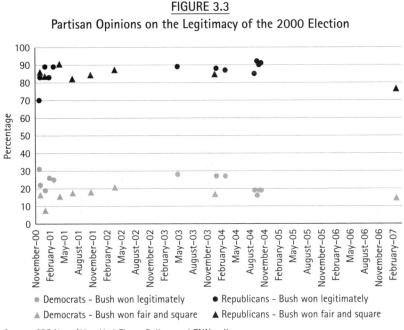

Source: CBS News/New York Times, Gallup, and CNN polls.

FIGURE 3.4
Partisanship and Approval of Newly Inaugurated Presidents

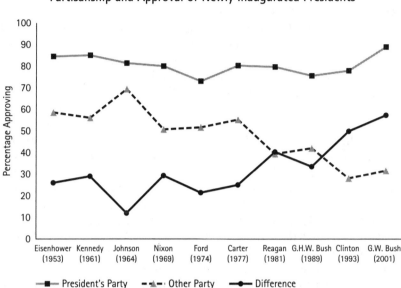

Source: Gallup polls taken during the first quarter of each administration (average).

points. His rating among his own partisans was the highest ever for this period, while Democrats were only slightly more positive about him than Republicans had been about Clinton in early 1993. Observe, though, that the partisan gap had been on the rise for at least two decades, almost entirely a consequence of declining approval ratings among rival-party identifiers. The data suggest that, even before George W. Bush, the presidential honeymoon was becoming a thing of the past, again reflecting the polarizing trends discussed in Chapter 2. Still, Bush's extraordinary path to the White House no doubt made things worse for him in this regard; in the ANES's postelection survey, Democratic voters interviewed during the first week after the election rated Bush at 50.4 degrees on the 100-degree feeling thermometer, during the second week 46.0 degrees, and thereafter 39.1 degrees (with no further trend).[17]

---

[17] The difference between the first one or two weeks and the rest is significant at $p < .01$. Gore's ratings among Democrats increased significantly as well; there was no significant postelection trend among Republican identifiers in ratings of either candidate.

CONCLUSION

Although George W. Bush's 2000 presidential campaign sought to shed the image of unbridled partisanship and conservative zealotry projected by the Republican Party's congressional wing, even before the postelection battle for Florida, seeds had been planted that could easily blossom into a continuation of intense partisan conflict after the election. While mostly avoiding head-on attacks on Bill Clinton, the campaign's attempt to exploit popular disgust with the moral tone of his administration to undermine Al Gore's support meant that the bitter legacy of impeachment politics was never far below the surface. The social and cultural differences that have increasingly come to distinguish Republicans and Democrats were clearly visible in the distribution of votes. And while some parts of the "compassionate conservatism" agenda could, properly packaged, attract bipartisan support, Bush's broader agenda advocated orthodox Republican economic and social policies on a range of issues that had divided the parties fundamentally since at least the Reagan administration. In particular, insofar as Bush's affinity with and obligations to the religious right guided his appointments and policies, he was certain to alienate most ordinary Democrats. Much would depend on how, once the Supreme Court had awarded him his victory, Bush intended to govern.

CHAPTER **4**

■ ■ ■ ■ ■

The First Two Years: Before and After 9/11

George W. Bush's disputed victory was part of a broader partisan stalemate in 2000. The same election left the Senate divided exactly in half, with Republicans and Democrats each holding fifty seats; vice president Dick Cheney would cast the tiebreaking vote. The Republicans held onto their slim majority in the House of Representatives, losing a net two seats but keeping control, 221 to 212 (the two independents also split on which party they routinely supported). With questionable legitimacy, no mandate, and the slimmest of Republican margins in the House and Senate (Republicans had actually lost seats in both chambers), more than a few postelection analysts predicted that Bush would have to govern from the center in bipartisan fashion or face almost certain failure.[1] Some wilder flights of fancy envisioned a kind of coalition government, with Bush bringing substantial Democratic representation into his cabinet and encouraging bipartisan power-sharing in Congress.[2] Had Bush moved in this direction after his inauguration, it is most doubtful that he

---

[1] See, for example, Gerald M. Pomper, "The Presidential Election," 148; Wilson Carey McWilliams, "The Meaning of the Election," 178; and Paul S. Herrnson, "The Congressional Elections," 155; all in Gerald M. Pomper, ed., *The Election of 2000* (New York: Chatham House, 2001); also, Gary C. Jacobson, "Congress: Elections and Stalemate," in Michael Nelson, ed., *The Elections of 2000* (Washington, DC: Congressional Quarterly Press, 2001), 206.

[2] "What's the Mandate? The Overriding Message for the Next President: All Roads Lead to the Center," *Business Week Online,* November 20, 2000, at http://www.businessweek.com/2000/00_47/b3708001.htm (accessed June 28, 2005).

would have become the most polarizing president in modern history, and this book would not have been written.

Of course, Bush did nothing of the sort. One reason is that congressional Republicans would have mutinied. Were it not for the Florida debacle, the big story of the 2000 election would have been that it gave the Republicans full, if tenuous, control of Congress and the White House for the first time since the first Congress of the Eisenhower administration (1953–1954). After six years of being stymied and outmaneuvered by Bill Clinton, Republicans on the Hill were scarcely in the mood for bipartisan compromises. A more important reason is that it is simply not in Bush's nature to concede ground without a fight. It would go against his conceptions of strategy and leadership as well as his conviction that his positions are the right ones. It is also unlikely that any of his closest advisors recommended caution; as Dick Cheney is reported to have said, "A notion of sort of a restrained presidency because it was such a close election, that lasted maybe 30 seconds. . . . We had an agenda, we ran on the agenda, we won the election—full speed ahead."[3]

THE BUSH AGENDA

The agenda was not, as I noted in the previous chapter, one to promote consensus. Polls taken in the spring of 2001 found that the early partisan split on Bush extended to most of his policies. Majorities of Democrats opposed and Republicans favored his proposals on taxes, energy development, Social Security, military spending, and budgeting more generally. Democrats joined Republicans in supporting only some elements of "compassionate conservatism": spending more on education, funding faith-based organizations to deliver social services, and providing a prescription drug benefit.[4]

The Bush administration's strategy for achieving legislative victories on its agenda also promised to be divisive. Bush's idea of legislative leadership

---

[3] Bob Woodward, *Plan of Attack* (New York: Simon and Shuster, 2004), 28.
[4] "Bush and the Democratic Agenda," CBS News/*New York Times* Poll, June 14–18, 2001, at http://www.cbsnews.com/htdocs/pdf/bushbac.pdf (accessed July 7, 2003); CBS News/*New York Times* Monthly Poll, March 2001; *Los Angeles Times* Poll #455: "Bush's Budget Speech to Congress," March 2001.

was, by his own and others' descriptions,[5] to stake out a firm position right at his own ideal point ("The moment I negotiate with myself, I lose," as he put it[6]), defend it against all objections, pursue it with focus and tenacity, and compromise only at the last minute and to the smallest extent possible to gain the victory. Backed by his unwavering commitment, the leader's "team" of strategists, aides, and congressional allies conducted a coordinated, disciplined, but tactically flexible campaign, with everyone speaking from the same prepared script. The payoff to this approach was clear in Bush's first important legislative victory, the $1.3 billion tax cut enacted by Congress on May 26, 2001; the administration compromised only far enough to peel off the handful of Senate Democrats needed to prevent a filibuster and got 80 percent of what it had initially proposed.[7] A legislative strategy aimed at winning all the Republicans and a few necessary Democrats made sense and could be effective, but it was also polarizing, with the degree of polarization mitigated only to the extent that policy had to be moderated to pick up the Democrats. Victories could be celebrated by ordinary Republicans but were not appreciated by ordinary Democrats; about two-thirds of Democrats opposed Bush's tax and budget proposals, while about 85 percent of Republicans supported them.[8] Bush did not invariably adopt a partisan legislative strategy; major bills dealing with education in 2001, prescription drug benefits in 2004, and the bank bailout in 2008 were truly bipartisan—by necessity, because some conservative Republicans in Congress opposed all three. But the partisan strategy was more common on domestic legislation, and partisans in the electorate divided in response to the results accordingly.

At least as divisive as Bush's legislative agenda was his administrative agenda, which amounted to a concerted effort to undo as much of the regulatory work of the Clinton administration and its predecessors as was politically feasible. On the environmental front, that agenda included

---

[5] Ivo H. Daalder and James M. Lindsay, *America Unbound: The Bush Revolution in Foreign Policy* (Washington, DC: Brookings Institution, 2003), 32–33; Charles O. Jones, "Capitalizing on the Perfect Tie," in Fred I. Greenstein, ed., *The George W. Bush Presidency: An Early Assessment* (Baltimore: Johns Hopkins University Press, 2003), 176–178; Bob Woodward, *Bush at War* (New York: Simon and Shuster, 2002), 256.
[6] Quoted in Jones, "Capitalizing on a Perfect Tie," 181.
[7] John C. Fortier and Norman J. Ornstein, "President Bush: Legislative Strategist," in Fred I. Greenstein, ed., *The George W. Bush Presidency: An Early Assessment* (Baltimore: Johns Hopkins University Press, 2003), 147–151.
[8] CBS News/*New York Times* Poll, March 8–12, 2001.

reopening public lands set aside for protection against commercial exploitation, weakening protection of endangered species, easing standards on air and water pollution (including those covering arsenic, mercury, selenium, and perchlorate), and rejecting the Kyoto protocols on global warming. The administration's attitude toward the environment was typified by its proposal to open the Alaskan National Wildlife Refuge to oil exploration as part of an energy program designed behind closed doors by lobbyists from the oil and gas industries and under the supervision of Vice President Cheney. Cheney's dismissive response to the criticism that the proposal ignored conservation—"Conservation may be a sign of personal virtue, but it is not a sufficient basis for a sound, comprehensive energy policy"[9]—set the tone.

Not all of these initiatives succeeded, but they made it clear where the administration stood when environmental values were at stake, squarely on the side of private industry and resource development. This obviously pleased an important Republican constituency (and major source of campaign funds) and was supported by ordinary Republicans, although not always by overwhelming majorities.[10] Environmental activists were predictably outraged and soon came to regard the Bush administration as the worst ever on environmental issues. Their opinion was widely shared by ordinary Democrats, and although environmental protection was not a top priority for most, it contributed to negative views of the president.[11] The regulatory tilt toward the business sector was repeated in other domains as well, generating divisions along predictable partisan and ideological fault lines between business interests and consumer groups.

TACTICS

George W. Bush's decision to pursue his agenda full throttle despite the lack of a popular mandate and with only the narrowest margins in Congress, combined with his conception of leadership, encouraged (if any encouragement was necessary) the adoption of tactics for dealing with

---

[9] Reported at http://www.usatoday.com/news/washington/2001-05-01-cheney-usat.htm (accessed March 16, 2010).
[10] In March 2001, for example, 55 percent of Republicans said they approved of drilling for oil in ANWR, compared to 27 percent of Democrats. See CBS News/*New York Times* Poll, March 8–12, 2001.
[11] In a June 2001 poll, only 23 percent of Democrats approved of Bush's handling of the environment; see the CBS News/*New York Times* Poll, June 14–18, 2001.

the public that contributed profoundly to deep partisan differences in evaluations of him and his administration. The full consequences of these tactics become clear only when we examine public views of the war in Iraq in the following two chapters, but their potential was evident from the beginning.

With some risk of caricature, the Bush administration's typical approach can be described like this: Policy proposals were designed in-house in great secrecy so that any internal disagreements were thrashed out and resolved (by Bush as final arbiter if necessary) before presenting a unified front to the outside world. The president then announced his proposal as "the right thing for the American people," and he and his team went to work turning it into policy. The public campaign took the form of a multifaceted sales exercise; the aim was not to explain the product, but to sell it. Everyone on the team was expected to "stay on message," reiterating with little variation arguments and rhetoric carefully vetted in advance. The message depended on what Bush's strategists thought would sway the public (and thereby other politicians in Washington) and might be altered as necessary as circumstances shifted (for example, the tax cut was first justified by the Clinton surplus and then, when recession erased the surplus, by the need to stimulate the economy). Contrary messages and messengers were denounced (a favorite ploy was to portray opposition as motivated solely by partisanship). Probing questions from reporters were ducked or ignored if straightforward answers might undermine the message. The idea was to control not only the agenda, but also the framing, language, and definition of what counted as relevant facts regarding the issue at hand.

All of this is understandable from the perspective of a president who entertained no doubts or second thoughts about the rightness of his goals and wanted to achieve major changes in public policy despite a narrow political base, widespread political resistance, and general public indifference or opposition to what he wanted to do. It may be difficult to imagine succeeding on any other basis. Yet in practice, this mindset and consequent emphasis on marketing bred a cavalier approach to truth: dishonesty not by lying, but by a deceptive selection of truthful but misleading statements. In pushing to get his tax cut enacted, for example, Bush repeatedly claimed that his plan would "reduce taxes for everyone who pays taxes," which was true only if you excluded Social Security and Medicare taxes (the biggest federal tax burden on millions of low-income workers). He also said it offered "the greatest help for those most in need" because "the highest percentage tax cuts got to the lowest income Americans." True, but only because the lowest income groups already paid so little; reducing a tax liability from $200 to $100 represents a large percentage cut but small substantive benefit for the taxpayer. Bush extolled the reduction of the top income tax bracket from 39.6 percent to 33 percent as a boon to America's 17.4 million small business owners without mentioning that only 1.4 percent of them were paying the top rate. In fact, about 72 percent of the total tax reduction would be enjoyed by the top 20 percent of taxpayers, 45 percent of it by the top 1 percent of taxpayers.[12] But anyone who brought this up was accused of fomenting "class warfare."

This kind of marketing is inherently polarizing. Republicans, positively disposed toward the president, tended to accept his "facts" and arguments uncritically because of both their source and their fit with prior attitudes; people do not devote cognitive resources to picking apart the statements of opinion leaders with whom they prefer to agree.[13] Unless the president's arguments were clearly false (as opposed to merely deceptive) and widely exposed in the news media as such, his supporters were under no psychological pressure to reject them; quite the contrary. In contrast, Democrats and others not inclined to follow the president's lead or accept his word were open to (and may have even sought out) analyses by critics busy parsing the rhetoric and pointing out the deceptions. And they were ready to recognize "facts" ignored by the president that undermined his case. Insofar as their initial reflexive doubts about the policy and its promoter appeared to be confirmed, these attitudes could only be strengthened. A president who pursues policy goals by deceptive rhetoric and careful selection of misleading facts may succeed in getting a Congress run by his partisans to do his bidding, but one price is the alienation of those on the losing side who resent the manipulation and deception and regard the victory as illegitimately won. It is, then, a polarizing victory.

The Bush administration applied the same kind of salesmanship to its administrative and regulatory policies. Again, decisions were made behind closed doors and, if likely to promote popular resistance, then carefully marketed to the public. Expert analyses and scientific findings

---

[12] Ben Fritz, Bryan Keefer, and Brendan Nyhan, *All the President's Spin: George W. Bush, the Media, and the Truth* (New York: Simon and Schuster), 75–78.
[13] Petty and Wegener, "Attitude Change," *Handbook of Social Psychology*, 344–348.

that did not support the policy were "off message" and routinely suppressed or rewritten by political appointees to conform to the administration's line. Rejecting the Kyoto Protocol, Bush acknowledged the reality of global warming but emphasized the uncertainties about how much and how fast it would happen—an accurate but misleading representation of the scientific consensus on the severity and immediacy of the threat—as the excuse for doing nothing beyond funding more research and encouraging voluntary action to reduce hydrocarbon emissions. The distortion of science for political ends became prevalent enough to provoke a public protest by sixty senior scientists, including twenty Nobel laureates.[14] Language was then reconfigured to soften opposition. On the advice of Republican strategist Frank Luntz, the administration replaced "global warming" with the more innocuous "climate change" in addressing the topic.[15] The administration's plan to open national forests to more extensive logging became the "Healthy Forests Initiative." The EPA's rollback of pollution control requirements for power plants was called the "Clear Skies Initiative." None of this contrived naming would bother people who agreed with the substance of the administration's policies, and it may have reassured people not particularly attuned to the issues involved. But to those who cared and disagreed with the policies, the language was infuriatingly Orwellian. Again, its effect was polarizing.

In both content and form, then, the Bush administration's actions in its first eight months were not calculated to reduce partisan divisions in Washington or in the broader public, and they did not. As Figure 4.1 shows, partisan differences in evaluations of Bush were wider during each of the first three quarters (prior to September 11 in the third quarter) of his first year in office than for any previous president. The gap was an average of 7.4 percentage points wider than for the former record holder, Bill Clinton.

Another consequence of Bush's approach was a temporary loss of the Senate. The administration's hard-line conservatism on most issues led one of the few remaining moderate Republicans, Senator James Jeffords of Vermont, to announce on May 24, 2001, that he would henceforth

---

[14] "Preeminent Scientists Protest Bush Administration's Misuse of Science," news release, Union of Concerned Scientists, February 18, 2004, at http://www.ucsusa.org/news/press_release.cfm?newsID=381 (accessed July 5, 2005).
[15] Fritz et al., *All the President's Spin*, 94.

FIGURE 4.1

Party Differences in Presidential Approval in the First Three
Quarters of a New Administration

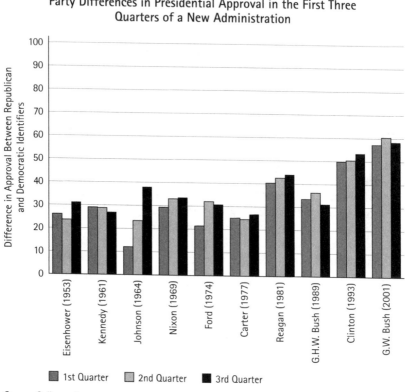

Source: Gallup polls.

serve as an independent who would vote on organizational matters with
the Democrats.[16] Jeffords's defection raised a new roadblock to the
administration's goals, giving Democrats a platform to resist the president
and to articulate a competing agenda. By late summer the Bush administration seemed stuck in the doldrums. Then, on September 11, 2001,
everything changed.

---

[16] Jeffords explained his decision as a direct reaction to the Bush administration's policies: "Looking
ahead, I can see more and more instances when I will disagree with the President on very fundamental
issues—issues of choice, the direction of the judiciary, tax and spending decisions, missile defense,
energy and environment and . . . other issues large and small"; see CQ Weekly, May 26, 2001, 1243.

AFTER SEPTEMBER 11

The Washington community responded to the terrorist attacks of September 11, 2001, on the World Trade Center in New York City and the Pentagon in Washington with a remarkable display of bipartisan unity. The day's events awakened human responses that transcended party; conservative Republican Dick Armey was observed draping a consoling arm around Maxine Waters, among the House's most liberal African American Democrats. Republican and Democratic leaders found themselves getting acquainted in a new way as they shared an emergency bunker while waiting out the immediate threat of further attacks.[17] President Bush received a thundering bipartisan ovation as he addressed a joint session of Congress on the crisis. In the days that followed, bipartisan consultation and cooperation flourished as Congress quickly complied with the president's requests for emergency legislation to deal with the consequences of the attack. Only a single member of Congress[18] voted against the joint resolution passed on September 14 authorizing the president "to use all necessary and appropriate force against the nations, organizations, or people that he determines planned, authorized, committed, or aided the terrorist attacks on the United States that occurred September 11, 2001" (PL 107-40). A week later, the airline relief bill (PL 107-42) passed 356 to 54 in the House, 96 to 1 in the Senate. A broad antiterrorism bill requested by the administration (PL 107-56) passed 357 to 66 in the House, 98 to 1 in the Senate during the last week of October.

The bipartisan unity displayed by Congress in its response to the president's call for action against terrorism was echoed in public, and Americans of all political persuasions rallied around their president.[19] As documented earlier in Figure 1.1, Bush's approval ratings shot up from the 50s to the highest levels ever recorded, topping 90 percent in some September and October polls. The largest change by far occurred among Democratic identifiers (Figure 1.2). Approval of Bush among Democrats

---

[17] Janet Hook, "Under the Shadow of War, Congress Declares a Truce," *Los Angeles Times,* September 22, 2001, A21.

[18] Democratic Representative Barbara Lee of California.

[19] The rally-round-the-flag phenomenon is discussed most thoroughly in John E. Mueller, *War, Presidents, and Public Opinion* (New York: John Wiley and Sons, 1973), 208–213, and Richard A. Brody, *Assessing the President: The Media, Elite Opinion, and Public Support* (Stanford, CA: Stanford University Press, 1991), ch. 3.

jumped almost overnight by more than 50 percentage points, from an average of less than 30 percent in the summer before September 11 to an average of 81 percent in the month following the attacks. Support also rose among Republicans (to 98 percent in polls taken through October), but it was already so high (89 percent) that the Republican contribution to the overall rise could be only modest. Independents approximated the national figures, going from an average of 52 percent approving before September 11 to an average of 86 percent approving over the next month.

The rally was by no means confined to the president, however. Approval of Congress reached 84 percent in one October Gallup poll, topping its previous all-time high by 27 percentage points (Figure 4.2). The proportion rating House Speaker Dennis Hastert's performance as "excellent" or "pretty good" rose from 27 percent in August to 52 percent

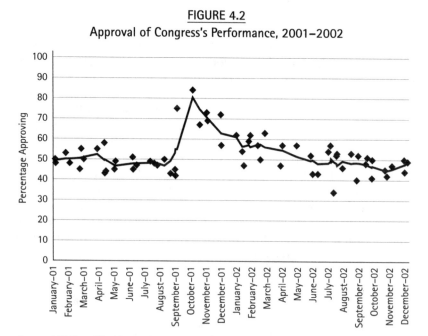

FIGURE 4.2
Approval of Congress's Performance, 2001–2002

Source: ABC News/*Washington Post,* CBS News/*New York Times, Los Angeles Times,* NBC News/*Wall Street Journal,* and Gallup polls, at http://www.pollingreport.com/CongJob1.htm (accessed March 22, 2005).

in October; the equivalent ratings of Senate majority leader Tom Daschle went from 26 percent to 60 percent.[20] There were also sharp increases in positive responses to questions about the direction of the country, trust in government, satisfaction with the United States, even assessments of the economy.[21] A naïve observer might wonder why a spectacular failure of a government to deliver that most basic of public goods, protection from foreign attack, would inspire a dramatic surge in approval of its leaders and institutions. But of course, the public's reaction reflected a radical change in the context in which people responded to such survey questions. The president was now to be evaluated as the defender of the nation against shadowy foreign enemies rather than as a partisan figure of dubious legitimacy. Congress stood for once as the institutional embodiment of American democracy rather than as the playground of self-serving politicians addicted to petty partisan bickering. For a time, politicians and government institutions enjoyed the kind of broad public support normally reserved for such national symbols as the flag and the Constitution. With Americans just coming to grips with the countless ways their society was vulnerable and, by way of illustration, being spooked by deadly anthrax spores mailed to news organizations and political leaders, this was not the moment to point fingers or to doubt their institutions and leaders.

The moment did not last, of course, and by the summer of 2002, the effects of the rally had all but disappeared—except for approval of the president, which remained on average above 70 percent into July and above 60 percent through the end of the year. Indeed, Bush's ratings remained above 60 percent for sixteen months, the longest streak at this level for any president in history. The terrorist attacks had completely redefined the priorities and purpose of his presidency; Bush was now first and foremost a war president, and in that capacity, he drew overwhelming bipartisan support for his initial responses to the attacks. The public was nearly unanimous in backing the president's decision to use military

---

[20] As reported in Harris polls, August 15–22 and October 17–22, 2001, at http://pollingreport.com/h-j. htm (accessed June 24, 2005).

[21] For data on evaluations of the direction of the country, see the Gallup, *Los Angeles Times*, NBC News/*Wall Street Journal*, Ipsos-Reid/*Cook Political Report*, and Fox News/Opinion Dynamics polls at http://www.pollingreport.com (accessed January 27, 2003); for data on satisfaction with the U.S, see the Gallup polls at http://www.pollingreport.com (accessed January 27, 2003); for trust in government, see *Washington Post* and CNN/*USA Today*/Gallup polls at http://www.pollingreport.com/institut.htm (accessed July 8, 2005).

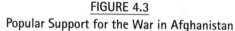

FIGURE 4.3
Popular Support for the War in Afghanistan

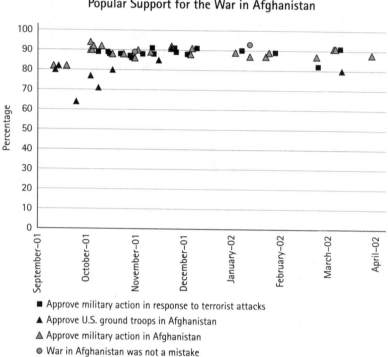

■ Approve military action in response to terrorist attacks
▲ Approve U.S. ground troops in Afghanistan
△ Approve military action in Afghanistan
◉ War in Afghanistan was not a mistake

Source: ABC News/*Washington Post*, CBS News/*New York Times*, Gallup, Pew Center for the People and the Press, Harris, Fox News, and *Newsweek* polls.

force to go after Osama bin Laden and his al Qaeda forces in Afghanistan when its Taliban government refused to hand them over (Figure 4.3). With nearly 90 percent of the public favoring military action against the terrorists, anything less might have actually cost him public support; the administration's main concern while preparing to fight in Afghanistan was to avoid the perception that it was reacting too slowly or with insufficient force.[22]

---

[22] Woodward, *Bush at War,* 150, 175, 207, 278.

Adopting the role of war president and taking decisive steps to retaliate against the attackers and their Taliban protectors, Bush began earning the comparatively high marks for his handling of the war on terrorism that buoyed his overall approval levels, albeit to varying degrees, until the end of his presidency. Initially, the shift in national focus to terrorism helped to insulate him from the full force of economic discontent that followed the dot.com crash and brief recession early in his term. Although the president sought to blame the terrorist attacks for the weak recovery, he could not escape generally negative views of his economic performance. But despite less than stellar grades on the economy, his leadership in the war on terrorism kept his overall ratings up. Normally, a president's overall job performance rating does not differ by much from his rating on handling specific policy domains, and economic perceptions help determine levels of presidential approval.[23] As Figure 4.4 indicates, this was the case with Bush before but not after September 11. Prior to the attacks, his overall rating was on average only 6 percentage points higher than his rating on the economy; for the year afterward, it averaged 18 points higher. The initial rally in approval of Bush's handling of the economy after September 11 had totally dissipated by the end of 2002, but his overall ratings continued to be bolstered for years by the higher ratings he received on terrorism.[24]

Approval of Bush's performance on terrorism also muted partisan differences on his overall performance. As we saw in Figures 1.5 and 1.6, partisans were much more sharply divided on Bush's handing of the economy than on his handling of terrorism during the year following September 11. On average, only 34 percent of Democratic identifiers approved of his handling of the economy during this period, while 69 percent approved of his handling of terrorism, helping to raise his overall rating among Democrats to an average of 58 percent. The difference between approval ratings of Republicans and Democrats was only 26 points on terrorism, compared with 45 points on the economy. High marks on terrorism—79 percent approving—also helped prop up independents' approval ratings of Bush, which averaged 72 percent overall

---

[23] Brody, *Assessing the President,* ch. 6.

[24] Unfortunately, no survey asked about his handling of terrorism after February 2008. Entries in Figure 4.4 are the lowess-smoothed data from the polls listed for Figure 1.1, based on 1,021 observations of overall approval, 323 on the economy, 411 on the Iraq war, and 254 on terrorism.

FIGURE 4.4
Approval of George W. Bush's Performance, by Policy Domain

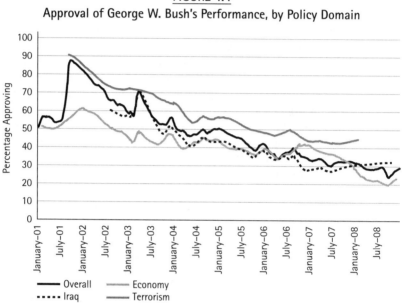

Source: ABC News/Washington Post, CBS News/New York Times, Los Angeles Times, Time, NBC News/ Wall Street Journal, Quinnipiac, Ipsos, Pew Center for the People and the Press, CNN, and Newsweek polls.

but only 51 percent on the economy. In year one of the war on terrorism, then, Bush did succeed in uniting the country behind his leadership in that mission.

Bush's strong bipartisan approval for his handling of terrorism did not, however, spill over into unrelated domestic matters. The administration's positions on energy development, taxes, abortion, prescription drug benefits, and Social Security did not become more popular after September 11; partisan divisions in the public on these issues remained as wide as ever.[25] Bush tried to use the unity generated by the war on terrorism to drum up bipartisan support for his economic stimulus proposal,

---

[25] Compare the responses to issue questions in the CBS News/New York Times polls conducted between February 2001 and January 2003.

renaming it the "economic security plan": "It's time to take the spirit of unity that has been prevalent when it comes to fighting the war and bring it to Washington, DC. The terrorists not only attacked our freedom, but they also attacked our economy. And we need to respond in unison. We ought not to revert to the old ways that used to dominate Washington, DC. The old ways is [sic]: What's more important, my country or my political party?"[26] But the attempt to delegitimize partisan opposition to the administration's economic policies fell flat; congressional Democrats felt no more pressure from their constituents to support the president's pre–September 11 domestic agenda after the attacks than they had before.

THE 2002 ELECTION

The political fallout from September 11 and its aftermath dramatically improved the Republicans' electoral prospects for 2002. Despite the steady decline from its lofty peak, Bush's approval level remained at an impressive 63 percent on election day.[27] While not as high as Bill Clinton's rating in November 1998 (66 percent), it tied Ronald Reagan's 1986 rating for the second highest in any postwar midterm election. Bush's high public approval, like that of Clinton and Reagan before him,[28] clearly helped his party's congressional candidates. Indeed, it helped in just the way that standard aggregate models of midterm congressional elections would predict.[29]

The crisis benefited Republicans in ways that went well beyond its contribution to the president's popularity. Bush's meteoric rise in public esteem shielded his administration from the consequences of financial scandals, epitomized by the collapse of Enron, involving Bush's political

---

[26] Speech on January 5, 2002, in Ontario, California, quoted in Fritz et al., *All the President's Spin*, 113.

[27] This was his rating in the final Gallup poll taken prior to the election—the measure used in standard referendum models of midterm elections—and also the average of the thirteen polls taken during the month leading up to the election.

[28] Democrats picked up five House seats in 1998; Reagan's Republicans lost only five seats in 1986, the best performance at the midterm for any Republican administration before 2002.

[29] For a discussion of such models, see Gary C. Jacobson, *The Politics of Congressional Elections*, 5th ed. (New York: Longman, 2001), 143–145, 158; for an application to 2002, see Gary C. Jacobson, "Terror, Terrain, and Turnout: Explaining the 2002 Midterm Election," *Political Science Quarterly* 118 (Spring 2003): 1–22, footnote 6.

cronies and campaign contributors.[30] It is easy to imagine how Democrats would have exploited the president's vulnerability on the issue had his status as commander in chief in the war on terrorism not put partisan criticism beyond the pale at the very time the scandals surfaced. The war on terrorism also helped deflect blame from the administration and its congressional allies for the return of budget deficits. The extraordinary expense of dealing with the physical and economic damage inflicted by the September 11 attacks and of tightening homeland security against future threats was unavoidable. Wars, after all, are always fought on borrowed money.

In addition, Bush's popularity scared off high-quality Democratic challengers. His uncommonly high approval ratings during the period when potential candidates had to make decisions about running evidently convinced politically experienced and ambitious Democrats that 2002 was not their year. As a result, Democrats fielded their weakest cohort of House challengers (in terms of prior success in winning elective public office) of any postwar election except the 1990 midterm.[31]

September 11 also shifted the political focus from domestic issues to national defense and foreign policy, moving the debates from Democratic turf to Republican turf. In preelection polls, most respondents thought the Democrats would do a better job dealing with health care, education, Social Security, prescription drug benefits, taxes, abortion, unemployment, the environment, and corporate corruption. Most thought Republicans would do the better job of dealing with terrorism, the possibility of war with Iraq, the situation in the Middle East, and foreign affairs generally.[32] Republicans held the advantage because voters put terrorism and the prospect of war at the top of the list of concerns. Without September 11,

---

[30] Enron, once the nation's seventh largest company, was a Houston-based energy conglomerate that collapsed into bankruptcy in late 2001 after the exposure of accounting schemes that had inflated its earnings by more than $1 billion. Enron's stockholders collectively lost billions of dollars, and thousands of former Enron employees had their pension savings wiped out. The head of Enron, Kenneth Lay, was a long-term supporter of fellow Texan George W. Bush and one of his leading campaign contributors. By one count Enron and its executives had contributed a total of $736,800 to Bush's various campaigns since 1993; see http://www.commondreams.org/views02/0215-01.htm (accessed March 17, 2010).

[31] Only 10.8 percent of Republican incumbents were opposed in 2002 by Democrats who had ever held elective public office, a Figure 1.9 standard deviations below the postwar mean of 24.9 percent. The postwar low was 10.1 percent in 1990.

[32] Jeffrey M. Jones, "Republicans Trail in Congressional Race Despite Advantage on Issues," Gallup News Service, September 26, 2002, at http://www.gallup.com/poll/releases/pr020926.asp?Version=p; Lydia Saad, "National Issues May Play Bigger-Than-Usual Role in Congressional Elections," Gallup News Service, October 31, 2002, at http://www.gallup.com/poll/7114/National-Issues-May-Play-BiggerThanUsual-Role-Congressional-Elections.aspx.

the election would have hinged on domestic issues, and the talk of invading Iraq, if any, would have seemed like "wagging the dog," a transparent ploy to deflect attention from the economy.[33] Instead, the Democrats' inept handling of legislation establishing a Department of Homeland Security (delaying passage until after the election in a dispute over personnel policy involving unionized government workers) gave Republicans an issue that played to their strength and that they exploited effectively in several close Senate races.

Bush's accusation that Senate opponents of his preferred version of the Homeland Security Department were "more interested in special interests in Washington and not interested in the security of the American people" provoked an outraged response and demand for an apology from Senate majority leader Tom Daschle, to which Republicans responded by accusing Daschle of being divisive.[34] With no apologies, the Republicans used the issue in Senate campaigns, most notoriously in Saxbe Chambliss's successful Senate challenge of Georgia Democrat Max Cleland, who had lost both legs and an arm in Vietnam. The Chambliss campaign featured a television ad that followed footage of Osama bin Laden and Saddam Hussein with an unflattering shot of Cleland and a voice-over claiming that he had "voted against the president's vital homeland security efforts." The ad, and Cleland's defeat, infuriated his Democratic colleagues in Washington and was arguably the single largest contributor to the post–September 11 revival of partisan acrimony on the Hill.

Bush's popularity—along with successful Republican gerrymanders in Michigan, Pennsylvania, Ohio, and Florida—helped Republicans pick up a net six House seats. They also gained a net two Senate seats, one essentially by a tragic accident.[35] Aside from reapportionment, what kept the election from duplicating the 2000 stalemate was turnout. Republicans did a better job of mobilizing their core supporters. Bush's near-universal approval among Republicans, his energetic fundraising, and his frenzied last-minute campaigning in competitive states, combined

---

[33] *Wag the Dog* is a 1997 film comedy in which a president's media advisor fakes a war in order to distract attention from the president's involvement in a sex scandal.

[34] "Gephardt Joins the Fray," at http://www.cbsnews.com/stories/2002/09/25/politics/main523246.shtml (accessed June 27, 2005).

[35] Senator Paul Wellstone of Minnesota died in a plane crash with his wife and daughters eleven days before the election; Republican Norm Coleman defeated his hastily chosen replacement, former Senator Walter Mondale, after Democrats' use of a memorial service as a partisan pep rally generated a public backlash.

with effective Republican grassroots drives to get out the vote, put Republicans over the top.[36] The election was a major victory for the president, as Republicans avoided the midterm losses usually suffered by the president's party. But it was won by mobilizing the base rather than broadening the party's appeal to independents and Democrats. The electorate was as polarized along party lines as it had been in 2000; the upsurge in national unity provoked by the war on terrorism had not brought Americans together on the issues that put them into opposite party camps prior to September 11.[37]

GOD'S INSTRUMENT

Religious conservatives were a key target of Republican mobilization efforts; by one estimate, their share of the electorate went from 14 percent in 2000 to 18 percent in 2002, foreshadowing even larger increases in 2004 (see Chapter 7).[38] Even before September 11, Bush had continued to display his religious commitments, for example, by letting it be known that he kneels in prayer every morning and studies the Bible daily and by opening cabinet meetings with a prayer.[39] He had also filled his cabinet with the faithful—most prominently Attorney General John Ashcroft, a devout Pentecostal—nominated many judges who were pro-life Catholics and evangelicals, and pursued a variety of policies pleasing to religious conservatives. These included banning federal funding for stem-cell research except for "existing lines" (of which there were far fewer available than the administration initially claimed), signing a ban on late-term abortion, and pursuing his faith-based initiatives. Bush did not always go as far as urged by leaders of religious conservatives—some wanted to ban all stem-cell research, for example—but on the whole, this part of his base had plenty of reason to be satisfied.[40]

---

[36] Mary Clare Jalonick, "Senate Changes Hands Again," *CQ Weekly,* November 9, 2002, 2907–2909; Rebecca Adams, "Georgia Republicans Energized by 'Friend to Friend' Campaign, *CQ Weekly,* November 9, 2002, 2892–2893.

[37] Gary C. Jacobson, "Terrorism, Terrain, and Turnout: Explaining the 2002 Midterm Elections," *Political Science Quarterly* 118 (Spring 2003): 3–12.

[38] Daron R. Shaw, "Door-to-Door with the GOP," *Hoover Digest* (Fall 2004) at http://www.hoover.org/publications/digest/3010066.html (accessed March 17, 2010).

[39] Judy Keen, "White House Staffers Gather for Bible Study," *USA Today,* at http://www.usatoday.com/news/washington/2002-10-13-bible-usat_x.htm (accessed June 27, 2005).

[40] James L. Guth, "George W. Bush and Religious Politics," in Steven Shier, ed., *High Risk and Big Ambition: The Presidency of George W. Bush* (Pittsburgh, PA: University of Pittsburgh Press, 2004), 129–134.

The tectonic shift in national politics generated by September 11 raised Bush's connection to conservative Christians to an entirely new level. Bush deliberately adopted Christian dualism's language of good and evil to refer to his new mission, most famously in his State of the Union address four months after the 9/11 attacks, in which he designated Iraq, Iran, and North Korea as an "axis of evil."[41] Although he stopped referring to the war on terrorism as a "crusade" after the term triggered a counterproductive backlash among Muslims, he left the sense that it was just that. An unnamed Bush family member is reported to have said, "George sees this as a religious war. He doesn't have a p.c. view of this war. His view of this is that they are trying to kill the Christians. And we the Christians will strike back with more force and more ferocity than they will ever know."[42]

Many conservative Christians, on their side, came to see Bush as God's chosen instrument in the battle between good and evil. Ralph Reed, one-time leader of the Christian Coalition and later a Republican official, told a reporter, "I've heard a lot of 'God knew something we didn't.' In the evangelical mind, the notion of an omniscient God is central to their theology. He had a knowledge nobody else had: He knew George Bush and the ability to lead in this compelling way."[43] Bush himself denied that he ever said he believed God had chosen him to lead the war on terrorism: "I think God sustains us, but I don't think I was chosen. I was chosen by the American people."[44] Yet others close to him have said otherwise: "I think, in his frame, this is what God has asked him to do."[45] And given his religious beliefs, it would be difficult to think otherwise. As he told a meeting of religious leaders in February 2002, "Events aren't moved by blind change and chance. Behind all of life and all of history there's a dedication and purpose, set by the hand of a just and faithful God."[46]

---

[41] Reported at http://transcripts.cnn.com/2002/ALLPOLITICS/01/29/bush.speech.txt/ (accessed July 5, 2005).

[42] Quoted in Peter Schweizer and Rochelle Schweizer, *The Bushes: Portrait of a Dynasty* (New York: Doubleday, 2004), 517.

[43] Dana Milbank, "Religious Right Finds Its Center in the Oval Office," *Washington Post*, December 24, 2001, A2.

[44] Quoted in Howard Fineman and Martha Brant, "This Is Our Life Now," *Newsweek,* December 3, 2001, 29.

[45] Unidentified "close friend" reported in Frank Bruni, "For President: A Mission and a Role in History," *New York Times,* September 22, 2001, A1.

[46] Quoted in Daalder and Lindsay, *America Unbound,* 89.

For people who believed Bush was God's chosen instrument to lead a global war pitting good against evil, it became a religious duty to give him unwavering, unquestioning support. In the five ABC News/*Washington Post* polls taken during the year following September 11 that asked if respondents considered themselves born-again or evangelical Christians, Bush's approval rating among white Republicans who did so (about 38 percent of all Republicans in these surveys) ranged from 98 to 100 percent. This was not so important in sustaining adequate public backing for the war in Afghanistan, which was nearly unanimous. But, as we shall see in future chapters, it became very important in sustaining support for the president and his venture in Iraq, especially after its original justifications, that Saddam Hussein possessed weapons of mass destruction and was in league with al Qaeda, became untenable.

CHAPTER 5

Going to War in Iraq

Well before September 11, the George W. Bush administration had been contemplating military action to take out Iraqi dictator Saddam Hussein and his regime. Savagely brutal to his own people, Saddam was also believed to be intent on acquiring weapons of mass destruction (WMD) in defiance of the United Nations and agreements made after the Gulf War in 1991. His past record of using chemical weapons and invading neighboring countries marked him as a continuing menace and had made "regime change" in Iraq a goal of United States policy even before Bush entered the White House. As the United States' archenemy in the Middle East, Saddam immediately became a prime suspect, second only to al Qaeda's Osama bin Laden, as the sponsor of the terrorist attacks on New York City and Washington. Some members of Bush's national security team, notably Deputy Secretary of Defense Paul Wolfowitz, argued for making Saddam's regime the first target in the war against terrorism but did not persuade the president. "I believe Iraq was involved," Bush reportedly told a meeting of his National Security Council on September 17, 2001, "but I'm not going to strike them now. I don't have the evidence at this point."[1]

The public shared the president's opinion of Saddam Hussein and was likewise ready to assume the worst. In a poll taken on September 13, 34 percent of respondents thought it "very likely" and another 44 percent thought it "somewhat likely" that Saddam was "personally involved in

---

[1] Bob Woodward, *Bush at War* (New York: Simon and Schuster, 2002), 99.

FIGURE 5.1
Support for War in Iraq Before It Began

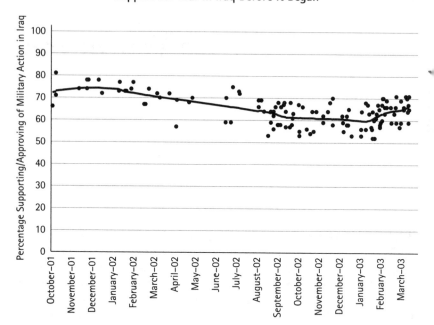

Source: 128 ABC News/*Washington Post,* CBS News/*New York Times,* Gallup, Fox News, NBC News/*Wall Street Journal,* Pew Center for the People and the Press, *Los Angeles Times,* Harris, Quinnipiac College, and *Time*/CNN polls.

Tuesday's terrorist attacks" (the comparable figures for bin Laden were 78 percent and 14 percent, respectively).[2] It is not surprising, then, that Americans generally backed military action against Iraq; in polls taken between September 2001 and March 2002, an average of 73 percent of respondents said they supported or approved of such a step (Figure 5.1).[3] Support for attacking Iraq was also largely bipartisan at this time (Figure 5.2). Large majorities of all political persuasions—on average, 80 percent of Republicans, 69 percent of Democrats, and 68 percent of independents—favored the action.

---

[2] *Time*/CNN Poll, September 13, 2001, at http://pollingreport.com/terror9.htm (accessed July 6, 2005).
[3] In a total of twenty-three polls taken by ten major media polling organizations, an average of 73.3 percent of respondents (standard deviation, 3.5 percent) approved of or supported military action in Iraq during this period; see http://pollingreport.com/iraq.htm (accessed July 6, 2005). See also Philip Everts and Pierangelo Isernia, "Trends: The War in Iraq," *Public Opinion Quarterly* 69 (Summer 2005), 291–294.

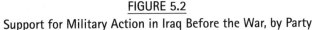

FIGURE 5.2

Support for Military Action in Iraq Before the War, by Party

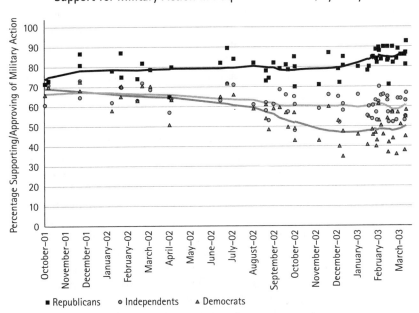

■ Republicans   ○ Independents   ▲ Democrats

Source: 57 ABC News/*Washington Post*, CBS News/*New York Times*, Gallup, Pew Center for the People and the Press, *Los Angeles Times*, Quinnipiac College, and *Time*/CNN polls.

As noted in Chapter 4, however, popular support for going after bin Laden in Afghanistan was even higher, reflecting the greater certainty of his involvement in the attacks. Bush also opted to focus on Afghanistan first, partly because the case for bin Laden's involvement was far easier to make and partly because military action could be initiated sooner, with wider international backing, and with better prospects for quick results.[4] But as early as November 21, 2001, the president told his secretary of defense, Donald Rumsfeld, to begin drafting a new war plan for Iraq. On April 7, 2002, Bush told a British television interviewer, "I made up my mind that Saddam needs to go," and in the June of that year, Bush formally announced he would order preemptive strikes against countries he considered serious

---

[4] Woodward, *Bush at War*, 49, 99.

threats to the United States.[5] Exactly when Bush made the final decision to invade Iraq remains in dispute. The administration's position was that the decision was not taken until after Secretary of State Colin Powell's speech to the United Nations on February 5, 2003, only weeks before the March 20 invasion. But other accounts, including Bob Woodward's *Plan of Attack,* leave a powerful impression that Bush had decided almost immediately after September 11 to use military force to effect regime change in Iraq if that is what it took to do it.[6] In any case, there is little question that the president believed strongly that removing Saddam and his regime was both important to American national security and morally justified by the regime's treatment of Iraq's people and neighbors. The question was how to justify initiating a preemptive (more accurately, preventive) war to Congress, the American public, and, if possible, the international community.

In May 2003, Wolfowitz told an interviewer that there were four main reasons for invading Iraq—Saddam's pursuit of WMD, his support for terrorism, the possibility that he might supply WMD to terrorists, and his brutality against his own people—but "the truth is that for reasons that have a lot to do with the United States government bureaucracy we settled on the one issue that everyone could agree on which was weapons of mass destruction as the core reason."[7] This became the centerpiece of the White House's characteristically carefully planned, tightly run campaign to persuade Americans that their security required military action to overthrow Saddam's regime. The campaign was coordinated by a high-level task force assembled by Andrew Card, the White House chief of staff, which included Karl Rove, the president's chief political advisor; communications specialists Karen Hughes, Mary Matalin, and James Wilkinson; national security advisor Condoleezza Rice; and I. Lewis Libby, Cheney's chief of staff. The group supervised a "strategic communications" staff charged with formulating and articulating the case for war. Its first fruits appeared in September 2002 because, as Card put it, "From a marketing point of view, you don't introduce new products in August."[8]

---

[5] Ibid., 131–133; Bob Woodward, *Plan of Attack* (New York: Simon and Schuster, 2004), 2, 119, 330.

[6] A *Time* article reported that Bush's response to a question on Iraq from one of three senators attending a March 2002 meeting with National Security Advisor Condoleezza Rice was "Fuck Saddam, we're taking him out"; see http://www.time.com/time/archive/preview/0,10987,1101030331-435907,00.html. The public believed Bush had made up his mind well before February 2003; in a Gallup poll taken November 22–24, 2002, 58 percent believed he had already decided to invade, while 38 percent thought he had not; see http://www.pollingreport.com/iraq4.htm (accessed March 31, 2003).

[7] Interview with Sam Tannenhaus, May 9, 2003, quoted at http://www.usatoday.com/news/world/iraq/2003-05-30-wolfowitz-iraq_x.htm (accessed July 7, 2005).

[8] Barton Gellman and Walter Pincus, "Depiction of Threat Outgrew Supporting Evidence," *Washington Post,* August 10, 2003, A01.

THE CASE FOR WAR

The administration's marketing strategy became clear immediately and was not subtle: Not only was Saddam hiding chemical and biological weapons but he was also pursuing nuclear weapons and, if successful, would use them to attack or blackmail the United States and its allies. On September 8, Rice said in an interview on CNN that "there will always be some uncertainty on how quickly he can acquire nuclear weapons, but we don't want the smoking gun to be a mushroom cloud."[9] Bush invoked the mushroom cloud again on October 7, as did General Tommy Franks, head of the United States Central Command, on November 12. Bush and Cheney also raised the specter of "nuclear blackmail" and the danger of Saddam giving nuclear weapons to terrorists.[10] The evidence that Iraq had an active program to produce nuclear weapons was, in fact, exceedingly thin, discounted by many intelligence experts, and, according to postwar investigations, specious. But the nuclear threat put the onus on Democrats or others in Washington skeptical about the need to invade Iraq to explain why the United States should take the risk of letting Saddam Hussein remain in power when the worst-case scenario was so horrific.

Bush and his spokespersons were even more adamant in claiming that, as the president put it in a Rose Garden address on September 26, "the Iraqi regime possesses biological and chemical weapons" and "is building the facilities necessary to make more biological and chemical weapons."[11] Cheney was equally unequivocal: "Simply stated, there is no doubt that Saddam now has weapons of mass destruction [and] there is no doubt that he is amassing them to use against our friends, against our allies, and against us."[12] This theme was repeated and elaborated upon until the war began; in his March 17, 2003, speech giving Saddam forty-eight hours to leave Iraq, Bush reiterated that "intelligence gathered by this and other governments leaves no doubt that the Iraq regime continues to possess and conceal some of the most lethal weapons ever devised."[13]

---

[9] Ibid.
[10] Ben Fritz, Bryan Keefer, and Brendan Nyhan, *All the President's Spin: George W. Bush, the Media, and the Truth* (New York: Simon and Schuster), 154–155.
[11] Dana Priest and Walter Pincus, "Bush Certainty on Iraq Arms Went Beyond Analysts' Views," *Washington Post*, June 7, 2003, A01.
[12] Ibid.
[13] Reported at http://www.whitehouse.gov/news/releases/2003/03/20030317-7.html.

SADDAM AND 9/11

The administration also wanted to tie Saddam to the terrorist attacks of September 11 or at least to al Qaeda more generally. The problem, as Bush had noted from the beginning, was the lack of evidence. And although the administration mobilized United States intelligence agencies to look for connections—Donald Rumsfeld, secretary of defense, reportedly asked the CIA on ten separate occasions for evidence linking Saddam to September 11—nothing tangible could be found.[14] Cheney and some of his staff claimed the link was a meeting in April 2001 between Mohammed Atta, the hijackers' leader, and an Iraqi agent in Prague, but the evidence that the meeting had taken place was weak and was eventually discredited in the *9/11 Commission Report*.[15] On somewhat more solid ground was the claim, articulated by Secretary of State Colin Powell in his February 5, 2003, speech to the United Nations asking its approval for removing Hussein, that al Qaeda allies, notably Abu Musab al-Zarqawi, were active in Iraq, suggesting a "potentially much more sinister nexus between Iraq and the al-Qaida terrorist network."[16] The problem here was that the sinister activities Powell described—mainly training al Qaeda recruits in use of poisons—went on in a Kurdish area of Iraq not under Saddam's control, although al-Zarqawi—a terrorist but not a member of al Qaeda—had been in Baghdad for medical treatment.

The thinness of the evidence for Saddam's complicity in the September 11 attacks and his plotting with al Qaeda did not stop the president and his team from repeatedly linking Saddam rhetorically with the terrorist attacks. For example, in an address to the nation on October 7, 2002, Bush put it this way: "Some citizens wonder, 'After 11 years of living with this [Saddam Hussein] problem, why do we need to confront it now?' And there's a reason. We have experienced the horror of September the 11th. We have seen that those who hate America are willing to crash airplanes into buildings full of innocent people. Our enemies would be no less willing, in fact, they would be eager, to use biological or chemical, or a nuclear weapon." In the same speech, he reminded Americans that

---

[14] Daniel Eisenberg, "We're Taking Him Out," *Time*, May 13, 2002, at http://archives.cnn.com/2002/ALLPOLITICS/05/06/time.out/ (accessed July 7, 2005).

[15] Official United States government version, 228–229.

[16] Remarks to the United Nations Security Council, at http://www.globalsecurity.org/wmd/library/news/iraq/2003/iraq-030205-powell-un-17300pf.htm (accessed July 7, 2005).

"after September the 11th, Saddam Hussein's regime gleefully celebrated the terrorist attacks on America."[17] Rice, asked if there was any hard evidence linking the Iraqi government to September 11 and al Qaeda, replied: "There is certainly evidence al Qaeda people have been in Iraq. There is certainly evidence that Saddam Hussein cavorts with terrorists," and then added, "I think if you asked, do we know that he had a role in 9/11, no we do not know that he had a role in 9/11. But I think that this is the test that sets a bar that is far too high."[18] House Speaker Dennis Hastert was even less equivocal: "There is no doubt that Iraq supports and harbors those terrorists who wish harm to the United States. Is there a direct connection between Iraq and al Qaeda? The president thinks so."[19] Rumsfeld told a Chamber of Commerce luncheon audience in September that the case for links between al Qaeda and Saddam's government was "bulletproof."[20]

Although, like Rice, Bush and others speaking for the administration admitted when questioned directly that there was no hard evidence that Saddam had a hand in September 11, they nonetheless conveyed to the public the impression that they believed it was true. In a poll taken in December 2003, just before Saddam's capture, 57 percent of respondents said they thought the Bush administration believed Saddam was involved in September 11, while only 25 percent thought the administration believed he was not.[21] Perhaps more revealing, of respondents asked in a January 2003 survey to estimate "how many of the September 11 terrorists were Iraqi citizens" and given a range of options, 21 percent chose "most," 23 percent, "some," 6 percent, "one," and only 17 percent got it right: "none."[22] Prior suspicions and all the rhetoric associating Iraq with al Qaeda evidently left half the public with the false impression that Iraqis had been in on the hijackings.

---

[17] "President George W. Bush's Address Regarding Iraq," White House press release, October 7, 2002, archived at http://www.johnstonsarchive.net/terrorism/bushiraq.html (accessed July 7, 2005).

[18] Interview with Condoleezza Rice conducted by Wolf Blitzer, *CNN Late Edition*, September 8, 2002, at http://www.mtholyoke.edu/acad/intrel/bush/wolf.htm (accessed July 7, 2005).

[19] Gebe Martinez, "Concerns Linger for Lawmakers Following Difficult Vote for War," *CQ Weekly*, October 12, 2002, 2673.

[20] Eric Schimtt, "Rumsfeld Says United States Has 'Bulletproof' Evidence of Iraq's Links to al Qaeda," *New York Times*, September 28, 2002, A1.

[21] CBS News/*New York Times* Poll, December 12–15, 2003.

[22] The remaining 33 percent did not know; see the Knight Ridder poll, January 3–6, 2003, at http://www.pollingreport.com/iraq4.htm (accessed March 31, 2003). Although there is some uncertainty about the identities of some of the hijackers, fifteen were evidently from Saudi Arabia, two from the United Arab Emirates, one from Lebanon, and one, the leader Mohammed Atta, from Egypt.

It is unclear whether Bush and his senior officials continued to believe Saddam was complicit in September 11 as, despite their best efforts, United States intelligence agencies continued to come up short in their search for a connection. Rumsfeld's maxim that "the absence of evidence is not evidence of absence"[23] was (and remains) available to anyone who wanted to believe in Saddam's involvement.[24] There is little doubt, however, that Bush and his advisors were certain that Iraq was hiding WMD, as were most outside experts, American and foreign. Saddam's history of producing and using such weapons, his government's evasive dealings with UN weapons inspectors, the biological and chemical weapons material Iraq possessed prior to the Gulf War in 1991 that was still not accounted for, and plenty of other circumstantial if inconclusive evidence made it easy to believe that hidden WMD must exist. When Bush reacted to the case for WMD presented by the CIA at a December 21, 2002, meeting with "This is the best we've got?" George Tenet, director of the agency, reassured him: "Don't worry, it's a slam dunk."[25] If there were skeptics, at home or abroad, they would be confounded when Iraq fell and the United States forces exposed Saddam's hidden caches.[26] More to the point, Bush and his advisors were far more worried about failing to do enough than about doing too much in defending the nation from further terrorist assaults. The worst-case scenarios used to bring the public and Congress on board, however unlikely, were certainly frightening enough to make leaders more cautious than Bush willing to initiate a war.

THE PUBLIC'S RESPONSE

The Bush administration's campaign to muster public support for a preventive war against Iraq ultimately succeeded, but to a greater extent with Republicans than with Democrats and independents, and Americans on the whole displayed a stubborn reluctance to go to war without the support

---

[23] "Rumsfeld Says Iraqis Growing More Confident About Country's Future," Defense Department report, August 5, 2003, at http://www.globalsecurity.org/wmd/library/news/iraq/2003/08/iraq-030805-usia03.htm (accessed July 8, 2005).

[24] Woodward, *Plan of Attack*, 290–292.

[25] Ibid., 249.

[26] As Bush told Woodward in an interview in Crawford, Texas, on August 20, 2002, "Confident action that will yield positive results provides kind of a slipstream into which reluctant nations and leaders can get behind and show themselves that there has been—you know, something positive has happened toward peace." In Woodward, *Bush at War*, 341.

FIGURE 5.3
The Public's Beliefs in Justifications for the Iraq War Before It Began

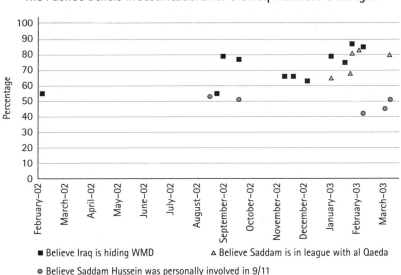

■ Believe Iraq is hiding WMD   △ Believe Saddam is in league with al Qaeda

● Believe Saddam Hussein was personally involved in 9/11

Source: ABC News/*Washington Post*, CBS News/*New York Times*, Gallup, Fox News, Knight Ridder, and CNN/*Time* polls.

of the United Nations or traditional allies. The chief justification for invading Iraq—that Saddam was hiding WMD—was accepted by a majority of Americans from the beginning, and acceptance rose to greater than 80 percent during the months leading up to the invasion (Figure 5.3). Partisan differences on this question were relatively small, on the order of 15 percentage points, and did not grow over the period leading up to the war. Beliefs about Hussein's personal involvement in September 11 remained essentially unchanged, with about half the public believing he was involved (again, partisan differences were small, fewer than 10 percentage points). However, the belief that Saddam was in league with al Qaeda was much more widespread, exceeding 80 percent in February and March 2003. An even larger share of respondents—86 to 88 percent—thought Saddam was "involved in supporting terrorist groups that have plans to attack the United States."[27] About three-quarters of the public believed

---

[27] CNN/*USA Today*/Gallup Poll, August 5–8, 2002, and March 14–15, 2003, at http://www.pollingreport.com/iraq.htm (accessed March 31, 2003).

that if Iraq acquired nuclear weapons, Saddam would use them against the United States[28] or his neighbors.[29] Four of five Americans accepted the general proposition that Iraq posed a threat to the United States.[30]

That most Americans believed that Hussein was hiding WMD, conniving with al Qaeda terrorists, and threatening the United States did not, however, necessarily mean that they believed the administration had made a convincing case for preventive war. Asked in six ABC News/ *Washington Post* polls taken between September 12, 2002, and February 1, 2003, "Do you think Bush has presented enough evidence showing why the United States should use military force to remove Saddam Hussein from power, or would you like him to present more evidence?" an average of only 41 percent thought he had presented enough evidence, while 57 percent wanted to see more.[31] Later, in February and March 2003, when the question did not include the option of seeing more evidence, a larger proportion said that the administration had produced enough evidence, but it still amounted to a modest majority, an average of 54 percent in eight surveys.[32] Partisan differences on these questions were substantial. In the first set of polls, an average of 59 percent of Republicans thought the evidence was sufficient, compared to only 28 percent of Democrats; in the second, the comparable figures were 77 percent and 37 percent.

Agreement with the premises of the war did not mean that Americans gave Bush an automatic green light to invade Iraq. Although the administration claimed it already had full authority to act,[33] large

---

[28] Fox News/Opinion Dynamics Poll, January 14–15, 2003, and CNN/*USA Today*/Gallup Poll, September 13–16, 2002, at http://www.pollingreport.com/iraq.htm (accessed March 31, 2003).

[29] *Newsweek* Poll, March 13–14, 2003, at http://www.pollingreport.com/iraq.htm (accessed March 31, 2003).

[30] In four ABC News/*Washington Post* polls taken in September and December 2002 and January and March 2003, the share of the public expressing this belief was 79 percent, 81 percent, 81 percent, and 79 percent, respectively. See http://www.pollingreport.com/iraq.htm (accessed March 31, 2003).

[31] ABC News/*Washington Post* polls, September 12–14, 2002; December 12–15, 2002; January 16–20, 2003; January 27, 2003; January 28, 2003; and January 30–February 1, 2003; at http://www.pollingreport. com/iraq.htm (accessed March 31, 2003). The distribution of responses showed no trend over these months.

[32] CBS News/*New York Times* polls February 5–6, 2003; February 10–12, 2003; March 4–5, 2003; March 7–9, 2003; and March 15–16, 2003; ABC News/*Washington Post* polls, January 30–February 1, 2003; February 5, 2003; and February 6–9, 2003; all at http://www.pollingreport.com/iraq.htm (accessed March 31, 2003). A slightly higher proportion—56 percent and 57 percent, respectively, in February and March Gallup polls—said they thought the Bush administration had "made a convincing case about the need for the United States to take military action against Iraq." See http://www.pollingreport. com/iraq.htm (accessed March 31, 2003).

[33] Miles A. Pomper, "Senate Democrats in Disarray After Gephardt's Deal on Iraq," *CQ Weekly*, October 5, 2002, 2606.

FIGURE 5.4

"Would you Support or Oppose United States Military Action [Against Iraq] in this Circumstance?"

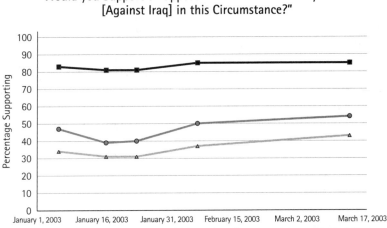

- ■ The United States joined together with its major allies to attack Iraq, with the full support of the United Nations Security Council

- ● The United States and one or two of its major allies attacked Iraq, without the support of the United Nations

- ▲ The United States acted alone in attacking Iraq, without the support of the United Nations

Source: Newsweek polls, at http://www.pollingreport.com/iraq2.htm, 11–12 (accessed March 31, 2003).

majorities—including majorities of Republicans—wanted the president to get Congress's approval first.[34] If the president and Congress disagreed on going to war, large majorities also wanted Congress rather than the president to have the last word.[35] Moreover, the public wanted the administration to get the backing of America's traditional allies and the United Nations before taking action. As Figure 5.4 shows, support for attacking Iraq was much higher if the United States was joined by allies and the UN; with only one or two major allies (the eventual case), support barely passed 50 percent on the eve of the war. Most did not

---

[34] In the four CBS News/*New York Times* polls taken between August 6 and October 10, 2002, an average of 69 percent of respondents wanted Bush to get congressional authorization first, including 57 percent of Republicans and 75 percent of Democrats.

[35] It was Congress over Bush, 59 to 37 and 61 to 34 in the ABC News polls of August 7–11 and August 29, 2002; see http://www.pollingreport.com/iraq5.htm (accessed March 31, 2003).

want the United States to go it alone if that was the only option, although support for unilateral action rose just before the onset of the war. In nineteen surveys taken between February 2002 and March 2003 (using a variety of question wordings), the option of invading Iraq without UN support was backed on average by only 33 percent of respondents and never received majority support; a majority (averaging 55 percent) always preferred invading only with UN approval, with the remainder not wanting to invade at all. These averages did not change much as the war approached; in the eight polls taken in February and March 2003, an average of 36 percent supported action without UN approval, and 58 percent, only with it.[36]

BRINGING CONGRESS ON BOARD

With public opinion as clear-cut, it was politically infeasible to ignore Congress and the UN in steering the course toward war, no matter what the administration believed about the president's existing authority to act. Bush had relatively little difficulty winning congressional support for a resolution giving him wide latitude in deciding whether or when to invade Iraq, which he requested in a prime-time speech on October 7, 2002. Although many Democrats were reluctant to give the president such broad authority, the resolution passed the House on October 10 by 296 to 133, with substantial Democratic support (81 to 126; among Republicans, the vote was 215 to 6). The Senate vote the next day was 77 to 23, with a majority of Democrats (29 to 21) and all but one of the 49 Republicans backing it.[37] Some Democrats justified supporting the resolution as a way of putting pressure on the UN to act more forcefully on renewing demands for weapons inspections in Iraq, with the ultimate goal of avoiding war.[38] Others feared political attacks questioning their devotion to national security in the upcoming midterm election, less than

---

[36] Philip Everts and Pierangelo Isernia, "The Polls—Trends: The War in Iraq," *Public Opinion Quarterly* 69 (Summer 2005): 302.

[37] Gebe Martinez, "Concerns Linger for Lawmakers Following Difficult Vote for War," *CQ Weekly,* October 12, 2002, 2671.

[38] Miles A. Pomper, "Senate Democrats in Disarray After Gephardt's Deal on Iraq," *CQ Weekly,* October 5, 2002, 2606.

a month away. (Many congressional Democrats suspected the preelection timing of the request for authority was not accidental, and their partisans evidently agreed, with 56 percent of Democrats but only 12 percent of Republicans believing that Bush was "deliberately using the talk of war in Iraq to distract attention from other issues in this year's congressional elections."[39]) But it was the memory of September 11 and the specter of mushroom clouds that produced greater Democratic support for the resolution than Bush's father had gotten for the Gulf War in 1991. In light of the dire threat depicted by the administration and genuine uncertainties about Saddam's weapons, associations, and intentions, prudence lay in not opposing the war. If it turned out to be unjustified, unnecessary, or disastrous in some way, Bush would get the primary blame. But if Democrats opposed the war and Saddam's complicity in September 11 and possession of WMD were confirmed, or if the Iraqi people welcomed Americans as liberators and democracy blossomed from the ashes of Saddam's sadistic regime, Democrats could face a political reckoning. Worse, if they succeeded in hindering the president's plans and another terrorist attack occurred on American soil, no matter what its provenance, they could wind up scapegoats.

Bush had a much tougher time getting United States allies and the UN on board and largely failed, although the effort helped to increase public support for the action that was eventually taken by his "coalition of the willing." Speaking at the UN on September 12, 2002, the president told the organization to enforce its resolutions against Iraq or else the United States would do so by itself; however, he also asked for further "necessary resolutions" from the UN Security Council authorizing action if Saddam refused full compliance. On November 8, the Security Council unanimously passed a resolution imposing tough new arms inspections on Iraq and threatening "serious consequences" if Saddam resisted, but the resolution did not include the automatic authority for war on any Iraqi failure to comply that the administration had wanted; a second resolution would be necessary to get the UN's approval to use force. Saddam backed down, and on November 18, UN weapons inspectors returned to Iraq for the first time since 1998. Their searches turned up

---

[39] *Newsweek* Poll, September 26–27, 2002, at http://www.pollingreport.com/iraq4.htm (accessed March 31, 2003).

no solid evidence of WMD, and Iraq denied having any, but there was enough missing information and uncooperative behavior to convince administration hawks that Saddam was continuing his cynical games of deception.

In his State of the Union address on January 28, 2003, the president announced that he was prepared to invade Iraq even without a UN mandate. Nonetheless, Secretary of State Colin Powell was dispatched to the UN to make the case for war on the basis of United States intelligence, which he did in a 76-minute speech on February 5. Powell was the administration's most popular figure—he enjoyed approval ratings at the time of around 75 percent and favorability ratings of around 85 percent, both figures substantially higher than the president's[40]—and Powell was known to be less eager for war than Rumsfeld, Cheney, and other administration hawks, so his presentation had an impact on American public opinion, if not on the Security Council. This may have been its principal objective: not only to have the administration's most credible voice articulate the most persuasive case it could muster for war, but also to show it had made every effort to get the UN's approval and help before taking the unpopular step of going to war without it.

POPULAR SUPPORT FOR A DISCRETIONARY WAR

A majority of Americans had supported military action to take out Saddam Hussein ever since September 11, but by margins that had been trending downward until early February 2003, after which the Bush administration's campaign succeeded in boosting support for the war by about 5 percentage points (see Figure 5.1). In polls taken in the final week before the war began, an average of about two-thirds of respondents backed going to war. But as Figure 5.2 indicates, partisan differences in support for war in Iraq grew over time, especially after September 2002, when the administration began its concerted effort to make the case for taking action. Large majorities of Republicans backed war all along; their support rose another 10 percentage points or so after the

---

[40] See his ratings for the period September 2002–February 2003 in various polls reported at http://pollingreport.com/p.htm (accessed July 14, 2005).

first of the year and stood at close to 90 percent just before the war began. Support for war declined among Democrats after September and typically remained below 50 percent until just before the onset of fighting. Even then, as late as March 16, 2003, 64 percent of Democrats (compared with 30 percent of Republicans) said the United States should "wait and give the United Nations and weapons inspectors more time" rather than "take military action against Iraq fairly soon."[41] The proportion of Republicans who thought that "Iraq presents such a clear and present danger to American interests that the United States needs to act now, even without support of its allies" grew from 34 percent in August–October 2002 polls to 58 percent in February 2003 polls, while the proportion of Democrats taking this view scarcely budged, moving from 20 percent to 22 percent.[42] In March 2003, 62 percent of Republicans answered a parallel question in which "United Nations" was substituted for "allies" by saying the United States should act rather than wait for UN approval, compared with only 22 percent of Democrats.[43] On all of these questions, independents were on average much closer to Democrats than to Republicans.[44] Clearly, even when they believed that regime change in Iraq was imperative, most Democrats and independents remained reluctant to resort to force and opposed to unilateral action on the part of the United States. People whose prior attitudes did not incline them to trust Bush or his advisors seemed to be looking to America's European allies and the UN weapons inspectors to provide independent confirmation of the administration's rationale for an invasion of Iraq before giving it their complete backing.[45]

Such as it was, support among Democrats and, to a lesser extent, independents for military action depended crucially on beliefs that Iraq possessed WMD and that Saddam Hussein had been personally involved in

---

[41] CBS News/*New York Times* Poll, March 15–16, 2003, at http://www.pollingreport.com/iraq2.htm (accessed March 31, 2003).

[42] CBS News/*New York Times* polls, March 4–5, 2003; August 6–7, 2002; September 2–5, 2002; October 3–5, 2002; February 10–12, 2003; and February 24–25, 2003; at http://www.pollingreport.com/iraq. htm (accessed March 31, 2003).

[43] CBS News/*New York Times* Poll, March 4–5, 2003, at http://www.pollingreport.com/iraq.htm (accessed March 31, 2003).

[44] The distribution of responses among independents typically falls about one-third of the way across the gap between the Democrats' and the Republicans' distributions on these questions.

[45] On the importance of international validation for public support of United States military actions, see I. M. Destler and Stephen Kull, *Misreading the Public: The Myth of a New Isolationism* (Washington, DC: Brookings Institution Press, 1999).

FIGURE 5.5

Beliefs About WMD and Saddam Hussein's Involvement in 9/11 and Approval of Military Action to Remove Hussein from Power (September 2002)

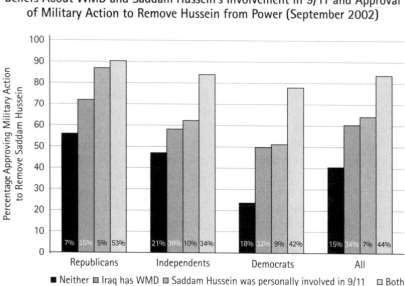

■ Neither ▨ Iraq has WMD ▨ Saddam Hussein was personally involved in 9/11 □ Both

Note: The percentage of respondents in each category is listed at the bottom of the column.
Source: ABC News/*Washington Post* Poll, September 23–26, 2002.

the terrorist attacks of September 11. Figures 5.5 and 5.6, based on polls taken at the beginning and end of the administration's campaign to mobilize support for attacking Iraq, illustrate this point. In September 2002, people who believed Saddam's regime was guilty on both counts were much more supportive of war than those who believed it was guilty on neither, but with effects far more pronounced for Democrats than for Republicans. Those believing in only one of the charges fell in between. By February 2003, large majorities of Republicans had come to support military action regardless of which charges they believed; moreover, 97 percent accepted at least one of the two grounds for going to war, and more than half accepted both. Substantial majorities of independents who accepted either one or both (about 85 percent of independents in this poll) also supported military action. Among Democrats, only the third that believed both charges favored going to war (slightly more than 70 percent of that group favored war); support for war among those

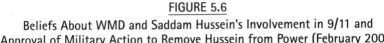

FIGURE 5.6
Beliefs About WMD and Saddam Hussein's Involvement in 9/11 and Approval of Military Action to Remove Hussein from Power (February 2003)

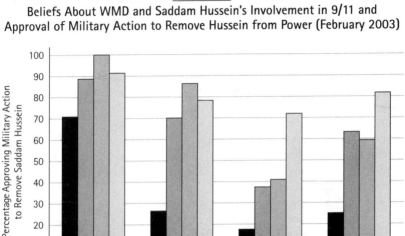

Note: The percentage of respondents in each category is listed at the bottom of the column.
Source: CBS News/New York Times Poll, February 10–12, 2003.

who believed only one of the charges was around 40 percent, and among the minority who believed neither, it was below 20 percent.

On the eve of the Iraq War, then, partisan divisions on its wisdom and necessity were substantial, on the order of 35–40 percentage points. As we shall see in the next chapter, this partisan gap was much wider than it had been for other military actions involving the United States since the Second World War. In part, this gap reflected the prior polarized evaluations of Bush himself; support for war was, of course, highly correlated with presidential approval.[46] But the gap also reflected the fact that, more than any of the other comparable United States military actions,

---

[46] The direction of causality is of course hopelessly ambiguous, but across partisan categories in the February 2003 poll used for Figure 5.5, support for the war was 36–49 points higher among those who approved of Bush's performance, and approval of Bush's performance was 33–50 points higher among respondents who supported going to war.

the Iraq War was discretionary and preventive. The Iraqi regime had not attacked the United States or any of its allies, nor was it currently engaged in a civil war against a faction backed by the United States. Although the war's proximate provocation was the terrorist attacks of September 11—and the administration's mobilization campaign did include insinuations of Saddam's involvement—the war's public justification was not retaliation but prevention, leaving both the need for war and the urgency of taking action open to question. The UN Security Council and major European allies, including France and Germany, were not convinced, so it is not surprising that Americans not predisposed by partisanship to follow George W. Bush's lead would also be inclined to doubt that war was necessary or, if it was, could not be put off while diplomacy was given more time.

The evidence justifying the war was underwhelming even for some of the president's staunchest supporters in Congress. After a meeting on February 5, 2003, in which Bush and Rice briefed twenty key members of Congress on war plans, Senator John Warner (R-VA.), chair of the Senate Armed Services Committee, reportedly told a senior aide to Rice, "You got to do this and I'll support you, make no mistake. But I sure hope you find weapons of mass destruction because if you don't you may have a big problem."[47] Not least, it could be added, with those segments of the American public whose support for the war depended on belief in this rationale.

---

[47] Woodward, *Plan of Attack*, 309.

CHAPTER **6**

Illusion, Disillusion, and Faith in the President After "Mission Accomplished"

The Iraq War began with the launch of Operation Iraqi Freedom on March 20, 2003. The initial military phase of the war was a swift and stunning success; the British took Basra on April 7, Baghdad fell to American forces on April 9, the Kurds took control of Kirkuk on April 11. The most fearsome consequences of invading Iraq envisioned before the war—burning oil fields, chemical or biological weapons used against United States forces, Iraqi attacks on Israel, uprisings in other Middle Eastern countries, terrorist operations in the United States homeland, bloody house-to-house combat in major Iraqi cities, thousands of United States casualties, mass destruction of Iraqi cities, widespread civilian deaths, millions of refugees—did not materialize.[1] The sense of relief among political leaders and ordinary Americans alike was palpable. Pictures of celebrating Iraqis and the exposure of mass graves of Saddam's victims and the torture chambers where they had suffered underlined the point that, no matter what else it may have accomplished, the war had at least deposed a sadistic tyrant. Bush celebrated the victory on May 1 by landing on the aircraft carrier *Abraham Lincoln* in full flight regalia to greet sailors returning from the Middle East. A huge sign reading "Mission Accomplished" served as

---

[1] The public had shared many of these fears; in a *Newsweek* poll taken March 13–14, 2003, 76 percent thought "Iraq would retaliate by using biological or chemical weapons against the United States," and 73 percent thought, against Israel; 82 percent thought war "would inspire terrorist attacks against American citizens," and 69 percent thought "it would cause serious problems for the United States throughout the Arab world"; see http://www.pollingreport.com/iraq2.htm (accessed March 31, 2003).

the backdrop for his nationally televised speech from the carrier's deck, in which he declared that "major combat operations in Iraq have ended. In the Battle of Iraq, the United States and our allies have prevailed."[2]

The battle may have been won, but the war was not over. Although the worst fears had not been realized, unanticipated troubles appeared immediately with the complete collapse of law and order, widespread and destructive looting, incidents of summary vengeance, and the beginnings of an insurgency that only intensified over the following months. Prewar testimony by administration officials that Iraqi oil revenues would pay for the war or that other nations would pitch in in a major way[3] turned out to be wildly optimistic, as did low-ball estimates of the war's drain on the United States treasury. Extensive corruption as well as lack of security hampered reconstruction; the trashed and looted infrastructure made life difficult for ordinary Iraqis, souring many on both their American liberators and the new Iraqi government being constructed under their sponsorship. More than two years after the main fighting had stopped, Iraqi oil production had yet to return to prewar levels, power and gas shortages continued to plague the country, and the Iraqi people were still beset with high levels of criminal and political violence.

Amid these difficulties, the Bush administration faced an escalating embarrassment: the search for Iraq's caches of WMD and evidence of Saddam's links to terrorists targeting the United States continued to come up empty handed. Any dreams Bush and his advisors may have entertained of a "told you so" reckoning with leaders of France, Germany, and other countries who had blocked UN support for the war melted away; that satisfaction (diplomatically implicit) belonged to those who had argued that the UN had Saddam contained, and it gave them an excuse to stint on help in dealing with the war's expensive aftermath.

It was many months before the administration publicly conceded that prewar intelligence on Iraq's WMD had been faulty. In an interview with Bob Woodward on December 10, 2003, the president acknowledged that WMD had not been found but only on the condition that Woodward not publish that information until his book came out months later.[4] On January 28, 2004, David McKay, former head of the United States weapons

---

[2] Text of speech displayed at http://www.cbsnews.com/stories/2003/05/01/iraq/main551946.shtml (accessed July 15, 2005).
[3] Warren Vieth, "War with Iraq: Iraq Debts Could Add Up to Trouble," *Los Angeles Times*, April 4, 2003, A1.
[4] Bob Woodward, *Plan of Attack* (New York: Simon and Schuster, 2004), 423.

inspection team in Iraq, told the Senate Intelligence Committee that no WMD had been found and that prewar intelligence had been "almost all wrong."[5] But he continued to regard Iraq as a threat because it retained the know-how and intent to produce biological and chemical weapons once UN sanctions were lifted. Bowing to strong political pressure after McKay's testimony, Bush reluctantly appointed a commission to look into the intelligence failures, admitting in a television interview on the subject in February that WMD caches had yet to be found. The commission was to report in March 2005, five months after the 2004 presidential election.[6] On March 2, 2004, the UN weapons inspection teams reported that Iraq had possessed no WMD of any significance after 1994. The CIA' s Iraq Survey Group's leader, Charles Duelfer, told the Senate Armed Services Committee on October 4, 2004, that they had found no evidence that Iraq had produced WMD since 1991, when UN sanctions had been imposed.[7] In January 2005, the United States military forces officially abandoned the search for WMD without having found any. Thus, the main *casus belli* was discredited, but gradually enough to allow the administration plenty of time to recast its prewar arguments and revise its public case for the war.

REVISING THE CASE FOR WAR

Revise it they did. Talk shifted from Saddam's WMD to his WMD *program*. In an April 25, 2003, interview, for example, Bush declared, "I think there's going to be skepticism until people find out there was, in fact, a weapons of mass destruction program," adding later, "we know he had a weapons of mass destruction program."[8] On May 6, responding to a question about evidence of a biological weapons lab, Bush repeated the phrase "weapons program" fourteen times. On June 9, when asked if United States credibility was on the line regarding WMD in Iraq, he replied, "I'm not exactly sure what that means. Iraq had a weapons program. Intelligence throughout the decade showed they had a weapons program. I am absolutely convinced that with time we'll find out they did have

---

[5] Ibid., 434.
[6] "Meet the Press with Tom Russert," February 7, 2004, at http://www.msnbc.msn.com/id/4179618 (accessed July 19, 2005).
[7] Testimony based on "Comprehensive Report of the Special Advisor to the DCI on Iraq's WMD," September 30, 2004, at https://www.cia.gov/library/reports/general-reports-1/iraq_wmd_2004/ index.html (accessed March 16, 2010).
[8] *Dateline NBC*, NBC, April 25, 2003, quoted in Ben Fritz, Bryan Keefer, and Brendan Nyhan, *All the President's Spin* (New York: Simon and Schuster, 2004), 192.

a weapons program."[9] On June 10, the president's press secretary, Ari Fleisher, said that "when the president talked about weapons programs, he includes weapons of mass destruction in that" and confirmed that he meant that Bush used the terms interchangeably.[10] In December, when Bush was asked by Diane Sawyer of ABC News about the distinction between "stated as a hard fact, that there were weapons of mass destruction" and "the possibility that [Saddam] could move to acquire the weapons still," Bush replied, "What's the difference?"[11]

At one point the president even claimed that biological weapons had been found, telling a Polish television interviewer, "We found the weapons of mass destruction. We found biological laboratories."[12] The evidence was the discovery of a pair of trailers that could have been used to make biological weapons, although there was no indication they had been used for that purpose and they had other legitimate uses. Several other administration voices, including that of Vice President Cheney, made the same claim—even after United States intelligence officials had publicly backed away from it.[13]

Postwar investigations also found little evidence of a meaningful al Qaeda connection. A few contacts between Iraqi officials and members of al Qaeda were documented, but investigators found no sign of any sustained or high-level cooperation and no evidence of Iraqi involvement in September 11. This did not stop the administration from continuing to imply a connection. In his address from the deck of the *Abraham Lincoln*, Bush declared, "The liberation of Iraq is a crucial advance in the campaign against terror. We've removed an ally of al Qaeda, and cut off a source of terrorist funding."[14] Asked by Tim Russert on *Meet the Press* in September 2003 if he was surprised that a large majority of Americans believed Saddam was involved in 9/11, Cheney replied, "No. I think it's not surprising that people make the connection." Asked further, "But is there a connection?" Cheney left it open: "We don't know."[15] Cheney also continued to refer to the unconfirmed prewar allegation of a meeting between the lead hijacker Mohamed Atta and an Iraqi intelligence official in Prague before the September 11 attacks as evidence of Saddam's complicity.

---

[9] "President Discusses Middle East, Iraq and the Dollar in Cabinet Meeting," White House news release, June 9, 2003, quoted in Fritz et al., *All the President's Spin*, 192.
[10] White House press briefing, June 10, 2003, quoted in Fritz et al., *All the President's Spin*, 196.
[11] *Primetime Live*, ABC, December 16, 2003, quoted in Fritz et al., *All the President's Spin*, 197.
[12] Interview of president by TPV, Poland, May 29, 2003, quoted in Fritz et al., *All the President's Spin*, 194.
[13] Fritz et al., *All the President's Spin*, 194.
[14] Text of speech displayed at http://www.cbsnews.com/stories/2003/05/01/iraq/main551946.shtml (accessed July 15, 2005).
[15] *Meet the Press*, NBC, September 14, 2003, quoted in Fritz et al., *All the President's Spin*, 211.

While conceding only slowly and with considerable backsliding that the case for war had been built on faulty intelligence, the administration was happy to highlight the one unassailable justification Paul Wolfowitz had listed (see Chapter 5) for forcing Saddam Hussein from office: Saddam's brutality against his own people. His regime's torture and murder of Iraqis on a grand scale was confirmed after the war, and few Iraqis appeared to be unhappy about his removal. As Bush put it at a press conference in April 2004, "I want to know why we haven't found a weapon yet. But I still know Saddam Hussein was a threat, and the world is better off without Saddam Hussein. . . . I know the Iraqi people don't believe that [they] . . . would be better off with Saddam Hussein in power."[16] Critics who said that the war was a mistake were open to the accusation that they wanted to see Saddam back in power. Even if the war's premises were mistaken, weren't its consequences worth it? Later, this approach broadened to emphasize the rationale that the war had set in motion a movement toward freedom and democracy across the Middle East; as Bush declared in his 2005 State of the Union address, "The victory of freedom in Iraq will . . . inspire democratic reformers from Damascus to Tehran, bring more hope and progress to a troubled region, and thereby lift a terrible threat from the lives of our children and grandchildren."[17]

The administration also argued for Saddam's guilt by geography. Condoleezza Rice, interviewed on July 30, 2003, noted that Saddam "was sitting astride one of the most volatile regions in the world, a region out of which the ideologies of hatred had come that led people to slam airplanes into buildings in New York and Washington."[18] Cheney said in September that "if we're successful in Iraq . . . we will have struck a major blow right at the heart of the base, if you will, the geographic base of the terrorists who have had us under assault now for many years, but most especially on 9/11."[19]

The geographical argument tied into what became the primary justification for the war and for continuing United States involvement, that Iraq was a central front in the war on terrorism. As Bush put it in a nationally televised speech on September 7, 2003, "Two years ago, I told

---

[16] Presidential press conference, April 13, 2004, at http://www.nytimes.com/2004/04/14/politics/14BTEX.html?pagewanted=all (accessed July 20, 2005).

[17] "State of the Union Address," February 2, 2005, at http://www.whitehouse.gov/news/releases/2005/02/20050202-11.html (accessed July 25, 2005).

[18] Interview with Gwen Ifil, *NewsHour with Jim Lehrer*, PBS, July 30, 2003, quoted in Fritz et al., *All the President's Spin*, 213.

[19] *Meet the Press*, NBC, September 14, 2003, quoted in Fritz et al., *All the President's Spin*, 213.

Congress and the country that the war on terror would be a lengthy war, a different kind of war, fought on many fronts in many places. Iraq is now the central front."[20] This claim became the main point of contention between Bush and his challenger, John Kerry, in the 2004 campaign and will be analyzed as such in Chapter 7.

Like the original, the revised case for war was persuasive—to Republicans. It was far less successful among Democrats and independents, and partisan divisions on the Iraq War became far wider than for any previous United States military action for which we have opinion survey data. Ultimately, partisan reactions to the war, its premises as articulated by the administration, and its consequences form the single most important explanation of why George W. Bush became the most divisive and polarizing president in the more than sixty years presidential approval has been surveyed.

THE IRAQ RALLY

As noted in Chapter 1, the onset of war in Iraq inspired a substantial rally in President Bush's overall job approval ratings (see Figures 1.1 and 1.2) and in evaluations of his handling of the situation in Iraq (see Figure 1.7). The rally was joined by partisans across the board but was naturally smaller among Republicans than among other citizens because Republican ratings of the president were already so high. The war was also the subject of its own rally, visible in Figure 6.1. Assessing support for the war is complicated by the diversity of questions used by pollsters to measure it; different questions elicit different levels of support, and the frequency with which each is asked has changed with evolving circumstances (a list of these questions may be found in the Appendix). Figure 6.1 displays the most general picture by including data from multiple variants of eleven different questions and using lowess smoothing to summarize the noisy trend.[21] As discussed in Chapter 5, support for invading Iraq was high right after September 11, when most Americans suspected Saddam Hussein

---

[20] "Transcript of State of the Union," at http://www.cnn.com/2005/ALLPOLITICS/02/02/sotu.transcript/ (accessed March 16, 2010).

[21] These data are from national polls sampling all adults or registered or likely voters; the polls were conducted by CBS News/*New York Times*, ABC News/*Washington Post*, NBC News/*Wall Street Journal*, *Los Angeles Times*, Gallup, Pew Center for the People and the Press, *Newsweek*, CNN/*Time*, Fox News, Quinnipiac College, National Annenberg Election Study, Knowledge Networks, and Democracy Corps and were reported at http://www.pollingreport.com or at the polling group's website. The various question wordings are shown in the Appendix.

FIGURE 6.1
Popular Support for the War in Iraq (All Question Wordings)

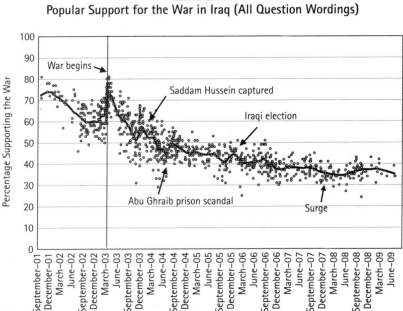

Source: 890 polls by fourteen survey organizations; see footnote 21.

was at least partly responsible. It declined as the focus turned to Osama bin Laden and Afghanistan, revived late in the administration's campaign to portray Iraq as a threat requiring immediate action, rose sharply after the onset of hostilities, and peaked in April just before the president's "Mission Accomplished" moment on the carrier.

The same trends appear when we examine separately those questions asked frequently enough for temporal comparisons. Support for the war was highest when respondents were asked if the United States had done the "right thing" in taking military action in Iraq or if the United States had made a mistake in going to war.[22] Support was as much as 20 points lower (sometimes in the same survey) when people were asked if the results of the war were worth the cost in American lives; the falloff was smaller, however,

---

[22] These questions typically read, "Do you think the United States did the right thing in taking military action against Iraq, or should the United States have stayed out?" or "In view of the developments since we first sent our troops to Iraq, do you think the United States made a mistake in sending troops to Iraq, or not?" See the first edition of this book (p. 129) for a graphic illustration of the question wording differences.

TABLE 6.1

Support for the War and Support for United States Troops in Iraq,
March 20, 2003 (Percentages)

	REPUBLICANS	INDEPENDENTS	DEMOCRATS	ALL
"As you may know, the United States went to war with Iraq last night. Do you support or oppose the United States having gone to war?"				
Support having gone to war	90.4	73.1	51.2	72.6
Oppose having gone to war	8.2	23.7	46.8	25.2
"Would you say you support the troops and you support the Bush Administration's policy on Iraq, or would you say you support the troops, but you oppose the Bush Administration's policy on Iraq?"				
Support both troops and policy	79.3	52.0	38.5	56.3
Support troops but oppose policy	9.8	20.5	12.1	14.6

SOURCE: ABC News/*Washington Post* Poll, March 2003.

if removing Saddam was specifically mentioned as the result. Although the levels differed, the trends in responses to these questions were generally parallel and consistent with the overall picture in Figure 6.1.

Expressed levels of support for the war depended not only on the way the question was worded, but also on the context in which it was asked. One reason for the observed rally in support for the war once it began was the change in what the question then meant to some respondents. The average level of support expressed in response to comparable sets of questions asked in the month of March 2003 (from twenty-five surveys in all) rose from 65 percent before March 20 to 74 percent after.[23] But the results of an ABC News/*Washington Post* survey taken just after the war started suggest that at least some of the increase reflected patriotic support for United States troops rather than approval of the war itself. Table 6.1 presents the evidence. About 20 percent of respondents who said they supported "having gone to war" also said they supported the

---

[23] These questions ask if respondents "support" or "approve of" military action in some format.

FIGURE 6.2
Party Identification and Support for the Iraq War (All Question Wordings)

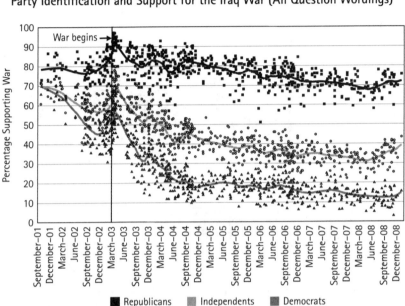

■ Republicans   ■ Independents   ■ Democrats

Source: 720 polls by fourteen survey organizations; see footnote 21.

troops but not the administration's policy on Iraq. This response was more common among independent (28 percent) and Democratic (24 percent) than among Republican (11 percent) war supporters.

Unfortunately, this follow-up question was not repeated in later surveys, but it is likely that support for the war policy itself grew during March and April with the military successes of United States forces on the ground, the remarkably low American casualties,[24] and televised images of joyful Iraqis toppling Saddam's statue. Thereafter, however, the continuing chaos, insurgency, and loss of American and allied lives began to sap support for the war, particularly among Democrats and independents. Figure 6.2 displays the data and lowess-smoothed trends in support for the Iraq War, disaggregated by party. The gap between Republicans and Democrats narrowed slightly in the first month of the war and then grew steadily

---

[24] American military deaths in Iraq numbered 139 in March and April 2003, along with 33 British fatalities; the number of wounded is listed as 542. See http://www.icasualties.org/Iraq/ByMonth.aspx (accessed July 19, 2005).

FIGURE 6.3

Partisan Differences in Support for the War in Iraq

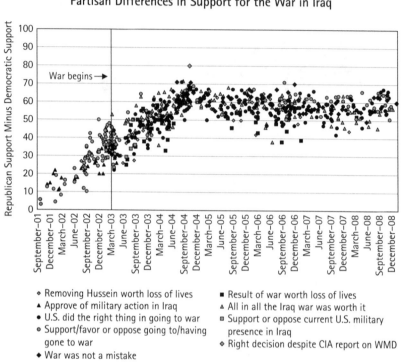

• Removing Hussein worth loss of lives   ▪ Result of war worth loss of lives
▲ Approve of military action in Iraq   ▲ All in all the Iraq war was worth it
● U.S. did the right thing in going to war ▣ Support or oppose current U.S. military
○ Support/favor or oppose going to/having   presence in Iraq
  gone to war   ◆ Right decision despite CIA report on WMD
▾ War was not a mistake

Source: 720 polls by fourteen survey organizations; see footnote 21.

wider for the next eighteen months. Figure 6.3 shows that the partisan gap widened regardless of how the war support question was posed. It reached an average of about 63 percentage points in the last quarter of 2004 before narrowing a bit to a stable average of about 57 points over Bush's entire second term. A *Los Angeles Times* poll question asking whether, in light of the CIA's report that Saddam had no WMD and no active program to produce them, Bush had made the right decision to go to war produced the biggest divergence of any survey, with 90 percent of Republicans but only 10 percent of Democrats answering "yes."[25]

These data stand in striking contrast to comparable data from previous wars. Figures 6.4 to 6.8 display the partisan differences in support

[25] *Los Angeles Times* Poll Alert, Study #510, October 25, 2004.

FIGURE 6.4
Partisan Differences in Support for the Korean War

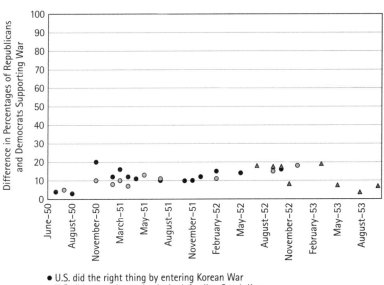

• U.S. did the right thing by entering Korean War
○ U.S. did not make a mistake in defending South Korea
▲ Korean War was worth fighting

Sources: John E. Mueller, War, Presidents, and Public Opinion (New York: John Wiley & Sons, 1973), 270; the 1952 ANES Survey; and National Opinion Research Center data from the Roper Center, University of Connecticut.

for United States involvement in five earlier conflicts, using the same scale as that in Figure 6.3. In none of the five is the gap anywhere nearly as large as it is for the Iraq War. Ironically, it is lowest in the most controversial of these engagements, Vietnam, averaging only 5 percentage points. The Vietnam War certainly divided Americans, but the division was within rather than between the parties, and support for the war declined at about the same pace for partisans in all categories. Party differences on Korea and Kosovo were of a similar magnitude, averaging 11 to 12 points, although the absolute levels of public support differed widely between these conflicts.[26] Bush's father's Gulf War inspired a somewhat wider partisan gap. Still, the party difference averaged only 20 points

---

[26] Partisan differences in support for military actions in Lebanon and Grenada in 1983 during the first Reagan administration averaged about 14 points, and differences on military action in Somalia in 1992–1993 during the G. H. W. Bush and Clinton administrations averaged about 5 points in the selection of CBS News/New York Times and ABC News/Washington Post polls I checked for these events.

FIGURE 6.5
Partisan Differences in Support for Vietnam War

◆ U.S. did not make a mistake in sending troops to fight in Vietnam
● U.S. did the right thing in getting into the fighting in Vietnam
▲ U.S. should have become involved in Southeast Asia

Sources: John E. Mueller, *War, Presidents, and Public Opinion* (New York: John Wiley & Sons, 1973), 271, and the 1964–1972 ANES surveys.

and never exceeded 31 points (and this observation, stemming from a question about whether the respondent approved of sending troops to defend Saudi Arabia, appears anomalously large). Ole Holsti, comparing these to earlier war support data, notes "rather substantial partisan differences,"[27] but they seem, in retrospect, quite modest compared with the partisan differences on Iraq.

The Afghan conflict initially enjoyed very high bipartisan support; in thirty-eight surveys taken from October 2001 through August 2002, an average of 94 percent of Republicans, 82 percent of Democrats, and 85 percent of independents favored it. The partisan gap, 12 points, was thus on par with that of Korea and Kosovo. Thereafter, the media polls' attention turned to the Iraq War, and none asked about support for the Afghan venture for the fourteen months spanning September 2002 to

[27] Ole R. Holsti, *Public Opinion and American Foreign Policy,* rev. ed. (Ann Arbor: University of Michigan Press, 2004), 174.

FIGURE 6.6
Partisan Differences in Support for the Persian Gulf War

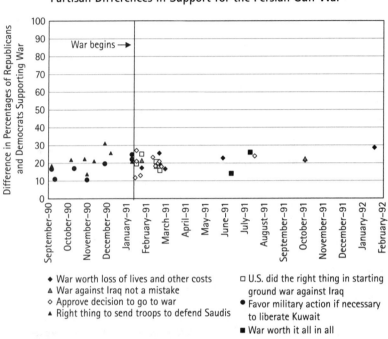

◆ War worth loss of lives and other costs
▲ War against Iraq not a mistake
◇ Approve decision to go to war
▲ Right thing to send troops to defend Saudis

□ U.S. did the right thing in starting ground war against Iraq
● Favor military action if necessary to liberate Kuwait
■ War worth it all in all

Sources: CBS News/*New York Times* polls; Gallup polls reported in Ole R. Holsti, *Public Opinion and American Foreign Policy*, rev. ed. (Ann Arbor: University of Michigan Press, 2004), 173; and ABC News/*Washington Post* polls.

November 2003. By the time it was next questioned, partisans had become sharply divided on Iraq and the president, and Democrats' disillusion with both had spilled over into their assessment of the Afghan effort. Still, for the rest of Bush's presidency, support among Democrats for the war in Afghanistan ran an average of 28 points higher than support for the Iraq War, and the partisan difference was on average about 17 points narrower.[28]

Not surprisingly, the party of the president determines whether support for military action is higher among Republicans or Democrats; in only

---

[28] Republicans' support was about 12 points higher for the war in Afghanistan (84 percent) than for the Iraq War (72 percent). For more on these comparisons, see Gary C. Jacobson, "A Tale of Two Wars: Public Opinion on the United States Military Interventions in Afghanistan and Iraq," presented at the Annual Meeting of the American Political Science Association, Toronto, Canada, September 3–6, 2009.

FIGURE 6.7

Partisan Differences in Support for Military Action in Kosovo

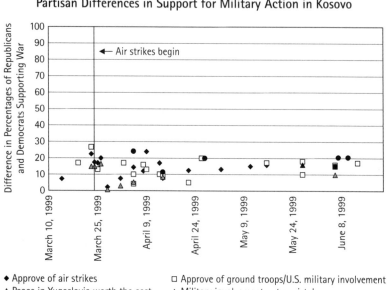

♦ Approve of air strikes   □ Approve of ground troops/U.S. military involvement
▲ Peace in Yugoslavia worth the cost   ▲ Military involvement not a mistake
  in American lives
● U.S. did the right thing in Kosovo

Source: CBS News/*New York Times*, Harris, Gallup, NBC News/*Wall Street Journal, Newsweek,*
CNN/*Time,* ABC News/*Washington Post,* and Pew Center for the People and the Press polls.

9 of the 211 observations displayed in these five charts do opposing-party identifiers support the action at higher levels than the president's party identifiers.[29]

For reasons discussed in Chapter 5, partisan divisions on the Iraq War were already substantial before it began. These narrowed in the early weeks of the war but soon widened again when the war's principal premises could not be confirmed and partisans responded to that emerging story quite differently. Most Republicans either refused to recognize that neither WMD nor a 9/11 connection could be substantiated or accepted the substitute justifications offered by the administration after the fact, whereas Democrats, with no inclination to miss the message or

---

[29] The 9 occurrences included 3 of the 28 observations for Vietnam, 2 of the 50 observations for Kosovo, and 4 of the 32 observations on Korea, all of the latter occurring after Eisenhower took over from Truman.

FIGURE 6.8
Partisan Differences in Support for the War in Afghanistan

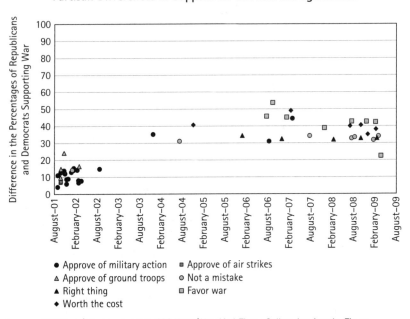

Sources: ABC News/*Washington Post*, CBS News/*New York Times*, Gallup, *Los Angeles Times*, *Newsweek*, Pew Center for the People and the Press, *Time*, and TIPP polls and the 2006 American National Election Study.

adopt new reasons for support, grew increasingly opposed to the war—and increasingly disaffected with President Bush.

BELIEF IN THE WAR'S PREMISES

Before the war, a large majority of Americans, regardless of party, believed Saddam was hiding WMD, and about half thought he was personally involved in 9/11. After the war, as time passed and the search for WMD and an al Qaeda connection continued to turn up nothing of substance, these beliefs became less common, but neither rapidly nor completely (Figure 6.9). Right after the war began, about a third of the public thought WMD had actually been found; a year later, a little less than 20 percent still clung to this misconception; by 2008, less than

FIGURE 6.9
Beliefs That Saddam Hussein Was Personally Involved in 9/11 and Iraq Had WMD

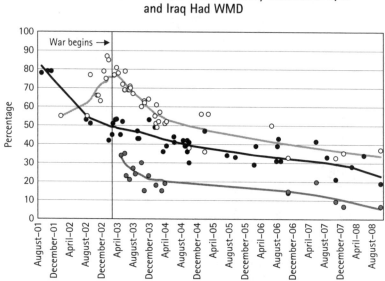

• Believe Saddam was involved in 9/11   ○ Believe Iraq possessed WMD before the war
• Believe WMD have been found

Source: ABC News/*Washington Post,* CBS News/*New York Times,* Gallup, Harris, PIPA/Knowledge Networks, *Newsweek,* Fox News, CNN, and CCES polls.

10 percent did so. The proportion who believed Iraq possessed WMD (even if they had not been found) also declined, but more than a year after the war began, a majority held this view, and as late as October 2008 more than a third continued to do so. The belief that Saddam had a hand in September 11 also declined, but gradually; more than eighteen months after Baghdad had fallen, about a third of the public still thought he had been involved, and nearly 20 percent still thought so by the end of 2008.

The data suggest that the main reason public opinion did not respond more sharply to postwar revelations is that they did surprisingly little to shake the faith of Republicans in Bush's original case for the war, even after the administration had officially abandoned it. Among Republicans, belief in Saddam's WMD peaked at 95 percent just before the war and has not fallen below 54 percent in any poll since; it stood at 63 percent at

FIGURE 6.10

Does (Did) Iraq Possess Weapons of Mass Destruction?

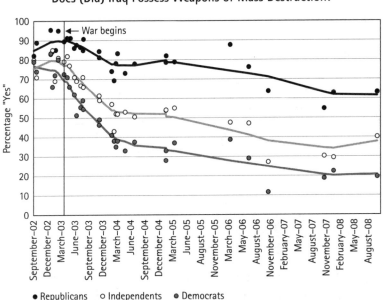

• Republicans ○ Independents • Democrats

Source: CBS News/New York Times, ABC News/Washington Post, Newsweek, PRSI, Harris, and Gallup polls and CCES and TESS surveys.

the end of Bush's presidency (Figure 6.10). In February 2003, 79 percent of Democrats thought Saddam possessed WMD; within about fifteen months, that figure had fallen to 33 percent, and by 2008 it was down to about 20 percent. Belief in Saddam's involvement in 9/11 also remained significantly higher among Republicans than among Democrats or independents (Figure 6.11). Among Republicans, it fell from a peak of 65 percent right after Baghdad fell in April 2003 to an average of 37 percent in the three surveys taken in 2008; the parallel decline among independents was from 51 percent to 29 percent, and among Democrats, from 49 percent to 20 percent.

Rather more surprising than these partisan differences is the extent to which even Democrats continued to believe the allegations long after well-publicized official reports had found no evidence to support them and the president and his administration had ostensibly disavowed them.

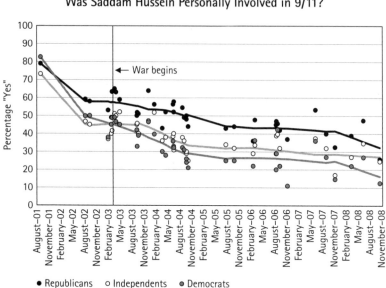

FIGURE 6.11
Was Saddam Hussein Personally Involved in 9/11?

● Republicans   ○ Independents   ● Democrats

Source: CBS News/*New York Times*, Gallup, *Newsweek, Time*, and CCES polls.

Evidently, Saddam's evil reputation continued to predispose Americans to think the worst and to ignore or forget exculpatory information. One important source of reinforcement for these continuing misperceptions is no doubt the Bush administration's continued use of artfully insinuating rhetoric. On March 19, 2005, the second anniversary of the United States invasion, the president put it this way: "We knew of Saddam Hussein's record of aggression and support for terror. We knew of his long history of pursuing, even using, weapons of mass destruction, and we know that September 11 requires our country to think differently."[30] With rhetoric like this—lumping together in two sentences Saddam Hussein, September 11, terror, and WMD—no wonder most Americans thought the administration was still advancing claims unsubstantiated by its own investigations despite having officially abandoned them.[31]

---

[30] Richard Boudreaux, "Insurgent Attacks Continue 2 Years After the United States Invasion," *Los Angeles Times*, March 20, 2005, A4.
[31] For evidence on this point, see Table 7.2 in Chapter 7.

The simplest interpretation of the patterns of belief in the two major justifications for the war is that Americans of all political persuasions tended to have strong prior beliefs about Saddam Hussein that led them to assume his complicity in September 11 and possession of illicit WMD, while Republicans also had a strong prior faith in the president and thus in his administration's version of Iraqi realities. Both sets of priors kept subsequent revelations from fully undermining existing beliefs in the war's original rationales, with their compound effect among Republicans explaining why the president's partisans were especially slow to acknowledge new, discordant information. A more detailed analysis of how such beliefs contributed to partisan polarization on the war will be presented in Chapter 9.

Republicans also were more likely to believe that the Iraq War was justified even if WMD were never found, and this view became more predominant after the war. In a survey taken on the day the war started, 31 percent of Republicans thought the war "was justified only if the United States finds conclusive evidence that Iraq has weapons of mass destruction," while 63 percent said it was justified even if conclusive evidence of WMD was not found. Ten days later the proportion of Republicans expressing the first view had dropped to 11 percent while the proportion expressing the second had risen to 83 percent, a pattern that was repeated in surveys taken in December 2003 and February 2004. Among Democrats, the proportion saying the war was justified even without conclusive evidence of WMD stood at 46 percent on March 20, rose to 56 percent ten days later, but by February 2004 had dropped to 35 percent; the proportion of Democrats saying the war was unjustified with or without WMD rose from 9 percent to 25 percent over the same period.[32] Asked in January 2005 whether the war "will have been worth the loss of American lives and other costs" if WMD are never found, 69 percent of Republicans said it still would be worth it, compared with 42 percent of independents and just 16 percent of Democrats.[33]

Belief in the Iraq War's primary rationales had a potent effect on support for the venture after as well as before its onset. Figure 6.12 replicates Figures 5.4 and Figure 5.5 from the previous chapter, except that

---

[32] ABC News/*Washington Post* polls—March 20, April 3, and December 18–21, 2003, and February 10–11, 2004—analyzed by the author. Among independents, the proportion saying WMD were not necessary to justify the war went from 50 percent on March 20 to 63 percent in April before declining to 58 percent in February 2004; the proportion saying the war was not justified regardless went from 6 percent to 19 percent.

[33] CBS News/*New York Times* Poll, January 14–18, 2005, at http://www.cbsnews.com/htdocs/CBSNews_polls/bush_back.pdf (accessed February 10, 2005).

FIGURE 6.12

Beliefs About WMD and Saddam Hussein's Involvement in 9/11 and Belief That Invading Iraq Was the Right Thing to Do (October 2008)

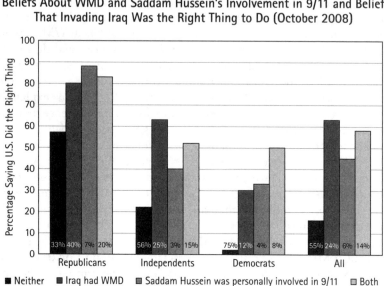

Note: Percent of respondents in each belief category is listed at the foot of the column.
Source: 2008 Cooperative Congressional Election Study, UCSD module.

support for the war is measured by whether the respondent believes "the United States did the right thing in taking military action against Iraq."[34] A comparison of Figures 5.5 and 6.12 is instructive. The proportion of Republicans who accepted as factual at least one of the war's primary justifications declined by 30 points between February 2003 and October 2008 but still stood at 67 percent. The decline was greater among Democrats (down 39 points, from 63 percent to 24 percent), with independents falling in between (down 36 points, from 80 percent to 44 percent). This is important, because support for the war remained much higher (59 percent) among respondents who believed either or both of the premises than among those who believed neither (16 percent). Note, however, that partisan differences in thinking the war was the right thing to do remained substantial even when controlling for belief in the war's

_____

[34] In Figures 5.4 and Figure 5.5, the question was "Do you approve or disapprove of the United States taking military action against Iraq to try to remove Saddam Hussein from power?"

premises. Among those still saying they believed in at least one premise, 82 percent of Republicans, 58 percent of independents, and 37 percent of Democrats said the war had been the right thing to do. Among those who now rejected both rationales, the figures were 57 percent, 22 percent, and 2 percent, respectively.

A naïve reading of these results would be that popular support for the war depended largely on misinformation and would have collapsed entirely had the public absorbed the reports of United States investigators who conceded that, despite their best efforts, they had found no convincing evidence of WMD or complicity of Saddam Hussein in September 11. But by itself, the widespread resistance to this information suggests that, for many Americans, particularly Republicans, support for the war came first, and the specifics of the factual case for it were of decidedly secondary importance. If forced to recognize that the war's original premises were faulty, these individuals would have been willing, as loyal followers of President Bush, to accept the other premises he proffered. I will have more to say in Chapter 9 about the psychological processes involved.

In sum, revelations that its main premises were faulty did little to undermine Republicans' support for the Iraq War because they were less likely than other Americans to get the message, less likely to withdraw support if they did, and more willing to adopt alternative rationales emphasized after the fact by the Bush administration. Among independents and Democrats, however, support for the war depended heavily on its original justifications and thus fell as these became increasingly untenable. As a consequence, on virtually every question concerning the premises, necessity, wisdom, and effect of going to war in Iraq, partisan differences grew very large.

THE PRESIDENT'S CREDIBILITY

Public reactions to the war and its aftermath amplified partisan differences in assessments of George W. Bush. The administration's campaign justifying the war, before and after Iraq was invaded, put Bush's credibility on the line. Republicans' faith was barely shaken, while the proportion of Democrats who thought the president had intentionally misled the country into war eventually exceeded 80 percent (Figure 6.13). Meanwhile, the proportion of Democrats deeming him "honest and trustworthy" fell from

FIGURE 6.13

Did the Bush Administration Intentionally Mislead the Public in Making the Case for the Iraq War?

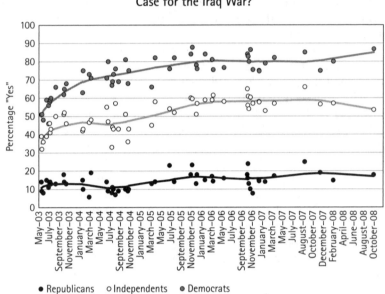

● Republicans   ○ Independents   ● Democrats

Source: 52 ABC News/*Washington Post,* Fox News, NBC News/*Wall Street Journal,* Gallup, *Los Angeles Times,* PIPA, and CNN polls and CCES surveys.

a high of 57 percent in May 2002 to an average of only 9 percent in the two polls taken in 2008 (Figure 6.14). Few Republicans came to believe that the Bush administration had intentionally misled the public in making the case for invading Iraq; very large majorities continued to think that the administration had actually believed its own alarums, although the data show some erosion, from 88 percent taking this position in July 2004 to about 74 percent in late 2008. A large majority of Republicans also maintained faith in Bush's integrity until the end of his administration, although again there were some signs of erosion during his last year in office.

Opinions on the administration's sincerity in arguing for military action in Iraq are, not surprisingly, strongly related to evaluations of Bush's overall performance as president. For example, among the Democrats in the 2008 CCES survey who thought they had been intentionally misled, 2 percent approved and 98 percent disapproved of Bush's performance; among the Republicans who thought the administration told what it

FIGURE 6.14
Is George W. Bush Honest and Trustworthy?

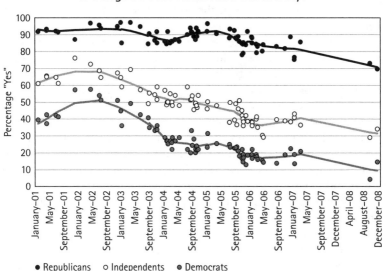

● Republicans   ○ Independents   ● Democrats

Source: 72 ABC News/*Washington Post*, Gallup, Pew Center for the People and the Press, *Los Angeles Times*, Harris, CNN, AP-Ipsos, and Quinnipiac polls and the 2008 CCES.

believed to be true, 79 percent approved, and 21 percent disapproved. Among the minority of trusting Democrats, 42 percent approved, and 58 percent disapproved; among the minority of distrusting Republicans, 3 percent approved, and 93 percent disapproved. The presidential evaluations of 87 percent of all respondents matched their views on whether the administration had been deliberately deceptive. The Republicans' continuing belief in the Bush administration's good faith in making its case for war, and the widespread sentiment among Democrats that they had been duped, thus contributed directly to the record partisan differences in assessments of President Bush.

THE RELIGIOUS FACTOR

The campaign to generate support for the Iraq War, both before and after the invasion, followed the Bush administration's archetypal script (see Chapter 4). Once Bush had determined that regime change in Iraq was

the "right thing for the American people," he and his associates under-
took a coordinated effort to assert claims about the danger Saddam
posed that were gauged to win the widest possible public backing for a
preemptive strike. Uncertainties about the factual grounds for these
claims were discounted, suppressed, or ignored. Doubts raised by intelligence analysts were never allowed to dilute the campaign's message.
Facts were deployed selectively and sometimes misleadingly; rhetoric
made connections when evidence did not. When neither WMD nor an
Iraqi alliance with al Qaeda could be documented, the administration
revised its rationale without acknowledging the change (attacking critics
who pointed out the revision as "revisionists"[35]—irony was not part of
the Bush administration mindset) or admitting any second thoughts. It is
not surprising that in response to these developments, public support for
the war and the president who initiated it would diminish. The puzzle is
why it did not diminish more than it did. After all, had Bush proposed to
spend hundreds of billions of dollars and sacrifice the lives of more than
4,000 American troops (and many times that number of Iraqi civilians)
to replace Saddam's regime with the shaky democratic experiment still
under way when Bush left office, it is hard to imagine that more than a
tiny minority of the public or Congress would have come on board.[36] Yet
the tenacious loyalty of most Republicans staved off the political debacle
threatened by unfolding events in Iraq, and the most tenacious of all
were white conservative Christians.

National surveys conducted for news media do not ask the extensive
array of questions designed to produce the detailed typologies of religious identity and beliefs developed by scholars of religion and politics
(see Chapter 2), but with some regularity the surveys have asked whether
the respondents consider themselves born-again or evangelical Christians. These admittedly imperfect data make it strikingly clear how powerfully religious identities shaped people's responses to Bush and his Iraq
policies, particularly after the original case for the war unraveled. White
born-again/evangelical Christians remained the most steadfast supporters

---

[35] Condoleezza Rice, for example, made this specific allegation on *Face the Nation* in June 2003; see
Fritz, Keefer, and Nyhan, *All the President's Spin,* 217.

[36] Even Bush might have decided otherwise; Scott McClellan, Bush's press secretary from 2003 to 2006,
wrote in his memoir: "I believe that, if he had been given a crystal ball in which he could have foreseen
the costs of war—more than 4,000 American troops killed, 30,000 injured, and tens of thousands of
innocent Iraqi citizens dead—he would never have made the decision to invade, despite what he may say
or feel he has to say publicly today." See Scott McClellan, *What Happened: Inside the Bush White
House and Washington's Culture of Deception* (New York: Public Affairs, 2008), 144.

FIGURE 6.15
Party, Religious Identity, and Support for the Iraq War

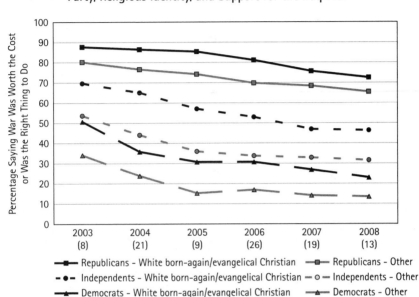

Republicans - White born-again/evangelical Christian
Republicans - Other
Independents - White born-again/evangelical Christian
Independents - Other
Democrats - White born-again/evangelical Christian
Democrats - Other

Note: The number of surveys averaged is in parentheses.
Source: CBS News/*New York Times* and ABC News/*Washington Post* polls.

of the war and the president, as is evident from Figure 6.15 and 6.16, which display the annual averages in support for the war and approval of Bush's overall job performance, broken down by party and religious identity (the number of polls used to compute the averages is in parentheses). They were the war and the president's most consistent backers and, while not completely impervious to unfolding events, displayed the least erosion of support of any of the groups. The combination of steadfast conservative Christian Republicans and increasingly disaffected Democrats who were not white born-again Christians clearly contributed to increasing partisan differences on the president and the war. By 2005, the opinions expressed by these two polar groups (together comprising about 40 percent of the public) differed by averages of 70 percentage points on whether the war was the right thing to do or worth the cost and by 79 points on Bush's overall performance. These differences remained very wide for the rest of Bush's presidency.

FIGURE 6.16

Partisanship, Religious Identity, and Presidential Approval (Annual Averages)

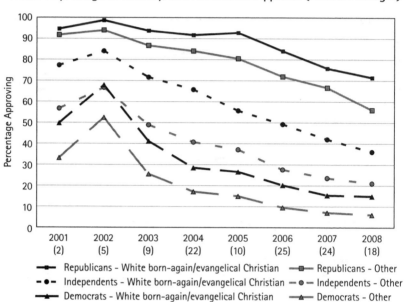

Note: The number of surveys averaged is in parentheses.

Source: CBS News/New York Times and ABC News/Washington Post polls.

FAITH IN BUSH

As I noted in Chapter 4, after 9/11 the idea that George Bush was God's chosen instrument in a global battle between good and evil had circulated in the conservative Christian community. Insofar as it was believed, it implied a religious duty to support him without reservation. To determine the extent and consequences of such beliefs, I designed a set of questions that were posed in sections of the 2006, 2007, and 2008 Cooperative Congressional Election Surveys.[37] After answering an initial question

---

[37] Gary C. Jacobson, Cooperative Congressional Election Study, 2006: UCSD Content (computer file), release 2(UCSD, 2007), at http://web.mit.edu/polisci/portl/cces/teamcontent.html; Stephen Ansolabehere, Cooperative Congressional Election Study, 2006: Common Content (computer file), release 2 (Cambridge, MA: MIT, November 14, 2007), at http://web.mit.edu/polisci/portl/cces/commoncontent.html; Gary C. Jacobson, Cooperative Congressional Election Study, 2008: UCSD Content (computer file), release 1 (UCSD, February 2009), at http://web.mit.edu/polisci/portl/cces/teamcontent.html.

FIGURE 6.17

Belief in G. W. Bush's Divine Selection and Opinions on the Iraq War

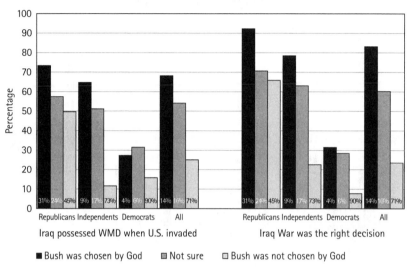

Source: 2006, 2007, and 2008 CCES surveys.

about belief in divine intervention in general,[38] respondents were asked, "Do you believe that George W. Bush was chosen by God to lead the United States in a global war on terrorism?" On average across the three studies, 31 percent of Republicans said they believed Bush was God's chosen instrument, and another 24 percent said they were not sure. A much smaller share of independents took either of these positions (9 percent and 17 percent, respectively), and nine of ten Democrats said that Bush was definitely not God's chosen instrument.[39]

As Figure 6.17 reveals, respondents who believed Bush was God's chosen instrument were much more likely to maintain the belief that Iraq possessed WMD (an average of 68 percent across the three surveys) than were those who did not see Bush in that way (25 percent), and

---

[38] The question was "Do you believe that God intervenes in human affairs and shapes historical events?" with possible answers of "Yes, regularly; history is determined by God"; "Yes, but only rarely; history is mostly made by human beings and natural events"; or "No, history is made by human beings without divine intervention." Among voters an average of 27 percent took the first option, 27 percent the second, 38 percent the third, and the remainder said they were not sure.

[39] The percentage of respondents taking each position is shown at the bottom of the columns in Figure 6.17.

FIGURE 6.18
Belief in G. W. Bush's Divine Selection and Approval
of Bush's Job Performance

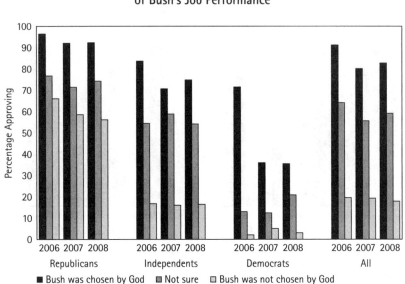

Source: 2006, 2007, and 2008 CCES surveys.

large differences between the two groups reappeared within all partisan categories (73 percent to 50 percent among Republicans, 65 percent to 12 percent among independents, and 27 percent to 16 percent among Democrats).[40] Believers in Bush's divine selection were also, not coincidentally, much more likely to support the Iraq War. More than 90 percent of Republicans holding this belief backed the war, compared with only 8 percent of Democrats who did not hold it. Notice that the distribution of responses of people who said they were unsure was much closer to that of believers, indicating that this response most often meant "maybe."

Not surprisingly, beliefs about Bush's relationship with the Almighty were strongly related to approval of his job performance (Figure 6.18). More than 90 percent of Republican believers continued to approve of his performance to the end. There was some falloff among the tiny fraction of Democratic believers, but they remained much more positive

---

[40] Believers in Bush's divine appointment were also much more likely to believe that Saddam Hussein was complicit in 9/11 (an average of 39 percent, compared with 12 percent of other respondents).

toward the president than did other Democrats. The effects were largest, however, among independents, where the approval gap between believers and nonbelievers averaged 60 percentage points.

Similar differences appear on other questions regarding the war and the president. In the 2008 CCES, among Republicans who believed in Bush's divine selection, 90 percent believed the Iraq War had helped the war on terrorism, 92 percent thought the United States should stay in Iraq as long as necessary for victory, 88 percent said the Bush administration had told what it believed to be the truth in making the case for war, and 94 percent deemed Bush honest and trustworthy. The equivalent distribution of opinions on these four questions among the huge majority of Democrats who did not believe Bush was divinely chosen were 8 percent, 5 percent, 4 percent, and 2 percent, respectively. These theological differences were thus another source of the deep partisan divisions on the war and the president. I will have more to say about this in Chapter 9.

CONCLUSION

The decision to invade Iraq was without question the most important of George W. Bush's presidency, and people's reactions to the venture powerfully shaped—and were shaped by—their assessments of the president and his administration. The war divided the public along party lines far more than any other United States military engagement undertaken since World War II, widening partisan differences in evaluations of Bush. Republicans, especially the conservative Christian faction, remained overwhelmingly supportive of the president and the war; Democrats and, to a lesser extent, independents became increasingly disenchanted with both. These differences reached their zenith during Bush's campaign for reelection in 2004, which turned into the most intensely partisan presidential contest in the past half-century.

CHAPTER 7

The 2004 Election: Mobilized Bases, Reinforced Divisions

President George W. Bush's triumphal airborne visit to the *Abraham Lincoln,* with the "Mission Accomplished" banner as backdrop, was immediately tagged "the mother of all photo ops" and widely acknowledged (not least by dispirited Democrats) as a superbly crafted opening to Bush's reelection campaign. The rally inspired by the swift military success gave Bush an advantage of about 15 percentage points over a generic Democratic opponent in polls taken from late March through May 2003, and he did even better matched against named Democrats.[1] The gravest of decisions of his administration, Bush's order to invade Iraq had carried political as well as military risks; as Colin Powell had warned the president, *"This will become the first term."*[2] In the spring of 2003, it looked like Bush's risk-taking would be richly rewarded come November 2004. A year later, with United States soldiers still dying, the violent insurgency showing no signs of fading, lawlessness continuing to plague ordinary Iraqis, and no evidence of WMD or operational Iraqi links to al Qaeda, the war threatened to become an electoral liability instead of an asset. The "Mission Accomplished" banner became an embarrassment, and administration spokespersons claimed for months

---

[1] In fourteen relevant generic polls reported for the period, Bush's advantage ranged from 10 points to 28 points, with an average of 15.2 and a standard deviation of 4.5. See http://www.pollingreport.com/wh04gen6.htm (accessed August 2, 2005).
[2] Bob Woodward, *Plan of Attack* (New York: Simon and Schuster, 2004), 150; emphasis in the original.

that the carrier crew had been responsible before they finally admitted that the idea and the sign had come from the White House.[3]

As we saw in Chapter 6, public reactions to the war became increasingly determined by party affiliation, with Republicans remaining overwhelmingly supportive and Democrats and, to a lesser extent, independents growing disenchanted with the venture. Partisan differences on the war intensified partisan differences in opinions on the president, setting the stage for the most partisan national election in at least fifty years. The election itself, in turn, magnified party differences on the war and the president as the campaigns focused public attention on both; it is no accident that in all of the relevant figures in earlier chapters, partisan differences peaked around election day.[4]

THE DEMOCRATIC NOMINATION

The growing disenchantment with the war and the president among Democrats strongly influenced the course of events leading to the nomination of Senator John Kerry to challenge Bush in the general election. Ordinary Democrats became increasingly eager to defeat Bush, and as signs that this might actually be possible grew more encouraging, the desire to nominate the Democrat with the best chance of winning also grew.

The initial beneficiary of Democrats' anger with Bush and his war was Vermont governor Howard Dean. In contrast to the other top-tier contenders, Dean, like Bush in 2000, was a Washington outsider who had no track record in national politics and could freely attack the president and his policies without the taint of having cooperated with him in the past. Among Dean's rivals, Senators Joseph Lieberman, John Edwards, and John Kerry and Representative Richard Gephardt had all voted to authorize the Iraq War; only Senator Bob Graham had voted against the authorizing resolution, and he did so because, he said, "it was too limited, too weak, and too timid."[5] Thus, Dean was able to separate himself

---

[3] David Paul Kuhn, 'Mission Accomplished' Revisited," CBS News, April 30, 2004, at http://www.cbsnews.com/stories/2004/04/30/politics/main614998.shtml (accessed August 8, 2005).

[4] See, for example, Figures 1.1, 1.4, 1.5, 1.6, 1.7, 1.8, 6.2, and 6.3.

[5] Michael Barone and Richard E. Cohen, eds., The Almanac of American Politics 2004 (Washington, DC: National Journal, 2003), 386. Second-tier Democratic candidates Dennis Kucinich, Carole Mosely Braun, and Al Sharpton also attacked Bush and his war, but none of them were regarded as viable.

FIGURE 7.1
Democrats' Preference for Democratic Presidential Candidates (Monthy Averages)

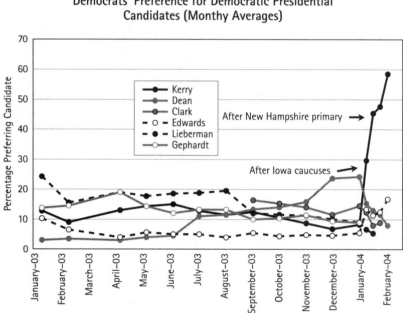

Source: CBS News/*New York Times,* Gallup, *Newsweek,* ABC News/*Washington Post,* NBC News/ *Wall Street Journal,* Fox News, Pew Research Center for the People and the Press, IPSOS, Quinnipiac University, and Harris polls, reported at pollingreport.com during 2003 and 2004.

from the pack by vigorously criticizing Bush and the war in a way that resonated among grassroots Democrats, especially the activists most likely to take part in nomination politics. Dean's pioneering Internet fundraising effort not only raked in more than $40 million for his campaign, but it also exposed the breadth and depth of opposition to the president among politically active Democrats.

Dean's rise in 2003 from obscurity to a lead in the Democratic horserace polls (Figure 7.1) served as an object lesson to his rivals, who began cranking up their own rhetorical assaults on the administration. Once Dean began to lose his comparative advantage on this dimension, his liabilities drew more attention. Democrats sought not only a candidate who would go after Bush but also one who could actually beat him. Dean's inexperience and brashness made him a comparatively risky choice, and his antiwar rhetoric[6] reminded some veteran Democrats of George McGovern's disastrous candidacy in 1972. Many Democrats seemed to recognize that, with terrorism a top public concern, no candidate could defeat Bush who was not credible on issues of national security and homeland defense. Perhaps more to the point, no Democrat could win without surviving the Bush campaign's inevitable charge (regardless of who was nominated) that the Democrat would not be tough enough in dealing with America's terrorist enemies. Hence, we see the boomlet for General Wesley Clark, a former NATO commander, immediately after he announced his candidacy on September 17 (see Figure 7.1). The boomlet faded as Clark's inexperience in electoral politics took its toll, leaving the mantle of military toughness to John Kerry, a decorated Vietnam veteran.

Kerry's astonishing comeback in the polls after his campaign for the nomination had been on the verge of collapse stands as the most eloquent testimony to Democrats' eagerness to defeat Bush. Kerry's support among Democrats was in single digits in most polls conducted during the three months preceding the Iowa caucuses; some surveys had even taken him off the list of candidates they asked about. But Kerry made an all-out effort in Iowa and managed to come out on top in the January 19 caucuses by mobilizing veterans and firefighters and sharpening his attacks on Bush while Dean and Gephardt were busy flailing at one another.[7] Both his military record and long experience in national politics helped Kerry persuade Iowa's activists that he was their best bet for November. According to a survey of caucus attendees, he attracted the most support from those for whom the most important quality was "right experience" or "can beat Bush."[8] The primal scream Dean unloosed during his televised Iowa concession speech reinforced doubts about his electability, moving many Democrats into Kerry's camp and ending Dean's hopes of winning the nomination.

---

[6] For example, his arguably accurate but ill-timed statement that "the capture of Saddam has not made America safer" while the United States was celebrating the event; see Associated Press, "Dean: America Not Safer After Saddam's Capture," December 16, 2003, at http://www.foxnews.com/story/0,2933,105789,00.html (accessed August 3, 2005).

[7] Barry C. Burden, "The Nominations: Technology, Money, and Transferable Momentum," in Michael Nelson, ed., The Elections of 2004 (Washington, DC: Congressional Quarterly Press, 2005), 29.

[8] Dean did best among those for whom the most important quality was "takes strong stands" and Edwards, best among those for whom the most important was "cares about people." See "Entrance Polls: Iowa," at http://www.cnn.com/ELECTION/2004/primaries/pages/epolls/IA/index.html (accessed August 2, 2005).

Kerry's victory in Iowa had a dramatic impact on Democrats across the nation, more than tripling his support virtually overnight and contributing to his victory in New Hampshire eight days later, which in turn inspired another sharp rise in the share of Democrats backing his nomination (see Figure 7.1).[9] Most ordinary Democrats were apparently ready to rally behind whichever of the contenders was best positioned to defeat Bush; their problem was figuring out who it was. Thus, they responded en masse when the Iowa Democrats sent a clear coordinating signal: "It's Kerry."[10] People knew little more about Kerry after New Hampshire than they had known before Iowa—other than that he had won in both states. Yet that was enough: In the three *Newsweek* polls taken before the Iowa caucuses, an average of 52 percent of Democrats viewed Kerry favorably, 16 percent unfavorably, and 32 percent didn't know enough to say; after the New Hampshire primary, the figures were 82 percent favorable, 7 percent unfavorable, and 11 percent unable to say.[11] In subsequent primaries, Kerry remained the overwhelming choice among Democrats for whom the most important candidate attribute was that "he can defeat George W. Bush."[12]

The Democrats' backing of Kerry was, then, more about Bush than about Kerry and remained so throughout the campaign. An election involving a sitting president is always largely a referendum on his performance, but Bush's centrality to the vote decision in 2004 was unique. As Figure 7.2 shows, a majority of Kerry supporters reported throughout the year that their vote would be more against Bush than for Kerry. This is unusual. Early in 1992, for example, 60 percent of Bill Clinton's supporters said that their vote would be more against George H. W. Bush than for Clinton, but by October only 36 percent gave this response. Early in 1996, 68 percent of Dole supporters said they were mainly

---

[9] These were substantially larger increases than usually follow victories in Iowa and New Hampshire; for a fuller discussion of this phenomenon, see Samuel L. Popkin, *The Reasoning Voter* (Chicago: University of Chicago Press, 1991), 117–129.

[10] This is not a message they could have gotten from polls; on average in the preprimary horse-race comparisons, Kerry matched up no better against Bush than did his major rivals. See http://www.pollingreport.com/wh04gen.htm (accessed February 3, 2004).

[11] Polls reported at http://pollingreport.com/k.htm (accessed August 5, 2005).

[12] Gary Langer, with Dalia Sussman, Cheryl Arenedt, and Maureen Michaels, "Electability Helps John Kerry, but Without Southern Comfort," ABC Exit Poll News Analysis, February 2, 2004, at http://abcnews.go.com/images/pdf/JrTuesdayAnalysis.pdf (accessed August 4, 2005); Gary Langer, Dave Morris, and Dalia Sussman, "The Electability Train Runs South," ABC Exit Poll News Analysis, March 11, 2004, at http://abcnews.go.com/images/pdf/VA-TNExitPollAnalysis.pdf (accessed August 4, 2005); "How Kerry Won, and the National Impact," Gallup Poll Analysis, January 28, 2004, at http://www.gallup.com/poll/releases/pr040128.asp?Version=p (accessed January 30, 2004).

FIGURE 7.2

George W. Bush's Centrality to Voting Decisions in 2004

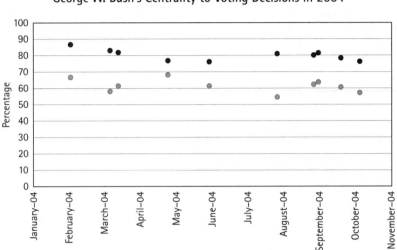

- Republicans saying their vote is more for Bush than against Kerry
- Democrats saying their vote is more against Bush than for Kerry

Source: Pew Research Center for the People and the Press Survey Report, October 31, 2004, at http://people-press.org/reports/display.php3?ReportID=232.

anti-Clinton, but only half were so by the end of the campaign. The proportion of Bush supporters who said their vote would be more for Bush than against Kerry—averaging about 80 percent and changing little over the course of the campaign—was also considerably higher than the equivalent percentage for previous presidents (66 percent for Clinton, and 60 percent for Bush senior).[13]

AN AVALANCHE OF MONEY

Kerry's momentum after New Hampshire carried him to a quick victory in the quest for his party's nomination; he clinched it on March 9, the same day as Bush, who had faced no primary opposition at all. Kerry

---

[13] Pew Center for the People and the Press, Survey Report, October 31, 2004, 10–11, at http://people-press.org/reports/display.php3?ReportID=232 (accessed August 4, 2005).

also began to run ahead of Bush in some horse-race polls. The tight race and high stakes in a sharply polarized context attracted an avalanche of campaign money for both campaigns. Both Bush and Kerry had rejected public money for the primary campaign and so were permitted to raise and spend unlimited sums until after the conventions. Their efforts and, more to the point, the political passions they were able to tap attracted an astonishing amount of campaign money, mostly from individual donors. Between them, the Bush and Kerry campaigns raised $847 million, nearly twice as much as was raised by the Gore and Bush campaigns in 2000 ($426 million) and nearly three times as much as the Clinton and Dole campaigns raised in 1996 ($288 million).[14] Independent expenditures, made mostly by national party organizations, amounted to another $245 million, and separate campaigns by so-called 527 groups (named after the section in the tax code applying to them) spent another $424 million, most of it on the presidential race.[15] Bush's prodigious fundraising prior to 2004—his campaign had nearly $100 million on hand as the election year began[16]—had been expected to given him a huge financial advantage over his Democratic opponent, but Democrats eager to defeat Bush filled Kerry's coffers, and with the additional help of 527 groups, Kerry's campaign enjoyed near financial parity with the president's, an altogether remarkable achievement.

THE WAR IN THE CAMPAIGNS

Although by no means the only issues, Bush's response to 9/11 in general and his invasion of Iraq in particular were inevitably a major focus of the 2004 presidential campaigns. The pivotal disagreement between Bush and Kerry concerned whether the war in Iraq was central to the war on terrorism or a distraction from it. Bush insisted that, regardless of mistaken assumptions about Saddam's WMD or complicity in 9/11, the war in Iraq was central to the war on terrorism, whereas Kerry argued that the

---

[14] "2004 Presidential Campaign Financial Activity Summarized," Federal Election Commission news release, February 3, 2005.
[15] Steve Weissman and Ruth Hassan, "BCRA and the 527 Groups," in Michael Malbin, ed., *The Election After Reform: Money, Politics and the Bipartisan Campaign Reform Act* (Lanham, MD: Rowman and Littlefield, 2005).
[16] "George W. Bush-Campaign Finances," at http://www.gwu.edu/~action/2004/bush/bushfin.html (accessed August 5, 2005).

FIGURE 7.3

Is the Iraq War a Major Part of the War on Terrorism, a Minor Part of the War on Terrorism, or Separate from the War on Terrrorism?

Republicans

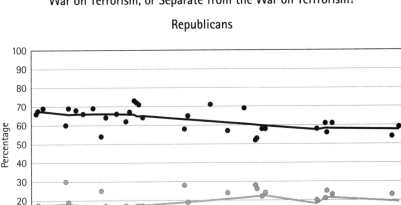

● War in Iraq is a major part of the war on terrorism
● War in Iraq is separate from the war on terrorism

Iraq invasion had unwisely taken resources from the pursuit of Osama Bin Laden and other al Qaeda terrorists who, unlike Iraq, had actually attacked the United States In the first televised debate between the two, for example, Kerry asserted that "Iraq is not . . . the center of the war on terror. The center is Afghanistan" and criticized Bush's decision to divert forces from there to Iraq. When Bush reiterated that "Iraq is a central part of the war on terror," Kerry came back with "Iraq was not even close to the center of the war on terror before the president invaded it." [17]

These opposing views were increasingly echoed by partisans in the general public as the campaigns progressed (Figure 7.3). From the war's beginning onward, large majorities of Republicans continued to accept Bush's

---

[17] "Transcript: First Presidential Debate," September 30, 2004, at http://www.washingtonpost.com/wp-srv/politics/debatereferee/debate_0930.html#c (accessed August 5, 2005).

FIGURE 7.3 *(continued)*

Democrats

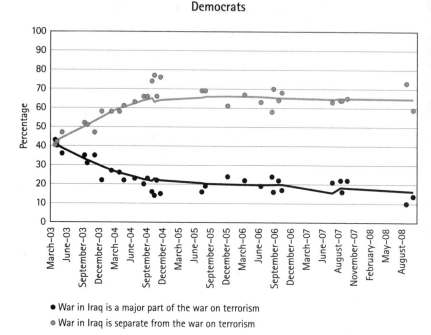

● War in Iraq is a major part of the war on terrorism
● War in Iraq is separate from the war on terrorism

Source: CBS News/*New York Times* polls and 2008 CCES.

argument that the Iraq War was a major part of the war on terrorism, and only a small and shrinking Republican minority thought it was separate from the war on terrorism.[18] Democrats increasingly took the latter position, and by the end of the campaign, more than 70 percent of them held this opinion. Thus, the gap between partisans on this issue widened steadily, reaching about 60 points in the final quarter of 2004. Thereafter, partisan opinions on this question remained stable until the end of Bush's second term. Both candidates, then, spoke persuasively to (or for) their own supporters on this issue but made no headway with those on the other side. Independents tended to move with Democrats on this question, going

---

[18] The third alternative was to consider the Iraq War a "minor" part of the war on terrorism; this option was taken by an average of 17 percent of Republicans, 14 percent of Democrats, and 18 percent of independents in these polls.

from an average of 49 percent "major part" and 34 percent "separate" in responses to polls taken in the spring of 2003 to an average of 51 percent "separate" and 32 percent "major part" in responses to polls taken close to the election. But among independents, this shift was completed by April 2004, before the campaigns had a chance to register.

There is, of course, no mystery about why Bush would want Americans to believe that Iraq was the central front in the war on terrorism despite the lack of evidence that it had anything to do with the attacks of 9/11. Not only did the argument offer a justification for a decision whose consequences were growing ever more troublesome, but it subordinated a domain in which Bush's approval was declining—his handling of Iraq—to the domain where his approval was highest—his handling of the war on terrorism (recall Figure 4.4). Surveys consistently found majorities believing that Bush would be better than Kerry in dealing with the terrorist threat, and to the degree that Bush could focus the electorate's attention on terrorism rather than on Iraq or convince people that the Iraq War and the war on terrorism were one and the same, he stood to benefit. The issue was an awkward one for Kerry; while arguing that America had been misled into a war that was unwise and unnecessary, he also had to say what he would do about it now that Colin Powell's Pottery Barn analogy ("You break it, you own it"[19]) had become all too apt. The consequences of abandoning Iraq before order had been restored and Iraqis had established some viable form of self-government were potentially disastrous now that the notion of Iraq as a center of anti-American Islamic terrorism had become a self-created reality. For all his criticism of the decision to invade Iraq, Kerry's ideas about what to do there now were hard to distinguish from the president's.

OPINION LEADERSHIP

The partisan reactions to the question of whether the Iraq War was central to or a distraction from the war on terrorism illustrate a feature of the relationship between public opinion and questions of war and peace that is heightened during presidential elections as the competing campaigns increase public awareness, articulate partisan cues, and accentuate partisan divisions: opinion leadership. Students of public

---

[19] Woodward, *Plan of Attack*, 150.

opinion have long recognized that, regarding most public issues and most especially issues pertaining to foreign affairs, a large majority of ordinary citizens are usually inattentive, uninformed, and thus largely dependent on cues from opinion leaders in deciding how to respond to survey questions. On matters of war and peace, national political elites are supposed to be the predominant cue-givers. Public responses, according to John Zaller's leading theory on the subject, depend on the interactive effects of predispositions and political awareness. The more politically aware an individual is, the more likely he or she is to get the message; the more consistent the message is with an individual's predispositions, the more likely it is to be accepted. This creates a distinction between "mainstream" and "polarization" effects, which have predictably different observable consequences. When a unified political elite sends a consistent message, then the more politically aware people are, the more likely they are to receive and accept the message (mainstream effect). When political leaders are divided by party (or ideology) on an issue, then the greater the level of awareness is, the more polarized the responses, as individuals follow the messenger they are predisposed to heed (polarization effect).[20]

Although my emphasis in this book has been on polarization, reactions to events during the Bush administration that were registered in the 2004 American National Election Study offer illustrations of both kinds of effects. Military action in Afghanistan received strong bipartisan support in Congress and among political leaders more generally. No important figure during the presidential campaign criticized the decision to use United States forces to pursue al Qaeda and drive its Taliban allies from power. Elite communications about the action thus generated mainstream effects, as Figure 7.4 demonstrates. The more politically aware the respondent was,[21] the more likely he or she was to believe that the war in Afghanistan was worth the cost. Support for the action increased with awareness regardless of party, with the most informed respondents showing the smallest partisan difference.

---

[20] John R. Zaller, *The Nature and Origins of Mass Opinion* (Cambridge: Cambridge University Press, 1992), ch. 6.
[21] Following Zaller, I use a simple information battery to measure political awareness. The ANES asked respondents to identify Dick Cheney, Tony Blair, Dennis Hastert, and William Rehnquist. Awareness is measured by the number of correct answers. The distribution was zero, 15 percent; one, 22 percent; two, 35 percent; three, 20 percent, and four, 8 percent.

FIGURE 7.4

Political Awareness and Support for Military Action in Afghanistan

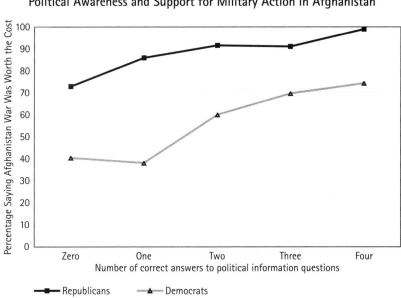

Note: Respondents were asked to identify Dick Cheney, Tony Blair, Dennis Hastert, and William Rehnquist.
Source: 2004 American National Election Study.

By the 2004 election, in contrast, Bush, Kerry, and other political leaders had become divided along party lines by the Iraq War, and consequently, belief that the venture was worth the cost was related positively to political awareness among Republicans but negatively to awareness among Democrats (Figure 7.5). Polarization thus increased steeply with political awareness: The least aware Republicans and Democrats were 31 points apart; the most informed, 77 points apart.

Opinion leadership was, of course, in evidence long before the election. George W. Bush was without question the dominant source of cues that shaped Republicans' opinions about the war in Iraq at this time, but he was backed by Secretary of State Colin Powell (more widely esteemed than the president) as well as virtually all Republicans of stature in or out of government. Ordinary Republicans thus had little inducement to break ranks, and they did not. But this raises the question of why solidarity among Republican elites was so high and why it generally survived the collapse of the original case for war. It is at least conceivable that the

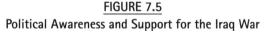

FIGURE 7.5

Political Awareness and Support for the Iraq War

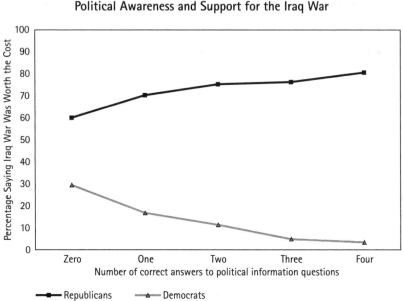

Note: Respondents were asked to identify Dick Cheney, Tony Blair, Dennis Hastert, and William Rehnquist.
Source: 2004 American National Election Study.

president's continued rock-solid support among ordinary Republicans had something to do with it: Republican opinion leaders who dissented might well have lost that status.

Among Democrats as well, it is not obvious that opinion leaders always led rather than followed. As we saw in Chapter 4, many Democrats in Congress had supported the war, including all who were prospective presidential aspirants. Indeed, Bush got a larger share of House and Senate Democrats' votes for the war against Iraq than his father had gotten for the Gulf War twelve years earlier, even though support for the second war was significantly lower among ordinary Democrats than it had been for the first.[22] Public delight with the American and British forces' rapid

---

[22] In five polls taken during the month before the start of the Gulf War in 1991, an average of 53 percent of Democrats supported going to war, with support dipping below 50 percent in only one survey; in fifteen polls taken during the month before the start of the Iraq War in 2003, an average of 44 percent of Democrats backed going to war, and in only four of the polls did support for it exceed 50 percent.

success and low casualties in the first month of the Iraq War discouraged vocal criticism or expressions of second thoughts among Democratic leaders for a considerable time afterward. No one was sorry to see Saddam gone, and, as noted in Chapter 6, criticizing the invasion invited the retort, "So, you'd rather have Saddam still in power?" Eventually, the persistent chaos and continuing violence, combined with the failure to find WMD or evidence of Saddam's involvement in 9/11, greatly reduced the political risks of questioning the war's wisdom or necessity, but it was not until Howard Dean found a receptive audience among ordinary Democrats for criticism of Bush's war that it became common among Democratic leaders. Just as in the case of Clinton's impeachment, mainstream Democratic politicians appeared to be taking cues from their followers, not vice versa.[23]

RATIONAL IGNORANCE?

Opinion leadership can be considered a species of delegation: Rationally ignorant citizens with neither the time nor inclination to understand the complexities of, for example, foreign policy delegate that task to trusted agents who supposedly command the necessary expertise. Ideally, this process enables people to achieve cognitive efficiency (substituting cheap, simple cues for complex, expensive information) while reaching the same conclusions they would have reached had they been as fully informed as their agents.[24] For the process to work benignly, people are supposed to use freely available information to monitor their agents, compelling them to maintain a minimum level of credibility lest they lose the trust essential to their status as opinion leaders. The example of the Iraq War, however, shows that opinions may be remarkably impervious to discordant information because people with strong priors are so ready to miss or deny its implications.

As we saw in Chapter 6, the absence of evidence that Iraq possessed WMD and that Saddam Hussein had been involved in 9/11 did not prevent large numbers of Americans, particularly Republicans, from continuing

---

[23] Gary C. Jacobson, "Public Opinion and the Impeachment of Bill Clinton," in Philip Cowley, David Denver, Andrew Russell, and Lisa Harrison, eds., *British Elections and Parties Review* 10 (London: Frank Cass, 2000), 1–31.

[24] Arthur Lupia and Mathew D. McCubbins, *The Democratic Dilemma: Can Citizens Learn What They Need to Know?* (Cambridge: Cambridge University Press, 1998), ch. 5.

TABLE 7.1
Bush and Kerry Supporters' Beliefs Concerning Justifications for the Iraq War (Percentages)

	BUSH SUPPORTERS	KERRY SUPPORTERS
Iraq had actual weapons of mass destruction or a major program for developing them.	72	26
Iraq's involvement with al Qaeda:		
Iraq was directly involved in 9/11	20	8
Iraq gave al Qaeda substantial support	55	22
Total	75	30
Experts now believe that before the war:		
Iraq had WMD	56	18
Iraq did not have WMD	23	56
Experts are divided on the question	18	23
Duelfer Report (ordered by President Bush) said:		
Iraq had WMD	19	7
Iraq had major program to build WMD	38	16
Total	57	23
9/11 Commission Report concluded:		
Iraq was directly involved in 9/11	13	7
Iraq gave al Qaeda substantial support	43	20
Total	56	27

SOURCE: PIPA/Knowledge Networks Poll: The American Public on International Issues, "The Separate Realities of Bush and Kerry Supporters," at http://zzpat.tripod.com/cvb/pipa.html.

to believe both of these rationales for the war. But a survey taken during the 2004 presidential campaign revealed a level of resistance to dissonant information more striking still. The PIPA/Knowledge Networks Poll conducted in September and October asked not only respondents' opinions about the war's main rationales, but also strictly factual questions about what well-publicized official reports issued after the war had concluded about their accuracy. Differences between Bush and Kerry supporters were predictably huge on the two basic justifications involving WMD and an al Qaeda connection (see the first two questions in Table 7.1). But substantial differences also persisted on strictly factual questions, with Republicans displaying a startling capacity to answer them wrong: Only 23 percent recognized that the consensus of experts analyzing postwar information was that Iraq had not possessed WMD immediately prior to the war; 57 percent and 56 percent, respectively, got the Duelfer Report and the 9/11 Commission conclusions exactly backwards. Kerry supporters appeared to be considerably better informed, but then the information was more consistent with their biases, and it is notable that from 23 percent to 41 percent of them also got the factual questions wrong.

Even knowing what was in the official reports did not necessarily convince Bush supporters that the war's premises had been wrong; 18 percent who acknowledged that the Duelfer Report, ordered by Bush from the CIA, had concluded that Iraq had no WMD and no active program to produce them still believed otherwise.[25] The survey also pointed to the explanation for Bush supporters' continuing acceptance of the discredited rationales: They thought that the Bush administration was sticking to them (Table 7.2). Large majorities of Bush and Kerry supporters alike believed that the administration was still making claims that the official reports, ostensibly accepted by administration officials as accurate, had concluded were unfounded; smaller majorities even believed that the administration was saying it had found clear evidence of WMD and a close al Qaeda connection. The strong, bipartisan agreement on these perceptions suggests that, if the Bush administration had indeed admitted that the original premises for the war were faulty, it had done it so quietly and equivocally that most of the public had missed the concession. Bush's categorical refusal to admit any mistake regarding the war, at least in public, thus probably helped keep his supporters loyal at the same time it reinforced the distrust and disdain of his opponents.

The survey also discovered high levels of misinformation among Bush supporters on other questions concerning the war and the election. Only 31 percent (compared with 74 percent of Kerry supporters) recognized that a majority of people surveyed in other countries opposed the Iraq War; only 9 percent acknowledged that most people in other countries preferred Kerry to Bush for president (69 percent of Kerry supporters got it right); 17 percent (compared with 86 percent of Kerry supporters) realized that world opinion of the United States had been made worse by

---

[25] "The Separate Realities of Bush and Kerry Supporters," the PIPA/Knowledge Networks Poll: The American Public on International Issues, 4, at http://zzpat.tripod.com/cvb/pipa.html (accessed November 24, 2004).

TABLE 7.2
Perceptions of the Bush Administration's Statements Concerning the Justifications for the Iraq War (Percentages)

	BUSH SUPPORTERS	KERRY SUPPORTERS
Believe the Bush administration is saying that prior to war:		
Iraq had WMD	63	58
Iraq had major program to build WMD	19	24
Total	82	82
Believe the Bush administration is saying that:		
Iraq was directly involved in 9/11	19	25
Iraq gave al Qaeda substantial support	56	49
Total	75	74
Believe the Bush administration is saying United States has found clear evidence Saddam Hussein worked closely with al Qaeda	55	52

SOURCE: PIPA/Knowledge Networks Poll: The American Public on International Issues, "The Separate Realities of Bush and Kerry Supporters," at http://zzpat.tripod.com/cvb/pipa.html.

Bush's foreign policies. Bush and Kerry supporters did indeed seem to exist in "separate realities,"[26] as a majority of Bush's supporters misperceived facts to keep their beliefs consonant with a commitment to the president. I will have more to say about this in Chapter 9.

MOBILIZING VOTERS

The deep partisan divisions inherited and reinforced by the Bush administration shaped the strategies of both the Bush and the Kerry campaigns, which put far more effort into mobilizing their own partisans than in reaching out to the dwindling number of uncommitted voters or to partisans on the other side. Both succeeded. Kerry's campaign actually surpassed its mobilization targets, producing a total Democratic vote 16 percent higher than Al Gore's 2000 total. But

---

[26] Ibid., 6–7.

Bush's campaign did even better, increasing his total vote by 23 percent over that of 2000 and delivering him a narrow but unambiguous victory—50.7 percent of the popular vote to Kerry's 48.3 percent.[27] The Bush campaign's most important targets were religious conservatives, notably the five million conservative Christians who Karl Rove, the president's chief strategist, estimated had sat out the 2000 election. Skirting the rules restricting partisan activities by tax-exempt organizations, the campaign organized "friendly congregations" and encouraged clergy to carry the Bush message. It was often an easy sell, for many conservative Christian groups were already organizing their own campaigns for the president. Their efforts were aided by the Massachusetts Supreme Court decision giving that state's same-sex couples the right to marry, which Bush had responded to by backing a constitutional amendment outlawing the practice.[28]

Republican strategists were, of course, fully aware of how strongly religious conservatives had bonded with the president. A preelection ABC News/*Washington Post* survey that, in addition to the usual political and demographic questions, asked respondents to classify themselves as "very religious," "somewhat religious," or "not religious" revealed just how totally the very religious Republicans (44 percent of the party's identifiers) belonged to the president (Table 7.3). They were most supportive of his war and gave him the highest performance ratings of any subgroup (ranging from 91 percent on his handling of Iraq to 98 percent on his handling of the terrorist threat). They were even overwhelmingly positive about the economy and Bush's handling of it, not the president's strongest suit at this juncture. And they were virtually unanimous in planning to vote for him later in the fall. Very religious respondents among independents and Democrats also usually viewed the president more positively than their less religious counterparts. Very religious Republicans and secular Democrats, together comprising about 20 percent of the adult population, could scarcely have been more polarized. As to

---

[27] According to the 2004 American National Election Study, presidential turnout among Democratic identifiers was 5.0 percentage points higher than that in 2000 and 5.5 points higher than their 1972–2000 average; among Republican identifiers, turnout was 8.5 points higher than that in 2000 and 7.5 points higher than their 1972–2000 average. ANES respondents always overstate their participation, but this does not prevent valid cross-election comparisons. ANES data for these elections are in the ANES Cumulative Data File, available at http://www.electionstudies.org/studypages/cdf/cdf.htm (accessed March 22, 2010).

[28] Alan Cooperman and Thomas B. Edsall, "Evangelicals Say They Led the Charge for the GOP," *Washington Post*, November 8, 2004, A01.

TABLE 7.3

Religiosity and Attitudes Toward George W. Bush and the Iraq War, September 2004 (Percentages)

	REPUBLICANS			INDEPENDENTS			DEMOCRATS		
	Very Religious	Somewhat Religious	Not Religious	Very Religious	Somewhat Religious	Not Religious	Very Religious	Somewhat Religious	Not Religious
Percentage in category (within party)	44	41	15	28	42	31	31	41	28
Iraq War was worth the cost	87	73	58	61	50	36	25	17	11
Approve Bush's handling of Iraq	91	84	55	61	52	37	18	20	9
Economy is excellent or good	85	75	65	48	46	40	22	19	22
Approve Bush's handling of the economy	95	86	74	56	41	38	20	14	10
Approve Bush's handling of terrorist threat	98	96	68	68	64	59	38	28	21
Approve of Bush's job performance	96	91	59	73	58	34	23	20	10
Plan to vote for Bush in November	98	96	79	68	48	29	22	16	6

SOURCE: ABC News/*Washington Post* Poll, September 23–26, 2004.

mobilization, Republicans who identified themselves as very religious in this survey were also the most likely to report having been contacted by organizations supporting Bush (32 percent, compared with 22 percent for somewhat religious and 11 percent for Republicans who were not religious); among Democrats, secular respondents were more likely to have been contacted by their candidate's supporters (31 percent, compared with 19 percent for other Democrats). The mobilization efforts, then, were skewed toward the extremes on this dimension.

THE VOTE

High turnout was only one manifestation of the polarized electorate in 2004. Surveys taken during the campaign season found that, compared with previous elections, fewer voters were undecided, fewer were open to changing their minds, more supported their candidate strongly, and more thought the election was "extremely important" and that it "really matters who wins."[29] The proportions of respondents in the 2004 American National Election Study (ANES) who said that there were important differences between the parties, who cared who won, and who tried to influence someone else's vote were the highest ever recorded.[30] The polarized atmosphere and partisan mobilization efforts produced the highest level of party-line voting in the fifty-two-year history of the ANES, eclipsing the previous record set in 2000. With leaners included as partisans, 89.0 percent of Democrats and 90.6 percent of Republicans voted for their party's candidates; excluding leaners, the respective figures are 92.0 percent and 94.0 percent. Because the proportion of purely independent voters in 2004 also matched its all-time low, the proportion of the electorate composed of loyal partisans—84.8 percent—was also the highest ever recorded by the ANES (the previous record, 81.3 percent, was set in 2000).[31]

---

[29] "Choice of President Matters More in 2004," news release, Pew Research Center for the People and the Press, July 8, 2004; "Swing Vote Smaller Than Usual, but Still Sizable," news release, Pew Research Center for the People and the Press, June 24, 2004; "Slight Bush Margin in Final Days of Campaign," news release, Pew Research Center for the People and the Press, October 30, 2004.

[30] Alan I. Abramowitz and Walter J. Stone, "The Bush Effect: Polarization, Turnout, and Activism in the 2004 Presidential Election," presented at the Annual Meeting of the American Political Science Association, Washington, DC, September 1–4, 2005.

[31] Data are from my own analysis of the 2004 American National Election Study. Exit polls documented equally high levels of party loyalty; see "Election Results" at http://www.cnn.com/ELECTION/2004/pages/results/states/US/P/00/epolls.0.html (accessed November 26, 2004).

FIGURE 7.6
Issues and Character in the 2004 Vote

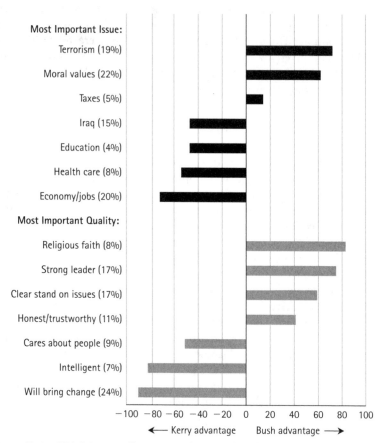

Source: National Exit Poll at http://www.cnn.com/ELECTION/2004/pages/results/states/US/P/00/epolls.0.html.

The electoral divisions exposed in 2000 (see Chapter 3) reappeared in 2004, and the voting patterns suggest little change in voters' preferences between the two elections. At the House district level, for example, the correlation between the major-party presidential vote in 2000 and 2004 was .98. The exit polls indicated that Bush and Kerry voters had quite different ideas about what issues and candidate characteristics were most important (Figure 7.6). Bush was the strong favorite among those who put terrorism or moral values at the top of their concerns and was a slight favorite among voters caring most about taxes; Kerry was preferred by people who thought education, health care, or the economy was most important. He was also preferred by those most concerned with Iraq. Bush was the overwhelming favorite of voters who thought religious faith was the most important quality in a president; he also dominated among voters who listed strong leadership, clear stands on issues, and honesty as most important. Kerry was preferred by those who believed caring about people was most important, and he was the overwhelming favorite among those for whom intelligence mattered most. Unfortunately for Kerry, only 7 percent of the electorate put the highest premium on intelligence. His largest margin came from the quarter of the electorate who thought what mattered most was bringing change—that is, those for whom the most important thing was making George W. Bush a one-term president.

Opinions on the Iraq War were, not surprisingly, strongly related to the vote (Figure 7.7). Relative support for Bush and Kerry varied dramatically according to whether or not voters approved of the war, believed it was part of the war on terrorism, believed it had made the United States safer, and thought it was going well. The ANES survey also found a tight relationship between support for the war and the presidential vote, which remains when party identification is taken into account (Figure 7.8); the relationship was particularly strong for the pure independents.[32] In total, 89 percent of Democrats and 82 percent of Republicans and independents cast a presidential vote consistent with their views on whether or not the Iraq War was worth the cost. It is also worth noting that the Iraq War question was asked in the preelection wave of the ANES survey, whereas the vote question was naturally asked after the election, reducing the likelihood that the answer to the former was merely a rationalization of the answer to the latter.

Opinion as to whether the Iraq War was worth the cost remains a strong predictor of the presidential vote when a variety of variables in addition to party identification are taken into account. The estimated coefficient of this variable in the first logit model in Table 7.4 shows its continued potency when party identification, ideology, income, religious

---

[32] The question was "Taking everything into account, do you think the war in Iraq has been worth the cost or not?"

FIGURE 7.7
Opinions on the Iraq War and the 2004 Vote

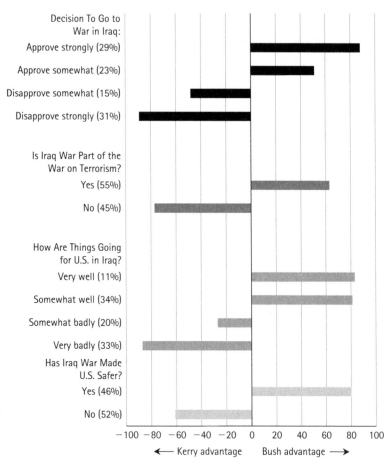

Source: National Exit Poll at http://www.cnn.com/ELECTION/2004/pages/results/states/US/P/00/ epolls.0.html.

service attendance, gender, and race and ethnicity are taken into account. The coefficient indicates that, for example, if values on the other variables predicted a .33 probability of voting for Bush, that probability would increase to .90 if the respondent believed that the Iraq War was worth the cost rather than the contrary; similarly, a .50 initial probability would become .95, and an initial .67 probability would become .97, if

FIGURE 7.8
Support for Iraq War and the Presidential Vote Choice

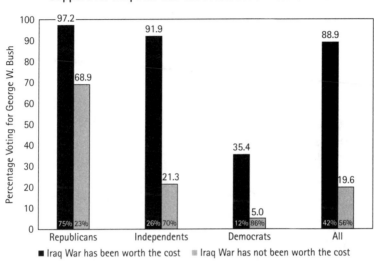

Note: The proportion of respondents in the category appears at the bottom of the column.
Source: 2004 American National Election Study.

TABLE 7.4
Multivariate Logit Models of Presidential Voting in 2004

	MODEL 1	MODEL 2	MODEL 3
Iraq War was worth the cost	2.97***	1.85***	1.48***
	(.34)	(.39)	(.43)
Party identification	.86***	.68***	.65***
	(.09)	(.11)	(.11)
Ideology	.80***	.43	.39
	(.24)	(.27)	(.27)
Income	.17	.34	.36
	(.19)	(.22)	(.23)
Religious service attendance	.21*	.26*	.25*
	(.10)	(.12)	(.12)

TABLE 7.4 (continued)

	MODEL 1	MODEL 2	MODEL 3
Male	−.11	−.11	−.12
	(.30)	(35)	(.35)
African American	−1.44***	−1.62***	−1.67***
	(.42)	(.45)	(.46)
Hispanic	.54	−.33	−.12
	(.50)	(.56)	(.56)
Approve of G. W. Bush's overall performance		2.87***	2.61***
		(.38)	(.39)
Approve of G. W. Bush's handling of Iraq			.95*
			(.44)
Constant	−4.14***	−4.71***	−4.64***
	(.50)	(.60)	(.61)
Log likelihood chi square	683.93	747.41	752.09
Pseudo R-squared	.68	.74	.75
Number of cases	726	726	726

NOTE: The dependent variable is 1 if the respondent voted for Bush, 0 if for Kerry; the Iraq War variable takes the value of 1 if the war was worth it, 0 otherwise; party identification is a 7-point scale from 0 (strong Democrat) to 6 (strong Republican); ideology takes a value of 1 for respondents placing themselves to the right of center on a 7-point liberal-conservative scale, −1 to the left of center, and 0 at the center; income takes the value of 1 if family income falls into the top third, 0 if in the middle third, and −1 if in the bottom third; religious service attendance is 1 = never, 2 = a few times a year, 3 = once or twice a month, 4 = almost every week, 5 = every week; male, African American, and Hispanic take 1 if respondent is in the category, 0 otherwise; the approval variables are scored 1 if respondent approved, 0 if not.; standard errors are in parentheses.

SOURCE: 2004 American National Election Study.

*$p < .05$
**$p < .01$
***$p < .001$

the respondent thought the war was worth it. We know that opinions on the war are strongly related to approval of the president overall and approval of his handling of Iraq in particular and that these variables should also be very strongly related to the vote, but opinion on the war remains a strong predictor of presidential preference even when the first (Model 2) or both (Model 3) of these approval variables are included in the equation. The coefficient of the war opinion variable in Model 3 indicates that if the values of the other variables produced an initial probability of voting for Bush of .33, it would double to .67 if the respondent also thought the war was worth it; under the same conditions, a .50 probability would become .81, and a .67 probability would become .89.

Party identification remains the most powerful predictor of the vote in all of these equations, and race always makes a substantial difference, reflecting the low level of regard for Bush (and other Republicans) among African Americans. Religiosity as expressed by service attendance also has a stable independent effect on the vote; for example, with other variables remaining unchanged, Model 3's predicted probability of voting for Bush would rise from .33 to .57 if religious attendance was in the highest rather than the lowest category. Income, gender, and Hispanic ethnicity, on the other hand, are not significantly related to the vote once the other variables are controlled (although all three are, by themselves, significantly related to it).

Bush's narrow victory was a product of higher Republican turnout and slightly greater party loyalty among Republican identifiers. His advantage over Kerry on the terrorism issue[33] was the principal source of Democratic defections; the 23 percent of Democrats in the ANES survey who approved of Bush's handling of terrorism defected to Bush at a rate twelve times greater than that of the 77 percent who did not approve (32.7 percent compared with 2.6 percent). The Kerry campaign's hesitant response to attacks on his Vietnam War record by the Swift Boat Veterans for Truth, a 527 group distinguishable from the Bush campaign only by a legal fiction, may have raised doubts about Kerry's reliability among enough Democrats nervous about homeland security to cost him the election. Unlike every previous winner except John Kennedy in 1960, Bush ran behind among independents, 48 percent to 49 percent in the

---

[33] For a summary of the polling data on this question, see James E. Campbell, "Why Bush Won the Presidential Election of 2004: Incumbency, Ideology, Terrorism, and Turnout," *Political Science Quarterly* 120 (Summer 2005): 225.

exit polls and 40 percent to 55 percent in the ANES study (excluding partisan leaners, 40 percent to 58 percent). In any close election, every contribution to victory is arguably decisive, but there is no question that the superior turnout and loyalty of Republicans was the sine qua none of Bush's reelection.

THE CONGRESS

The intensely partisan presidential contest found echoes in the 2004 House and Senate elections, much to the advantage of Republican candidates, for the unusually high Republican turnout and high levels of party-line voting served to magnify the already-formidable structural advantage Republicans enjoy in the battle for congressional seats.[34] The advantage stems from the greater efficiency with which Republican voters are distributed across districts and states, most clearly evident in the major-party vote for president in 2000. Short-term political forces were evenly balanced that year, and party-line voting was the highest it had been in decades, so both the national- and the district-level presidential vote reflected the electorate's underlying partisan balance with unusual accuracy.[35] The Democrat, Al Gore, won the national popular vote by about 540,000 of the 105 million votes cast. Yet the distribution of these votes across current House districts yielded 240 in which Bush won more votes than Gore but only 195 in which Gore outpolled Bush. Part of the reason for this Republican advantage is demographic: Democrats appeal to a disproportionate share of minority and other urban voters, who tend to be concentrated in districts with lopsided Democratic majorities.[36] But it is also a product of successful partisan gerrymanders brought about by the Republicans in states where they controlled the redistricting process after the 2000 census.[37] Democrats actually ran stronger in House races in

[34] Gary C. Jacobson, "Polarized Politics and the 2004 Congressional and Presidential Elections," *Political Science Quarterly* 120 (Summer 2005): 211.

[35] Gary C. Jacobson, "A House and Senate Divided: The Clinton Legacy and the Congressional Elections of 2000," *Political Science Quarterly* 116 (Spring, 2001): 5–27.

[36] For example, according to the CBS News/*New York Times* Poll of August 20–25, 2004, Democratic identifiers outnumbered Republicans nearly five to one in New York City. See "New York City and the Republican Convention" at http://www.cbsnews.com/htdocs/CBSNews_polls/nyc.pdf (November 6, 2004).

[37] The most important of these states were Florida, Michigan, Ohio, Pennsylvania, and, after 2002, Texas.

2004 than they had in 2002,[38] yet the high levels of party polarization and loyalty reinforced the Democrats' structural handicap, leaving them no chance of making significant gains. They lost a net three seats but would have gained a like number had it not been for the Republicans' remapping of Texas after they took control of the state in 2002.[39] Very few House seats changed party hands in 2004, but 80 percent of them went to the party winning the most presidential votes in the district. The number of districts with split House and presidential outcomes dropped to 59 (14 percent of all seats), the lowest in the half-century such data have been available. [40]

Republicans enjoy a similar structural advantage in pursuing Senate seats, an edge that was enhanced by the class of seats up for election in 2004. Despite running behind Gore nationally, Bush had carried thirty of the fifty states in 2000, including twenty-two of the thirty-four states with Senate contests in 2004. Democrats had to defend ten seats in states Bush had won, including five left open by retirements, all in the South, where support for Democrats has been eroding for several decades (see Chapter 2). Meanwhile, Republicans were defending only three seats in states won by Gore. In the end, Republicans won all five of the southern Democratic seats and made a net gain of four; eight of the nine Senate seats that changed party hands conformed to the red state–blue state presidential division. After the election, three-quarters of Senate seats were held by the party whose presidential candidate had taken the state in 2004, the highest level of partisan consistency of this sort in at least five decades.[41]

High turnout and high party loyalty, combined with the Republicans' structural advantage and the mix of Senate seats contested in 2004, thus served to strengthen the Republican grip on Congress despite the absence of any pro-Republican trend in public opinion. Indeed, the Bush administration's strategy of serving the party's base while in office and putting most of its energies into mobilizing core supporters during the reelection campaign was arguably even more productive for congressional Republicans than it was for the president. Under the circumstances prevailing in

---

[38] Their total vote increased by 1.0 percent from 48.1 to 49.1; their average district-level vote increased by 1.4 percentage points in districts contested in both 2002 and 2004; in nearly two-thirds of these districts, Democrats improved on their 2002 vote.
[39] Jacobson, "Polarized Politics," 201–202.
[40] Ibid., 207.
[41] Jacobson, "2004 Election," 209.

2004, a partisan standoff with both sides highly motivated and loyal to their parties assured Republican control of Congress.

The results of the congressional elections promised little mitigation of the intensely partisan atmosphere in which they took place. The turnover of congressional seats pointed in the opposite direction. All six of the Senate Democrats replaced by Republicans had been more moderate than their party's average (based on DW-Nominate scores). Four of the six newly elected Republican senators who had served in the House were more conservative than their party's average in that body. Moreover, the two retiring Republican senators whose seats were won by Democrats had voted to the left of their party's mean. Thus, in the Senate, both parties lost moderates and, at least on the Republican side, gained more extreme ideologues. Changes brought about by the House elections had a similar thrust, though the effect was smaller because a much smaller proportion of House seats changed party hands. The five Texas Democrats who were pushed out by redistricting and replaced by Republicans had been more conservative than the average for their party, as was Ralph Hall, who had taken one look at the new district lines and decided he was really a Republican. However, the net ideological effect of the other six party turnovers in the House was, by the same standard, neutral.[42]

AFTERMATH

National campaigns always intensify partisan differences, but issues, campaign strategies, and the fact that the election was a referendum on an especially divisive administration engaged in an especially divisive war magnified their effect in 2004. Bush won reelection by the smallest margin of any president in history, and few Democrats were satisfied with the outcome; in one postelection survey asking about feelings rather than opinions, 88 percent of Kerry voters said they felt disappointed, 74 percent, worried, 35 percent, angry, and 29 percent, depressed.[43] The election left

---

[42] Ibid., 213–214.

[43] Bush voters, in contrast, felt relieved (90 percent), reassured (90 percent), safer (88 percent), and elated (64 percent); see "Voters Liked Campaign 2004, but Too Much 'Mud-Slinging,'" Research Report, Pew Center for the People and the Press, November 11, 2004, at http://people-press.org/reports/display.php3?ReportID=233 (accessed November 12, 2004).

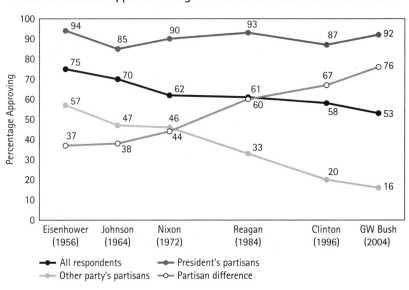

FIGURE 7.9

First Postelection Approval Ratings of Presidents Elected to Second Terms

Source: First postelection Gallup poll.

the nation as widely divided along party lines in their assessments of the winner as they had been before. As a result, Bush received the lowest overall Gallup job approval rating of any newly reelected president for whom survey data are available, as his near-unanimous approval among Republicans was offset by extraordinarily low approval among Democrats, producing the largest partisan gap (76 percentage points) in the series (Figure 7.9).[44] The 2004 election thus consolidated George W. Bush's status as "a divider, not a uniter," and nothing in the conduct or substance of his campaign suggested that his second term would do anything to change it.

---

[44] Note also the downward trend over time in approval by the loser's partisans, another manifestation of the long-term trend in out-party presidential approval discussed in Chapter 2.

CHAPTER **8**

■ ■ ■ ■ ■ ▓▓

President of Half the People

I n his first press conference after his reelection in 2004, George W. Bush
let it be known that he planned an aggressive second-term domestic
agenda—partial privatization of Social Security, making the 2001 tax
cuts permanent, tax "simplification," cutting social programs, pursuing proindustry tort reform and energy and environmental policies—
that was likely to be even more divisive than his first. "I earned capital
in the campaign, political capital," he told reporters, "and now I intend
to spend it. It is my style . . . I've earned capital in this election—and
I'm going to spend it for what I told the people I'd spend it on, which
is—you've heard the agenda: Social Security and tax reform, moving
this economy forward, education, fighting and winning the war on terror."[1] It certainly was his style; despite losing the popular vote in 2000,
Bush had acted in his first term as if he had won a mandate, so it was
inconceivable he would do otherwise after his undisputed victory in
2004. Moreover, the election had given him Republican reinforcements
in the House and Senate, enlarging his ambitions by making it easier
for him to prevail on the Hill, at least as long as Republicans stuck
together.

---

[1] Dan Froomkin, "Bush Agenda: Bold but Blurry," November 5, 2004, at http://www.washingtonpost.
com/wp%2Ddyn/articles/A27833%2D2004Nov5.html (accessed August 12, 2005).

A MANDATE?

All winners like to claim popular mandates, although more often than not, the claim commits the classic logical fallacy—*post hoc, ergo proctor hoc* ("after this, therefore because of this"). As Bush expressed it, "After hundreds of speeches and three debates and interviews and the whole process, where you keep basically saying the same thing over and over again, that when you win, there is a feeling that the people have spoken and embraced your point of view, and that's what I intend to tell the Congress, that I made it clear what I intend to do as the President, now let's work to—and the people made it clear what they wanted, now let's work together."[2] In the afterglow of victory, such assertions are understandable if empirically dubious,[3] but as Bush's statement makes clear, they are also tactical, intended to persuade other politicians that their constituents want what the president wants.

But how much political capital did Bush actually gain from the election? And what popular mandate did he receive, other than to continue keeping terrorists at bay? The answer to the first question is, not much, if any at all. The election left Americans as evenly and widely divided along party lines in their opinions of the president as they had been before it (recall Figures 1.2 and 7.9). The president's high job approval ratings among Republicans, and their high turnout and loyalty at the polls, left no doubt that he had amassed a generous stock of political capital among his own partisans. But there was little postelection softening of Democratic hostility, and his approval among independents remained well below 50 percent. In terms of popular approval, Bush was actually in a stronger position after his first election than after his second. In the first quarter of his first term, Bush's job approval rating averaged 89 percent among Republicans, 55 percent among independents, and 32 percent among Democrats; in the first quarter of his second term, the comparable averages were 90 percent, 43 percent, and 18 percent, respectively.[4] If "political capital" means popular support that can be drawn upon to win legislative victories,[5] Bush's was in a currency honored only in Republican territory.

---

[2] Ibid.
[3] One systematic analysis identified only three "mandate elections" since 1960: 1964, 1980, and 1994. See David A. M. Peterson, Lawrence W. Grossback, James A. Stimson, and Amy Gangl, "Congressional Response to Mandate Elections," *American Journal of Political Science* 47 (July 2003): 416–417.
[4] Calculated from the data in Figure 1.2.
[5] And popular support does help in this regard; see Gary C. Jacobson, "Partisan Polarization in Presidential Support: The Electoral Connection," *Congress and the Presidency* 30 (Spring 2003): 29.

Neither is there much plausible evidence of a mandate for Bush's domestic agenda. Had terrorism not been in the picture and had the election hinged on domestic issues, Kerry would almost certainly have won. Asked specifically about mandates in the *Time* Magazine/SRBI Poll taken in December 2004, only 33 percent of respondents said Bush had won a mandate to partially privatize Social Security, and only 38 percent said he had won a mandate to change the tax structure.[6] Majority support for his Social Security and tax proposals was limited to Republicans.[7] Again, if he had a mandate, it was from only his own partisans.

As a practical matter, however, neither of these things would matter for the second term as long as the president could count on overwhelming support from ordinary Republicans and, consequently, the Republicans on the Hill. The first term had demonstrated that playing to the base could be a successful legislative strategy; Democrats could be ignored or co-opted with minor concessions as long as Republican leaders kept the troops together, as they usually did. If Republicans were to split, however, Bush could not expect much help from Democrats. Quite the opposite: The hostility of their core supporters to the president, along with his tepid support among independents, left congressional Democrats with little incentive to help Bush in any way and every reason to obstruct administration proposals for which their electoral constituencies expressed little enthusiasm. The prime example is, of course, Bush's effort to reform Social Security.

THE CAMPAIGN TO REVAMP SOCIAL SECURITY

The campaign for Social Security "reform" during Bush's second term repeated many of the patterns set in the first term, but its results offer a telling illustration of the potential liabilities of being a "divider." The decision to take on the nation's most venerable and popular middle-class entitlement program was characteristically bold and self-congratulatory. Moving Social Security reform to the top of his agenda after the election, Bush presented himself as a leader who dared to touch this lethal "third

---

[6] "Post-election Political Study," *Time* Magazine/SRBI, December 13–14, 2004, at http://www.srbi.com/time-dec152004.pdf (accessed August 10, 2005).
[7] Cf. "The George W. Bush Presidency: Four More Years," CBS News/*New York Times* Poll, January 14–18, 2004.

rail of American politics" when other politicians lacked the courage.[8] He went public with an elaborate campaign, orchestrated by Karl Rove, to drum up support for action that began with a highly publicized "60 stops in 60 days"[9] tour of the country. The tour, which eventually extended beyond the planned sixty days, took Bush to a series of local meetings where he spoke before carefully screened audiences to carefully screened panelists who could be depended on to stay on message. The message was that the Social Security system was in crisis, on its way to bankruptcy in fewer than forty years, and that younger workers would eventually be stiffed. Bush's one positive proposal for changing the system, highlighted at every juncture, was to allow workers to put up to one-third of their Social Security contribution into an investment account they would own and control. Returns from these investments would, under optimistic scenarios, more than offset the reduction in guaranteed Social Security benefits accepted by people who opted for private accounts.

The problem was that private accounts (Bush and then the entire Republican establishment took to calling them "personal" accounts after that adjective got a better reaction from focus groups[10]) did nothing to address Social Security's solvency crisis. Indeed, they would make it worse by taking money out of the system and adding an estimated $2 trillion in transition costs to the national debt. Actually solving the crisis would require something the president avoided mentioning as long as possible: cutting benefits or raising the age of eligibility (from the start, Bush had ruled out the third option for making the arithmetic work, raising Social Security taxes).

For most of his sixty-day blitz, Bush refused to offer any specifics beyond advocating partial privatization while challenging his Democratic critics to put their ideas on the table. They refused to bite. Other than rejecting private accounts—indeed, demanding that they be taken off the table before they discussed anything—Democrats offered nothing. And

---

[8] See, for example, the White House's transcript of his address to the American Society of Newspaper Editors Convention on April 15, 2005, at http://www.whitehouse.gov/news/releases/2005/04/20050414-4.html (accessed August 12, 2005). The third-rail metaphor refers to the electrified third rail on subway lines: "Touch it and you die."

[9] This was the administration's title for the campaign; see http://www.treas.gov/press/releases/js2287.htm (accessed August 28, 2005); the number of stops never reached 60.

[10] Liberal Texas columnist Molly Ivins wrote an amusing column on the switch; in order to avoid being convicted of liberal bias for using the old term once Bush had abandoned it (which Republican strategist Frank Luntz actually said would be justified), she said, " I shall refer to them as 'the accounts formerly known as private.'" Molly Ivins, "'Private Accounts' Versus 'Personal Accounts,'" *The Free Press*, January 27, 2005, at http://www.freepress.org/columns/display/1/2005/1052 (accessed August 12, 2005).

why would they have? Any effective step toward making the system solvent was guaranteed to be unpopular. Republicans controlled the agenda
and everything else, so why would Democrats have taken the lead? Just
as the Republican minority had made sure that only Democrats' finger-
prints were on the unpopular budget-balancing provisions included in
Bill Clinton's 1993 budget,[11] Democrats in Congress saw no reason to
shield Republicans from heat for proposing the painful steps required to
make the Social Security system solvent.

The careful vetting of audiences and participants left no doubt that
the Social Security meetings were strictly marketing exercises designed
for local news media; the president did not go to listen but to persuade.
As he put it at one of the meetings, "In my line of work you got to keep
repeating things over and over and over again for the truth to sink in, to
kind of catapult the propaganda."[12] And as a sales campaign, "Strengthening Social Security" again played fast and loose with the truth. Bush
kept talking about how the system would be bankrupt by 2042 without
mentioning that this meant only that available funds would cover 70 percent to 75 percent of currently promised benefits rather than the whole
amount and that these benefits would still be appreciably higher in real
terms than present-day retirees were receiving.[13] He did not correct panelists who took bankruptcy to mean that no money at all would be left in
the program for younger workers, a common misperception the administration never tried to dispel.[14] Bush avoided any mention of costs—either
to workers whose benefits would be reduced, to the nation's fiscal health,
or to future recipients if the system were really to be made actuarially
sound. In talking up private retirement accounts as a step toward an
"ownership society," the president glossed over the fact that the accounts
would be subject to stringent mandatory guidelines about how the
money in the accounts could be invested and accessed.[15] The campaign

---

[11] Not a single Republican in either chamber voted for Clinton's 1993 budget, which aimed to reduce
the projected deficit by $500 million over the ensuing five years through a combination of politically
unpopular tax increases and spending reductions.
[12] "Remarks by President Bush in a Conversation on Strengthening Social Security," Greece, New York,
March 24, 2005, PR Newswire at http://www.prnewswire.com/cgibin/stories.pl?ACCT=109&STORY
=/www/story/05-24-2005/0003685801&EDATE=(accessed August 11, 2005).
[13] Scheduled benefits rise faster than inflation because they are indexed to wages, not prices.
[14] In the February 24–28 CBS News/*New York Times* Poll, 46 percent of respondents thought that by
bankruptcy, Bush meant there would be no money at all; 40 percent thought he meant reduced benefits;
at http://www.pollingreport.com/social2.htm (accessed August 12, 2005).
[15] "Bush's State of the Union: Social Security "Bankruptcy?" FactCheck.org, February 3, 2005, at http://
www.factcheck.org/article305.html (accessed August 12, 2005).

relied on two mutually exclusive economic scenarios to make the private accounts a better deal than the current system: slow economic growth (an average of 1.9 percent over seventy-five years) to generate the crisis and, at the same time, investments appreciating at 6.5 percent per year (after inflation). As critics pointed out, in no plausible economic model could both scenarios be true.[16]

WHY THE CAMPAIGN FAILED

Bush's Social Security road show succeeded in raising public awareness of the program's long-term problems, but it failed signally to generate support for the president's proposals or for the president himself. Part of the reason is that the administration could not control the terms of debate. Critics were quick to point out what they saw as the flaws in the administration's claims and harped on Bush's refusal, for several months, to propose any concrete changes in the system that actually addressed the bankruptcy threat. The town meetings got as much attention from national news reporters for their artifice as for their message. Democrats and their allied interest groups mounted in op-ed pieces, blogs, and TV ads an energetic defense of the New Deal's greatest and most popular achievement.

More important, large portions of the public, cool to both the singer and the song, formed a receptive audience for critics of Bush's proposals. Before the president began his traveling campaign, most Americans liked the idea of investing some of their Social Security contributions in the stock and bond markets. At the time Bush put his proposal at the top of his second-term agenda, most polls found the public split fairly evenly on the question, but with considerable variation depending on question wording. No matter how the question was asked, however, support for the idea declined during Bush's national campaign for it. Seven variants of the question were asked three or more times between December 2004 and June 2005; for six of the seven variants, support declined between

---

[16] If the economy did well enough to support such high investment returns, the Social Security shortfall would disappear; if it grew at the pace projected by the system's trustees, investments could not deliver returns that would make private accounts superior; see Paul Krugman, "Many Unhappy Returns," *New York Times,* February 1, 2005, at http://www.pkarchive.org/column/020105.html (accessed August 12, 2005).

the first and last survey in the series by between 4 and 7 percentage points; for the seventh variant, there was no change. Overall, support for Bush's proposal fell from an average of 46.1 percent to an average of 41.7 percent from the first to the last of these polls.[17]

The devil was, as always, in the details. When people were asked if they supported the idea of private accounts without mention of any of the costs, they divided nearly evenly, with an average of about 45 percent supporting the idea.[18] When asked if they backed the idea if it was accompanied by a reduction in guaranteed future benefits, average support dropped to 39 percent.[19] In surveys that specified that the cut in guaranteed benefits could be up to one-third, matching the proportion of Social Security taxes diverted into private accounts, support dropped to an average of 22 percent.[20] And if the program was to add $2 trillion to the national debt over the next ten years, on average only 27 percent of respondents favored it.[21] Both of these latter two conditions were part of the package, so over time, as more people came to understand what establishing the private accounts would entail, support for the idea declined. So, too, did approval of the president's handling of the Social Security issue, which by early August 2005 was down to about 30 percent, improving a bit only after Bush stopped talking about it (Figure 8.1). His job performance rating on this issue consistently fell well below his ratings in other major issue domains (for comparison, see Figure 4.4).

The campaign also ran up against the reality that people who were not already Bush loyalists did not believe the president's proposals for reforming the system were offered in good faith. Asked in January 2005 if they thought Bush was "trying to help more, average Americans or Wall Street investment companies," 75 percent of Democrats and 54 percent

---

[17] From data in CBS News/*New York Times*, ABC News/*Washington Post*, NBC/ *Wall Street Journal*, Gallup, and Pew Center for the People and the Press polls, at http://www.pollingreport.com/social.htm (accessed August 12, 2005).

[18] In thirty-one polls asking the question in this form, an average 45.2 percent supported and 46.6 percent opposed the idea; support ranged from 35 percent to 56 percent with a standard deviation of 5.3; see footnote 17.

[19] From eleven polls, with an average of 38.6 percent supporting (standard deviation, 7.3) and 54.6 percent opposing; see footnote 17.

[20] From three polls, with an average of 21.7 percent supporting (standard deviation, 0.6) and 69.0 percent opposing; see footnote 17.

[21] From four polls, with an average of 27.0 supporting (standard deviation, 13.0) and 64.0 percent opposing; support in three of these four ranged from 17 percent to 21 percent, with the fourth an outlier at 46 percent; see footnote 17.

FIGURE 8.1
Approval of George W. Bush's Handling of Social Security During His Second Term

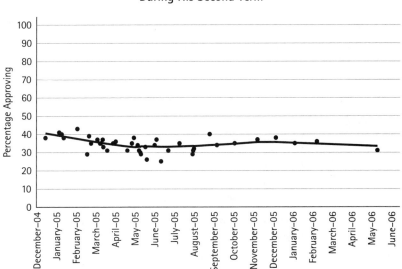

Source: ABC News/*Washington Post,* CBS News/*New York Times,* AP/Ipsos, Harris, Gallup, Pew Center for the People and the Press, *Newsweek,* and *Time* polls, most at http://www.pollingreport.com/ social.htm and, in some cases, the poll's own website.

of independents answered "Wall Street."[22] Asked in May if the president's real agenda was to "save and strengthen Social Security" or to "dismantle Social Security as we know it," 76 percent of Democrats and 54 percent of independents chose "dismantle."[23] Asked in June if they were confident or uneasy about "Bush's ability to make the right decisions about Social Security," 88 percent of Democrats and 70 percent of independents said they were "uneasy."[24]

---

[22] Only 19 percent of Republicans expressed this view; 73 percent said "ordinary Americans." See "The George W. Bush Presidency: Four More Years," CBS News/*New York Times* Poll, January 14–18, 2005, 20.
[23] Only 16 percent of Republicans picked "dismantle"; 72 percent chose "save and strengthen." See "Why So Many People Oppose the President's Social Security Proposals," *The Harris Poll #41,* May 13, 2005, at http://harrisinteractive.com/Insights/HarrisVault8482.aspx?PID=570 (accessed May 13, 2005).
[24] One third of Republicans were also "uneasy," while 59 percent were "confident"; see "The President, Social Security, and Iraq," CBS News/*New York Times* Poll, June 10–15, 2005, 4.

FIGURE 8.2
Opinions on the Iraq War and Social Security Reform

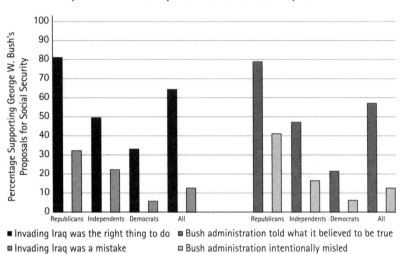

■ Invading Iraq was the right thing to do   ▣ Bush administration told what it believed to be true
▣ Invading Iraq was a mistake   ▣ Bush administration intentionally misled

Source: ABC News/*Washington Post* Poll, March 10–13, 2005.

Some of this cynicism may have reflected public statements by some of Bush's allies in the campaign who really did want to dismantle Social Security.[25] And although the causal linkages are hopelessly entangled, some of the cynicism was also almost certainly a legacy of the Iraq War. At least, support for the president's ideas on Social Security was strongly related to opinions on whether the war was worth the cost and whether the administration was deliberately deceptive in making the case for it (Figure 8.2). Regardless of party, respondents who believed they were misled on the war or who thought the war was a bad idea were much less likely to support the president's Social Security proposals. Only 37 percent of all respondents in this poll voiced support for the president's plan; it was backed by 64 percent of those who thought the United States

---

[25] For example, Stephen Moore, former president of the Club for Growth, an antitax group backing Bush's plans for private accounts, was widely quoted when he said, "Social Security is the soft underbelly of the welfare state. If you can jab your spear through that, you can undermine the whole welfare state." See John Tierney, "Can Anyone Unseat FDR?" *New York Times*, January 23, 2005, at http://www.nytimes.com/2005/01/23/weekinreview/23tier.html?ex=1264136400&en=9bc1372a4e3f8022&ei=5090&partner=rssuserland (accessed August 15, 2005).

had done the right thing in going to war in Iraq but by only 13 percent who thought the war was a mistake. Of course, critics of Bush's Social Security plans were fond of pointing out what they claimed were parallels between the misleading campaign to rally support for the Iraq War and the equally deceptive effort to "catapult the propaganda" to win public backing for privatizing Social Security; the polling data suggest that this charge resonated with a substantial segment of the public.

As Figure 8.2 indicates, Republicans were considerably more supportive of Bush's proposal than were Democrats—no shock here—and over time, partisan differences widened.[26] Partisan differences were also larger when it was labeled Bush's plan rather than simply described. In the survey that was the basis of Figure 8.2, 42 percent of Democrats supported "a plan in which people who chose to could invest some of their Social Security contributions in the stock market," but only 11 percent said they supported "George W. Bush's proposals on Social Security"; 83 percent said they opposed his proposals, 59 percent "strongly." In the same survey, 85 percent of Democrats and 59 percent of independents also said that the more they heard about Bush's proposals, the less they liked them. Among Republicans, 77 percent backed the stock market option, 73 percent supported the president's proposals, and 64 percent said that the more they heard about the proposals, the more they liked them.

Republicans were generally supportive of the president's ideas for Social Security, but not by margins large enough to offset the strong Democratic opposition to any proposal with Bush's name attached to it. Furthermore, when the downside of privatizing part of the system was mentioned—cuts in scheduled benefits, adding to the national debt—most Republicans no longer supported the idea.[27] In six surveys taken between March and August 2005, an average of only 60 percent of Republicans approved of Bush's handling of Social Security, 27 points below his average overall rating for the period. Among Democrats,

---

[26] Asked by the CBS News/*New York Times* Poll in January 2005 if they thought "allowing individuals to invest a portion of their Social Security taxes on their own is a good idea or a bad idea," 58 percent of Republicans and 30 percent of Democrats said it was a good idea. Asked the same question in June, 70 percent of Republicans but only 26 percent of Democrats said it was a good idea (support among independents also dropped 4 points, from 48 percent to 44 percent); see "The George W. Bush Presidency: Four More Years," CBS News/*New York Times* Poll, January 14–18, 2005, 20, and "The President, Social Security, and Iraq," CBS News/*New York Times* Poll, June 10–15, 2005, 4.

[27] See the CBS News/*New York Times* polls, January 14–18, May 20–24, and June 10–15, 2005.

Bush's average approval rating on Social Security was in single digits, 9 percent, and among independents, it was 24 percent.[28] It is not hard to fathom why congressional Democrats saw no reason in following the president's lead on this issue and why it made many Republicans in Congress very nervous.

THE BIPARTISAN CONSENSUS

Ironically, there actually was a bipartisan public consensus on what to do (or, more accurately, what not to do) about Social Security. The difficulty for politicians was that the consensus opposed virtually all of the changes that might assure the program's long-term solvency. In the March 2005 ABC News/*Washington Post* Poll, for example, majorities of Republicans, Democrats, and independents said they opposed increasing the Social Security tax rate, raising the retirement age for receiving full benefits, further reducing benefits for early retirees, reducing guaranteed benefits for future retirees, or changing the formula for calculating benefits to reduce their rate of growth. The only proposal that won majority support—again across party lines—was collecting Social Security tax on all wages, not just the first $90,000. Unfortunately, that would not raise enough money to solve the problem. In the face of such numbers, Bush's strategy of avoiding specifics, aside from promoting the upside potential of private accounts for many months, was understandable, as was the Republicans' insistence that reform had to have bipartisan support to proceed.

At the end of April, under pressure to fill out his proposal, Bush sought to win over some Democrats by suggesting that reductions in promised future benefits be calibrated to fall most heavily on the highest income groups and not at all on the lowest. Or, as he spun it, "I propose a Social Security system in the future where benefits for low-income workers will grow faster than benefits for people who are better off."[29] The idea by itself was attractive to ordinary Democrats, although a bit

---

[28] ABC News/*Washington Post* polls, March 10–13, April 21–24, and June 2–5, 2005; CBS News/*New York Times* polls, May 20–24, June 10–15, and July 29–August 2, 2005.

[29] Richard W. Stevenson and Elizabeth Bumiller, "Bush Cites Plan That Would Cut Social Security," *New York Times,* April 29, 2005, at http://www.nytimes.com/2005/04/29/politics/29bush.html? (accessed August 11, 2005).

less so to Republicans. When the Pew Center poll described such a policy to half their sample without mentioning it was Bush's idea, 54 percent of Democrats and 47 percent of Republicans favored it. But when it was described to the other half of the sample as Bush's proposal, it drew support from 62 percent of Republicans but only 34 percent of Democrats. Thus, the Bush cue cut sharply both ways, boosting Republicans' support by 15 points but reducing Democrats' by 20 points. Support also dropped 12 points among independents, from 55 percent to 43 percent, and 8 percent overall, from 53 percent to 45 percent, when the proposal was identified as the president's.[30] Being a divider can have its downside.

OTHER ISSUES

The president had greater success with other parts of his agenda where he could count on stronger Republican support. The 109th Congress (2005–2006) enacted a bankruptcy overhaul bill, class-action tort reform, an extension of tax breaks enacted in 2003, and an energy bill the administration had been pursuing since the beginning of Bush's presidency, and it ratified the Central American Free Trade Agreement (CAFTA). All were notable victories for the administration. The first three were won with unanimous or near-unanimous support from congressional Republicans; the minority of Democratic votes they received were superfluous (beyond the handful of Senate votes needed to preclude a filibuster).[31] The energy bill needed a bit more Democratic support to pass because of Republican defectors (31 in the House, 6 in the Senate); this was achieved by a judicious distribution of pork and the omission of a provision opening the Alaskan National Wildlife Refuge to drilling. CAFTA was the closest call; it passed the House by a single vote after the count was delayed to allow a few more Republican arms to be twisted. Democrats were much less supportive than they had been of previous free trade agreements, but the 15 who voted for it were just enough to offset the 27 Republicans who resisted the pressure and defected. None

---

[30] "Economy, Iraq Weighing Down Bush Popularity," Survey Report, Pew Center for the People and the Press, May 19, 2005, at http://people-press.org/reports/display.php3?ReportID=244us (accessed May 19, 2005).
[31] There were not more than two Republican votes against any of the three in either chamber.

of these was a great popular victory, but all of them were welcomed by core Republican supporters in the corporate sector, who were the prime beneficiaries.

THE TERRI SCHIAVO CASE

The president ran into a bit more trouble trying to please his other pillar of support, religious conservatives. The legal struggle between the husband and parents of Terri Schiavo, a Florida woman who had been in a persistent vegetative state for fifteen years, over whether to remove a feeding tube that was keeping her alive had emerged as an issue of great symbolic importance to religious conservatives, who viewed hers as a right-to-life case. Responding to their outcries, Congress passed a law giving federal courts jurisdiction to intervene to take the case from the state courts, which had sided with the husband and ordered the tube removed. President Bush took the rare step of interrupting his vacation in Texas to fly back to Washington to sign the legislation, which he later celebrated as bipartisanship in action: "Democrats and Republicans in Congress came together last night to give Terri Schiavo's parents another opportunity to save their daughter's life."[32] The vote was, in fact, fairly bipartisan; in the House, 97 percent of Republicans and 47 percent of Democrats who cast votes supported the measure (the measure passed the Senate by voice vote).

The public's reaction was also bipartisan: Majorities of Republicans as well as of Democrats thought Congress and the president had had no business intervening. Most people could imagine themselves facing this kind of wrenching decision some day, and the last thing they would want would be to have a federal case made of it.[33] Polls taken at the time found from 70 percent to 82 percent of respondents saying that the action was "not right" or "inappropriate" and that Congress and the president "should have stayed out." Partisan differences on these questions

---

[32] "Bush Signs Law Letting Parents Seek Restoration of Feeding Tube," CNN.com, March 22, 2005, at http://www.cnn.com/2005/LAW/03/21/schiavo/ (accessed August 18, 2005).

[33] Given a choice of who should make such decisions, only 9 percent of respondents to the CBS News/*New York Times* Poll of March 21–22, 2005, said "federal government"; 13 percent said "state government," and 75 percent said the government should stay out. See "The Terri Schiavo Case," CBS News poll report, March 23, 2005, at http://www.realclearpolitics.com/Polls/cbs_schiavo.pdf (accessed August 18, 2005).

were small, and a majority of Republicans (as large as 72 percent in one survey) panned the action. Majorities nearly as large (from 65 percent to 74 percent) said that Congress and Bush had been motivated by political advantage, with only 13 percent to 25 percent saying they had acted on principle or out of real concern for Schiavo.[34] Even Republicans were as likely as not to take this view, although Democrats were much more uniformly cynical.

The extraordinary intervention by Republican congressional leaders and the president in the Schiavo case underlined the powerful influence of religious conservatives in their party's coalition. It suggested that the real political capital accumulated in the 2004 election belonged to conservative Christian activists who could claim, not implausibly, that their efforts had kept Bush in the White House. It also suggested the difficulties a payback could pose for Republican politicians who, in scrambling to respond to a vocal and passionate minority of key supporters, failed badly to anticipate how the rest of their coalition, not to mention the rest of the electorate, might react. And it reinforced the image of Republicans in Washington as either right-wing religious zealots or their thralls.

HURRICANE KATRINA

Just how reflexive partisan responses to Bush had become was underlined by public evaluations of the administration's response to devastation caused by Hurricane Katrina in late August 2005. The disaster itself challenged the whole tenor of Bush's presidency. No upbeat spin or show of confidence could offset televised images and stories of bodies floating in the flooded streets of New Orleans, of hungry and thirsty refugees neglected for days, of fires and looting in abandoned neighborhoods. No amount of blame leveled at state and local officials, however well deserved, or at citizens of New Orleans itself could hide the fact that the federal government's response had been slow, disorganized, badly informed, poorly led, and, for an inexcusably long time, ineffectual. For once, the president had to admit his own and his appointees'

---

[34] Pew Center for the People and the Press, *Time*, CBS News/*New York Times*, ABC News/*Washington Post*, Harris, and Gallup polls reported at http://pollingreport.com/news.htm#Schiavo (accessed August 18, 2005).

mistakes, for to claim otherwise would have marked him as delusional. Worse for Bush, the failure was in a domain that was supposed to be his strong suit, homeland security; the government's flawed response to Katrina raised pointed questions about how well prepared the United States was, fully four years after 9/11, to deal with the consequences of a major terrorist attack. Katrina also brought issues of race, class, and poverty to the forefront, for among the worst hit and slowest to receive help were African Americans from New Orleans' poorest neighborhoods. Most of the victims were not part of the Republican coalition nor of the class served by the Bush administration's usual domestic policies.

Natural disasters are usually occasions for national unity. Katrina was not. Democratic leaders saw no reason to restrain their criticism of the administration's shaky performance in the crisis; administration critics linked it to other policies they opposed, including Bush's Iraq policy (arguing that it had crippled the government's response by thinning the ranks of the National Guard back home), his stance on global warming, and his budget priorities. Republicans reflexively counterattacked, accusing Democrats of "playing the blame game" while trying themselves to shift the blame to mostly Democratic state and local officials. Issues of race and class also quickly became the grist of partisan debate, as did the question of who—Congress? an independent commission? the White House?—would investigate the government's failures.[35]

The public took part in the blame game. An ABC News/*Washington Post* poll taken five days after the hurricane hit found 74 percent of Republicans but only 17 percent of Democrats approving of Bush's handling of the crisis.[36] In a Gallup poll taken a few days later, only 10 percent of Republicans rated Bush's response negatively, and only 10 percent of Democrats rated it positively.[37] Still, Katrina drove Bush's overall performance ratings to the lowest point yet of his presidency among

---

[35] Isaiah J. Poole, "Partisan Finger-Pointing over Katrina," CQ *Weekly*, September 12, 2005, 2414–2415.

[36] Dan Balz, "For Bush, a Deepening Divide," *Washington Post*, September 7, 2005, A19.

[37] Independents sided with the Democrats, 47 percent negative, 29 percent positive. The remaining respondents said the response was neither good nor bad. See David W. Moore, "Public Skeptical New Orleans Will Recover," Gallup News Service, September 7, 2005, at http://gallup.com/ (accessed September 7, 2005). In the Zogby America Poll taken a couple of days later, 67 percent of Republicans rated Bush's handling of Katrina as "excellent" or "good," while 71 percent of Democrats rated it "poor." Another 18 percent of Democrats rated his performance as "fair"; only 10 percent rated it as "excellent" or "good." See Zogby America Poll, September 5–6, 2005, at http://pollingreport.com/ disasters.htm (accessed September 8, 2005).

all partisan categories. Perhaps more ominous for the administration, support for keeping troops in Iraq also fell in some polls as domestic needs took priority in respondents' minds.[38] The public's preferred way to pay for reconstruction at home was, by a wide margin over any other option, to "cut spending for the war in Iraq."[39]

The modest decline in Republican support and unambiguous evidence that a large majority of Americans, leaders and ordinary citizens alike, were critical of Bush's initial response to Katrina's devastation prompted the administration to change its approach. In a nationally televised speech on September 15, the president acknowledged his administration's failures and took formal responsibility. He also acknowledged the class and racial disparities exposed by the disaster. And he sought to reclaim the initiative by proposing a hugely expensive federal program to completely rebuild New Orleans and the devastated Gulf Coast region, restoring communities and upgrading the poorest areas.[40] Such a massive, if unspecified, undertaking enjoyed broad public support,[41] and later Congress provided more than $85 billion in reconstruction and other aid by large bipartisan majorities. Although some administration opponents initially feared that reconstruction would be used to further a conservative agenda—the rumor that Karl Rove would be put in charge circulated briefly[42]—reconstruction policy did not end up adding fuel to the partisan fires. Although Bush's approval ratings recovered a bit after the post-Katrina dip, the administration's handling of the crisis raised questions about its competence that never completely dissipated and that bled over into judgments about its management of the Iraq War.

---

[38] "Iraq and Its Impact Back Home," CBS News/*New York Times* Poll, September 9–13, 2005, at http://www.cbs.news.com/htdocs/CBSNews_polls/Iraq_916.pdf (accessed September 19, 2005).

[39] In the September 16–19, 2005, CNN/*USA Today*/Gallup Poll, 54 percent took this option; 17 percent wanted to raise taxes, 6 percent wanted to cut domestic spending, and 15 percent wanted to increase the deficit; at http://pollingreport.com/disasters.htm (accessed September 21, 2005).

[40] "President Discusses Hurricane Relief in Address to the Nation," White House press release, September 15, 2005, at http://www.whitehouse.gov/news/releases/2005/09/20050915-8.html (accessed September 19, 2005).

[41] For example, asked if the proposed $200 billion to be appropriated by Congress for rebuilding was the right amount, 52 percent of respondents to an Associated Press/Ipsos poll (taken September 16–18, 2005) said it was the right amount, 15 percent it was too little, and only 24 percent said it was too much; see http://pollingreport.com/disasters.htm (accessed October 6, 2005).

[42] Dan Froomkin, "Mr. Big Government," *Washington Post* online edition, September 16, 2005, at http:// www.washingtonpost.com/wp-dyn/content/blog/2005/09/16/BL2005091601005.html (accessed September 19, 2005).

THE IRAQ WAR IN 2006

During the first half of 2006, George W. Bush went through the roughest patch of his presidency up to that time. The year began on a relatively positive note on signs of progress in Iraq. Elections to the National Assembly on December 15, 2005—celebrated by the president as "a landmark day in the history of liberty"[43]—were followed by Defense Secretary Rumsfeld's announcement of a planned troop reduction during the coming year. Popular support for the war rose a few points (see Figure 6.1). The proportion of Americans believing that the United States was "making significant progress in establishing a democratic government in Iraq" jumped from 47 percent in November 2005 to 65 percent after the election; 71 percent said they thought the election brought closer "the day United States forces can be withdrawn from Iraq."[44]

But the favorable news gave the president little durable traction because new troubles continued to arise. Revelations by the *New York Times* in December that the president had authorized the National Security Agency to monitor international email and telephone calls of American citizens provoked bipartisan criticism in congressional hearings, although the public's view of the monitoring divided predictably along party lines.[45] In February, the president met stubborn resistance from his own party over the proposed transfer of operational control of terminals at some United States ports to a company based in Dubai, a part of the United Arab Emirates. A strong bipartisan consensus opposed the move, and it was soon effectively killed.[46] Bush's coalition was also fractured by his proposals for immigration reform, with conservative House Republicans objecting to its guest worker provisions and what they saw as a thinly disguised amnesty program. They had also concluded that advocacy of an enforcement-only approach to border control would inspire their base for the 2006 elections. By May, more Republicans surveyed disapproved (42 percent) than approved (41 percent) of the president's handling of

---

[43] "Transcript of Bush Speech," December 18, 2005, at http://www.cnn.com/2005/POLITICS/12/18/bush.transcript/, (accessed March 22, 2010).

[44] ABC News/*Washington Post* polls, October 30–November 2 and December 15–18, 2005, at http://pollingreport.com/iraq3.htm.

[45] In the January 5–8 CBS News/*New York Times* Poll, 82 percent of Republicans but only 31 percent of Democrats said they approved of Bush's authorizing of warrantless wiretaps.

[46] Questioned in the February 22–26 CBS News/*New York Times* survey, 70 percent said they opposed the deal, including 58 percent of Republicans, 78 percent of Democrats, and 71 percent of independents.

the issue.[47] Conservatives in the party also continued to grow more vocally critical of the growth of government spending under Bush.[48] Finally, a sharp rise in the price of crude oil produced a sharp rise in the price of gasoline, which rose by an average of $.76 per gallon between January and July, surpassing $3.00 per gallon during the summer travel season,[49] and led the public to take a more negative view of the economy than the usual indicators such as GDP growth, inflation, and unemployment would seem to have warranted.[50]

Meanwhile, the news from Iraq soon dampened whatever sense of optimism the parliamentary elections had generated. It took five months for the four leading parties to agree on a government of national unity;[51] while they were haggling, the violence worsened and grew increasingly sectarian, raising the prospect of civil war. The escalating violence and absence of visible progress in establishing order in Iraq more than three years after the United States invasion were hard to overlook, even among leaders who had fully supported the action. If not the original policy, then its execution was certainly open to criticism, and plenty was forthcoming, notably from some retired senior military officers.[52] Few Republican politicians openly challenged the president, but the defense secretary was fair game, and calls for Rumsfeld's resignation eventually became part of some Republican reelection campaigns.[53]

The cumulative effects of these developments drove Bush's job approval ratings to their lowest point of his presidency thus far (see Figure 1.1), down to an average of 33.5 percent in the eleven national polls in May 2006. More ominous for the president, the largest drop occurred among Republicans (see Figure 1.2), with independents not far

---

[47] Among Democrats, the figures were 18 percent approve, and 69 percent disapprove. See the CBS News/*New York Times* Poll, May 4–6, 2006.

[48] John Cochran, "The End of the Republican Revolution," *CQ Weekly*, April 10, 2006, 965– 972.

[49] Data from http://www.eia.doe.gov/oil_gas/petroleum/data_publications/wrgp/mogas_history.html.

[50] In the seven Gallup polls taken between January and June 2006, an average of 37 percent rated the economy "excellent" or "good" while 63 percent called it only "fair" or "poor." At http://pollingreport.com/consumer2.htm (accessed September 22, 2006).

[51] And by then, the percentage of Americans who believed that the United States was "making significant progress in establishing a democratic government in Iraq" had dropped back to about where it had been before the Iraqi elections, 49 percent; ABC News/*Washington Post* Poll, March 2–5, 2006, at http://pollingreport.com/iraq3.htm.

[52] For example, see Anne Plummer, "Getting Down to Brass Attacks," *CQ Weekly*, April 17, 2006, 1014–1015.

[53] Adam Nagourney and Mark Mazzetti, "Candidates of Both Parties Turn Criticism of Rumsfeld into Political Chorus," *New York Times*, September 6, 2006, at http://www.nytimes.com/2006/09/06/washington/06rumsfeld.html (accessed March 22, 2010).

behind. His standing among Democrats was so low it could not have fallen much further; from early 2006 onward, it remained in single digits for the rest of his presidency. The average partisan gap in the Gallup polls fell below 70 points in the second quarter of 2006 for the first time since the first quarter of 2004, but this was surely not the way Bush wanted to see polarization diminish.

The slide ended after the Iraqi Assembly finally chose a government in May and Americans could celebrate the killing in Baghdad of Abu Musab al-Zarqawi, a viciously brutal al Qaeda leader, in early June. Again, however, the relief was temporary, for neither the new government nor al-Zarqawi's death reduced the violence. United States battle deaths did not decline, and monthly Iraqi casualties were actually more than 20 percent higher in June through September than they had been in January through May.[54]

The public's opinions on the war changed relatively little through the first nine months of the year but became increasingly negative thereafter. Overall support for the war rose after the legislative elections in December 2005 but soon fell back to where it had been before and then stayed basically flat until late summer, when it headed downward again. Partisan differences in support for the war remained wide and stable. Opinions on how the war was going grew more pessimistic, with especially notable downturns among Republicans and independents at the end of 2006, although, reflecting the administration's repeated claims that progress was being made, Republicans remained far more optimistic than Democrats (Figures 8.3 and 8.4). Conflicting reports and the high level of uncertainty about the direction of developments in Iraq created conditions in which partisan priors strongly shaped people's responses to these questions.

Support for staying the course eroded only a little during this period although the overall trend was downward until late 2007 (Figure 8.5). Its expressed level depended on question wording. Questions giving the alternatives of staying until the situation in Iraq has stabilized or withdrawing troops "as soon as possible" or "immediately" (the black markers in Figure 8.5) produced a higher level of support than questions giving the option of withdrawing some or most troops or doing so "next year" (the gray markers in Figure 8.5). Even among Democrats, support for

---

[54] The monthly average of United States battle deaths was an identical 58 for January–May and June–September; among Iraqi police and civilians, the average rose from 969 to 1186. See http://icasualties.lorg/Iraq/index.aspx (accessed March 22, 2010).

FIGURE 8.3
How Well Is the War in Iraq Going?

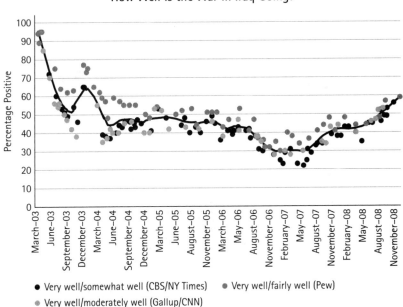

● Very well/somewhat well (CBS/NY Times)   ● Very well/fairly well (Pew)
● Very well/moderately well (Gallup/CNN)

Source: CBS News/*New York Times,* Pew Research Center for the People and the Press, and Gallup polls, at http://pollingreport.com/iraq.htm.

staying the course did not decline much during this period, remaining close to 40 percent in response to the questions represented by the black markers in Figure 8.5 (Figure 8.6).

The president's problem—and source of grumbling among Republican politicians—was that the effectiveness of this effort was coming into question. All along, majorities of the public were not persuaded that the Bush administration had a clear plan for achieving its goals in Iraq, regardless of how these goals were stated; by 2006 less than a third of Americans thought it did have a clear plan. Even Republicans expressed less than overwhelming faith that the administration had a coherent strategy for achieving its goals in Iraq; in twelve surveys taken in 2006, about 59 percent said they believed it did, compared with 24 percent of independents and 12 percent of Democrats.[55]

---

[55] See the first edition of this book, 225–226.

FIGURE 8.4

Evaluations of How Well the War in Iraq Is Going, by Party

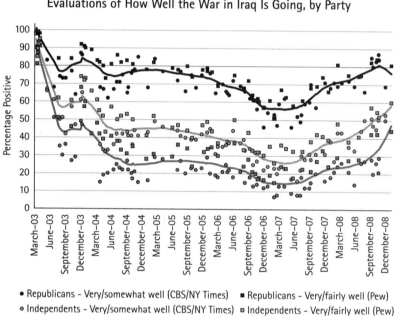

- Republicans - Very/somewhat well (CBS/NY Times)   ■ Republicans - Very/fairly well (Pew)
- Independents - Very/somewhat well (CBS/NY Times)   ▣ Independents - Very/fairly well (Pew)
- Democrats - Very/somewhat well (CBS/NY Times)   ▪ Democrats - Very/fairly well (Pew)

The president's conception and style of leadership made it difficult to deal with such sentiments. Whether or not he ever entertained doubts about the rightness of his decision to invade Iraq or the soundness of his advisors' strategy for winning the war—Bush claimed he had not[56]—he could never have admitted mistakes or second thoughts because doing so would have contradicted his idea of leadership. As he told Bob Woodward, "A president has got to be the calcium in the backbone. If I weaken, the whole team weakens. If I'm doubtful, I can assure you that there will be a lot of doubt. If my confidence level declines, it will send ripples throughout the whole organization."[57] The need to display resolution and confidence required continual upbeat pronouncements that, in the face of the bad news regularly coming out of Iraq in the months

[56] Bob Woodward, *Plan of Attack* (New York: Simon and Schuster, 2004), 420.
[57] Bob Woodward, *Bush at War* (New York: Simon and Schuster, 2002), 259.

FIGURE 8.5
Support for Keeping United States Troops in Iraq

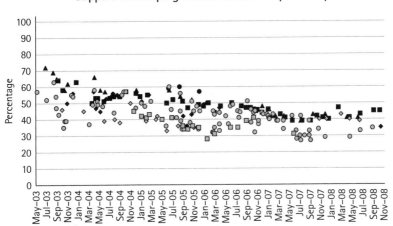

♦ Stay as long as it takes to make Iraq a stable democracy, or withdraw troops as soon as possible
■ Keep U.S. troops in Iraq until situation has stabilized, or bring troops home as soon as possible
▲ Keep troops until civil order restored despite U.S. casualties, or withdraw forces even if civil order not restored
● Keep U.S. troops in Iraq until situation has stabilized, or bring troops home immediately
◇ Keep troops in Iraq until there is a stable government, or bring most troops home next year
◎ Send more troops/same as now or withdraw some/all troops
▯ Maintain troop level to secure peace and stability, or reduce number of troops

Source: ABC News/*Washington Post,* CBS News/*New York Times, Time,* Pew Research Center for the People and the Press, IPSOS, Harris, Gallup, CNN, and NBC News/*Wall Street Journal* polls at http://pollingreport.com/iraq.htm.

following Bush's second inauguration, seemed increasingly detached from reality. Vice President Dick Cheney's assertion in late May that the insurgency was "in its last throes" was not credible even to Republicans.[58] Expressing confidence and optimism without appearing delusional became something of a challenge for Bush and his spokespersons.

Perhaps more ominous for the president, the public was becoming increasingly doubtful that the Iraq War was making the United States more rather than less secure from terrorist attacks. As usual, different question

---

[58] In the June 23–26 ABC News/*Washington Post* Poll, only 42 percent of Republicans said the insurgency was "on its last legs"; 55 percent said it was not, as did 68 percent of Democrats and 70 percent of independents (analysis by author).

FIGURE 8.6
Support for Keeping United States Troops in Iraq, by Party

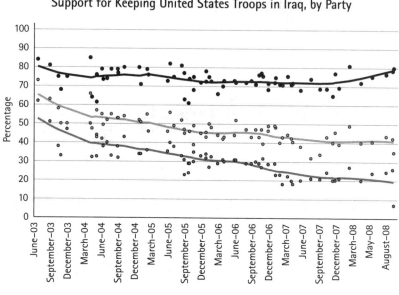

• Republicans   • Independents   • Democrats

Source: ABC News/*Washington Post,* CBS News/*New York Times,* and Pew Research Center for the People and the Press polls and CCES surveys.

wordings produced (in this case modestly) different distributions of opinion, but the overall trend was clearly downward (Figure 8.7). These surveys do not tell us whether people believed the risk of terrorism would be even greater if the United States pulled out of Iraq, but they do indicate an erosion of belief in the administration's most important remaining rationale for staying there. The usual partisan differences emerged on these questions, although they were not as wide as on many of the other questions regarding the war at this time (Figure 8.8).

GOING PUBLIC AGAIN ON THE WAR

Although opinions on the war and the president did not change much during the first half of 2006, they were already sufficiently negative to threaten Republican control of Congress. On average, generic House

FIGURE 8.7

The Effect of the Iraq War on Terrorism and United States Security

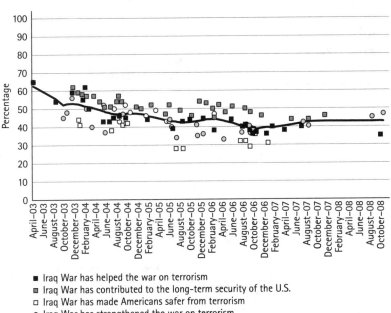

■ Iraq War has helped the war on terrorism
▣ Iraq War has contributed to the long-term security of the U.S.
□ Iraq War has made Americans safer from terrorism
o Iraq War has strengthened the war on terrorism
o Iraq War has made the U.S. safer from terrorism

Source: ABC News/*Washington Post, Time,* and *Newsweek* polls at http://pollingreport.com/iraq.htm; also 2008 CCES.

election polls (asking which party's candidate respondents would vote for if the election were held today) gave Democrats a 56 to 44 advantage during this period, compared with 51 to 49 in the equivalent period prior to the 2002 midterm.[59] Large popular majorities also thought that the country was on the wrong track, offered negative reviews of the economy, and disapproved of Congress's performance.[60] The prospect of losing one or both chambers to the Democrats was not a pleasant one for the president; not only would Democratic control obstruct his remaining

---

[59] Calculated from generic House poll data reported at http://pollingreport.com/2006.htm (accessed September 27, 2006).
[60] See data at http://pollingreport.com/right.htm, http://pollingreport.com/consumer2.htm, and http://pollingreport.com/CongJob.htm (accessed September 27, 2006).

FIGURE 8.8
The Effect of Iraq War on Terrorism and United States Security, by Party

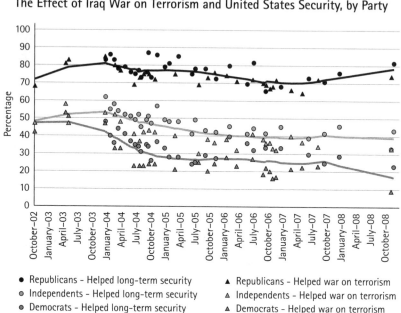

● Republicans - Helped long-term security   ▲ Republicans - Helped war on terrorism
◎ Independents - Helped long-term security   △ Independents - Helped war on terrorism
◉ Democrats - Helped long-term security   △ Democrats - Helped war on terrorism

Source: ABC News/*Washington Post,* CBS News/*New York Times, Time,* and Pew Center for the People and the Press polls; also 2008 CCES.

domestic agenda, but, more importantly, it would also expose his adminis-tration to endless probes into its responses to the terrorist threat, conduct of the war in Iraq, and management of the government more generally. Thus, the president and his allies orchestrated a coordinated, no-holds-barred counterattack against Democratic critics of Bush and the war.

The campaign's rhetorical sweep reveals how embattled the president and his supporters felt. Taking advantage of the public's attention to events commemorating the fifth anniversary of the September 11 attacks, Bush and his allies sought not only to reassert their claim that the war in Iraq and the war on terrorism were one and the same but also to elevate the con-flict to the equivalent of World War II and the Cold War. After ignoring Osama bin Laden for several years, Bush took the risk of reminding Ameri-cans that their prime enemy was still at large five years after he had attacked the United States; Bush quoted him at length in a September 6, 2006, speech justifying administration policies in Iraq and elsewhere. Describing bin Laden's fantasy of using terrorist violence to create an Islamic caliphate ranging from Spain to Indonesia and to "crush and destroy" America, and citing bin Laden's designation of the war in Iraq as the "Third World War" in which the only outcomes could be "victory and glory or misery and humiliation," Bush drew cautionary parallels to Lenin's *What Is to Be Done* and Hitler's *Mein Kampf.* [61] Implicitly evoking the "greatest generation" in his speech commemorating 9/11 a few days later, Bush asked, "Do we have the confidence to do in the Middle East what our fathers and grandfathers accomplished in Europe and Asia?" and went on to adopt the mantles of Franklin Roosevelt and Harry Truman as presidents who had stood fast in the face of global threats.[62]

In addresses delivered around the same time, Vice President Cheney and Secretary Rumsfeld also variously quoted Roosevelt, took the fight against Nazism and fascism as precedent, and, more to the political point, charged that critics of the administration's policies believed that "vicious extremists can be appeased"[63] and that "retreat from Iraq would satisfy the appetite of the terrorists and get them to leave us alone"[64]—in other words, that the critics were Neville Chamberlains to Bush's Winston Churchill. Cheney also sought to put any but upbeat assessments of the war beyond the pale, asserting that *"there is a difference between healthy debate and self-defeating pessimism."*[65] Republican Senator Charles Grassley of Iowa combined the themes: "It's my recall that in World War II we didn't have Republicans criticizing Franklin Roosevelt and how he was conducting the war." Grassley warned further that criticism of the Iraq War "gives comfort to the enemy" and "has a demoralizing effect on the troops."[66]

---

[61] "President Discusses the Global War on Terror," transcript of speech delivered September 6, 2006, at http://georgewbush-whitehouse.archives.gov/news/releases/2006/09/20060905-4.html (accessed March 23, 2010).

[62] "Text of President's Address to the Nation," transcript of speech delivered September 11, 2006, at http://www.washingtonpost.com/wp-dyn/content/article/2006/09/11/AR2006091100775.html (accessed March 23, 2010).

[63] "Address to the 88th Annual American Legion National Convention," delivered by Donald Rumsfeld, August 29, 2006, at http://www.defenselink.mil/Speeches/Speech.aspx?SpeechID=1033.

[64] "Vice President's Remarks at the Veterans of Foreign Wars National Convention," transcript of speech delivered August 28, 2006, at http://georgewbush-whitehouse.archives.gov/news/releases/2006/08/20060828-4.html (accessed March 23, 2010).

[65] Ibid; emphasis in the original.

[66] Mike Glover, "Iowan Says War Critics Embolden Enemy," AP wire story September 13, 2006, at http://news.aol.com/elections/story/_a/Iowan-says-iraq-war-critics-embolden/2006091313260999000 (accessed October15, 2006).

The central message was clear: Islamic jihadists were as profound a threat to the existence of the United States as the Axis powers and the Soviet Union had once been. Democrats (transparently the targets of this rhetoric), by questioning the wisdom of the Iraq War or the administration's conduct of the fight against terrorism more generally, revealed themselves as appeasers who were blind to the terrorist threat and, if given control of Congress, would put the security of the United States at grave risk. As Ken Mehlman, chairman of the Republican National Committee, put it, "The president's effort to keep Americans safe will grind to a halt with Democrats in control. . . ."[67]

The public's response to the campaign's motivation and rhetoric broke predictably along party lines, albeit with an interesting exception (Table 8.1). More than 80 percent of Republicans thought Bush's speeches and activities marking the anniversary of 9/11 were appropriate, while 62 percent of Democrats did not. Democrats (66 percent) thought the administration's talk about terrorism was "mostly for their own political gain," while more than three-quarters of Republicans thought the administration was sincerely worried about the terrorist threat. Independents divided evenly on these questions. The comparison of the war on terrorism to the fight against Nazis and fascists seemed appropriate to Republicans (66 percent), but large majorities of Democrats and independents were not buying it. Democrats were particularly inclined to cynicism when asked if the comparison was "appropriate" or "only being made to justify the Bush policy in Iraq"; only 4 percent said the former, and 91 percent, the latter. The appeasement analogy, however, fell flat; even most Republicans did not consider it a fair comparison, and Democrats and independents dismissed it by huge margins.

The campaign's message also received a decidedly mixed reaction. Majorities of Americans regardless of party agreed that al Qaeda's ultimate goal was to destroy the United States, and even larger majorities believed that the terrorist threat from Islamic fundamentalists was real and immediate.[68] Yet there was no consensus that the war in Iraq was helping to reduce it. For example, 60 percent of respondents to a *Los Angeles*

[67] Quoted in Dan Froomkin, "Off Message," at http://www.washingtonpost.com/wp-dyn/content/linkset/2005/04/11/LI2005041100879.html.

[68] In the September 15–19 CBS News/*New York Times* Poll, for the first question, the partisan breakdown was 74 percent of Republicans, 55 percent of Democrats, and 61 percent of independents; for the second, it was 85 percent, 68 percent, and 76 percent, respectively, for these subgroups; at http://www.cbsnews.com/htdocs/pdf/poll_president_092006.pdf (accessed September 22, 2006).

TABLE 8.1

Public Responses to Rhetoric Justifying the Iraq War on the Fifth Anniversary of 9/11 (Percentages)

	REPUBLICANS	INDEPENDENTS	DEMOCRATS	ALL

1. George W. Bush gave a number of speeches and personal appearances to mark the 5th anniversary of September 11, 2001. Some people say he used the occasion for his own political gain; other people say his actions were appropriate. Do you think George W. Bush used the 5th anniversary of September 11, 2001, for his own political gain, or do you think his actions were appropriate?[a]

	REPUBLICANS	INDEPENDENTS	DEMOCRATS	ALL
Used for own gain	11	42	62	40
Actions appropriate	81	43	24	48
Don't know	8	15	14	12

2. These days, when members of the Bush administration talk about the threat of terrorism, do you think they are doing it mostly because they are worried about the threat of terrorism or mostly for their own political gain?[a]

	REPUBLICANS	INDEPENDENTS	DEMOCRATS	ALL
Worried about the threat	78	44	24	48
Own political gain	15	43	66	42
Both (volunteered)	4	10	8	7
Don't know	3	3	2	3

3. President Bush has compared the war against terrorism to the fight against the Nazis and fascism. Do you believe that this is an appropriate comparison that reflects the danger of the current situation, or an inappropriate comparison that is only being made to *justify the Bush policy in the war against terrorism?*[b]

	REPUBLICANS	INDEPENDENTS	DEMOCRATS	ALL
Appropriate comparison	66	25	13	35
Inappropriate comparison	26	70	82	59
Not sure	8	5	5	6

4. President Bush has compared the war against terrorism with the fight against the Nazis and fascism. Do you believe that this is an appropriate comparison that reflects the danger of the current situation, or an inappropriate comparison that is only being made to *justify the Bush policy in Iraq?*[c]

	REPUBLICANS	INDEPENDENTS	DEMOCRATS	ALL
Appropriate comparison	63	27	4	32
Inappropriate comparison	28	67	91	61
Not sure	9	5	6	7

(continued)

TABLE 8.1 *(continued)*

	REPUBLICANS	INDEPENDENTS	DEMOCRATS	ALL
5. As you know, there are those in the Bush administration who have compared people who oppose the Iraq War to people who sought to appease the Nazis before World War II. Do you think this is a fair or unfair characterization of those who oppose the war? [d]				
Fair characterization	19	10	4	11
Unfair characterization	66	79	89	79
Don't know	15	11	7	10

[a] CBS News/*New York Times* Poll, September 15–19, 2006.

[b] NBC News/*Wall Street Journal* Poll, September 8–11, 2006; registered voters, half sample; emphasis added.

[c] NBC News/*Wall Street Journal* Poll, September 8–11, 2006; registered voters, other half sample; emphasis added.

[d] *Los Angeles Times*/Bloomberg Poll, September 16–19, 2006.

Times/Bloomberg poll taken after the campaign was in full swing took the Democrats' position that the Iraq War was diverting resources that would be better used to fight terrorism elsewhere; only 27 percent thought the war "is the most effective way to reduce the risk of terrorism."[69] There was little perceptible change in the distribution of beliefs about whether the war in Iraq was or was not part of the war on terrorism (Figure 8.9).[70]

Other survey data also turn up little evidence that minds were changed by the administration's efforts; the campaign appears, at most, to have simply reinforced existing partisan divisions. That may have been its primary goal: not to win bipartisan backing for continuing the war, but to revive support among Republican voters who had been showing signs of disillusionment with the war and thus the president. In that regard the campaign may have worked, for Bush's approval ratings among Republicans moved back up a few points during the second half of 2006 (see Figure 1.2). Democrats and independents were by then a

[69] Fifty-one percent of Republicans took this latter view, compared with 16 percent of Democrats and 17 percent of independents; see *Los Angeles Times*/Bloomberg Poll, September 15–17, 2006, at http://www.latimes.com/media/acrobat/2006-09/25492565.pdf (accessed September 25, 2006).

[70] The familiar partisan differences apply; in nine surveys taken during 2006, 73 percent of Republicans, 43 percent of independents, and 30 percent of Democrats agreed with the administration's position that the Iraq War was part of the war on terrorism.

FIGURE 8.9
Is the Iraq War Part of the War on Terrorism?

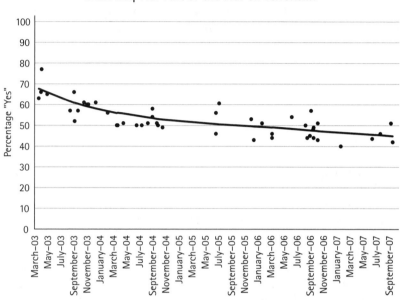

Source: CBS News/New York Times, NBC News/Wall Street Journal, CNN, Gallup, Los Angeles Times, and Fox News polls.

much harder sell; most of them had long since stopped believing what Bush and members of his administration were saying about the war and its justifications. Before the administration's September campaign, a large majority of Democrats (72 percent) already thought Bush was "using the threat of terrorism or the terrorism alerts for political reasons."[71] And as we saw in Chapter 6, an even larger majority of Democrats (about 80 percent) and most independents (60 percent) had come to believe that he had deliberately misled the nation into the war (see Figure 6.13); and fewer than 20 percent of Democrats and only about 40 percent of independents still considered the president "honest and trustworthy" (see Figure 6.14). Republicans, in contrast, continued to believe and trust the

---

[71] Fifty percent of independents but only 17 percent of Republicans held this view; see *Time* Poll, August 22–24, 2006 (party breakdowns were graciously supplied by Mark A. Schulman of Schulman, Ronca & Bucuvalas, personal communication, September 5, 2006).

president as consistently as before. Given the partisan distributions of these attitudes, it is not surprising that the administration's preelection effort to revive public support for the war was largely an exercise in preaching to and, at best, mobilizing the converted.

THE TACTICAL COMPONENT

The Bush administration's campaign also included a tactical component in the form of legislation, submitted to Congress in September 2006, to put terrorist suspects outside the protection of the Geneva Conventions, legalizing undefined coercive methods of interrogation that, according to one's sensibilities, may or may not amount to torture. With typical spin, the administration claimed to be "clarifying" rather than carving out exceptions to the Geneva Conventions in such cases as the president chose. The administration also sought congressional authorization for military tribunals to try terrorist suspects, including fourteen recently brought to the Guantanamo Bay military prison from secret detention centers overseas. The tribunals would operate without the usual constitutional protections, allowing hearsay evidence, unnamed witnesses, and no recourse to habeas corpus (the right to challenge detention in court) or the federal court system. Legislation permitting the president to authorize the interception of telephone and email messages between American citizens and contacts abroad without a court order was also placed on the docket.

This agenda was designed to put Democrats on the spot; any sensitivity to the human rights or civil liberties issues raised by these proposals— indeed, any opposition to giving the president unchecked powers to deal with anyone suspected of links to terrorists as he saw fit—would invite the charge of being soft on terrorists. Thus, for example, discussing the legislation a day after the 9/11 anniversary, the House Republican leader John Boehner told reporters, "I listen to my Democratic friends, and I wonder if they are more interested in protecting terrorists than in protecting the American people," and he went on to charge that "they certainly don't want to take the terrorists on to defeat them."[72]

The effort to paint Democrats opposing any component of the legislation as soft on terrorism briefly ran into a snag when several Republican

---

[72] Dana Milbank, "A Reprise of the Grand Old Party Line," *Washington Post,* September 13, 2006, A2.

senators, led by John McCain and backed by the testimony of Colin Powell and senior military officials, objected to the "clarification" of the United States's obligations for treating enemy combatants under the Geneva Conventions, on the grounds that it would put United States troops in danger of torture. But McCain and the other Senate Republicans quickly accepted a compromise that avoided tinkering with the Geneva Conventions and banned "outrages upon personal dignity, in particular, humiliating and degrading treatment" but then left it to the president to decide what constituted such treatment. Ultimately, Republicans pushed through a bill that gave the president broad authority to name foreign nationals, including legal United States residents, as "enemy combatants," who would then lose the normal protections afforded by the judicial system: They could be arrested and held indefinitely without recourse to habeas corpus and subject to whatever coercive interrogation methods the president deemed acceptable under his interpretation of the law's vague language. People so designated could be tried before military tribunals, in which the usual rules of evidence did not apply, with only the most limited rights of judicial appeal. If not brought to trial, they could be locked up for as long as the government deemed it expedient.

Those Democrats who balked at this extraordinary delegation of power to the executive were accused by Boehner in the floor debate on the bill of being opposed to "giving President Bush the tools he needs to protect our country."[73] The legislation was also necessary, according to Wisconsin Republican James Sensenbrenner, Jr., to "bring justice before the eyes of the children and widows of September 11."[74] Democrats countered that the abrogation of fundamental rights for persons accused of terrorism was un-American, invited international condemnation, and was not needed to combat and prosecute terrorists. Nonetheless, fear of being labeled soft on terrorism or willing to "coddle" the perpetrators of 9/11 was enough to induce thirty-four House and twelve Senate Democrats to vote for the bill on final passage.

If anyone was still naïve enough to harbor doubts about the terrorism agenda's electoral motivation, Republican leaders' comments after passage laid them to rest. Senate Majority Leader Bill Frist asked: "Do [voters] want to be voting for a party that does unabashedly say, 'We're

---

[73] Charles Babington, "House Approves Bill on Detainees," *Washington Post,* September 28, 2006, A1.
[74] Ibid.

going to have victory in this war on terrorism,' or a party that says, 'We've got to surrender'"? And according to House Speaker Dennis Hastert: "[Democrats] were so bent on protecting criminals . . . they're not allowing us to prosecute these people. The 130 most treacherous people probably in the world, and they want to . . . release them out into the public eventually."[75] Of course, no Democratic leader had even remotely advocated either surrender to or releasing terrorists; as in earlier coordinated campaigns of persuasion mounted by Bush and his Republican allies (see Chapters 4, 5, and 7), a fetish for accuracy was not allowed to dilute the message.

What did the American people think of the legislation? The public's responses to survey questions on the issues raised by the Republicans' September agenda suggested considerable ambivalence about weakening civil liberties to enhance domestic security (Table 8.2). A majority of Americans thought the Bush administration was right to tap international communications without a judge's warrant, with partisan differences on this question as wide as usual; 86 percent of Republicans but only 33 percent of Democrats backed the president's position. On questions regarding secret evidence and adherence to the Geneva Conventions, however, most Americans of all partisan persuasions disagreed with the administration, and partisan differences on these questions were unusually small (in part, perhaps, because Bush's name did not appear in the question). A plurality preferred accused terrorists to be tried in criminal rather than military courts, and a solid majority said torture was never justified to get information from them. Ordinary Republicans were more supportive of military trials and the use of torture, but in both instances a substantial minority of them took the opposite position. The details of the administration's legislative program for dealing with terrorists did not, then, attract broad public support, and it was in no sense a response to widespread popular demand. But for a short time it did shift public focus from a domain where Bush's policies seemed to be failing, Iraq, to the one area where the president and his party still enjoyed an advantage over the Democrats, protecting the United States against terrorists.[76]

---

[75] Doyle McManus, "Detainee Bill Boosts the GOP," *Los Angeles Times,* September 30, 2006, A1, A14.
[76] As has been the case since September 11, 2001 (see Figure 4.4 in Chapter 4), Bush's job approval rating on handling terrorism continued during his sixth year in office to run well ahead of his overall job rating, averaging 48 percent January–September as compared with 38 percent for the overall rating.

TABLE 8.2
Support for the Bush Administration's Antiterrorism Agenda (Percentages)

	REPUBLICANS	INDEPENDENTS	DEMOCRATS	ALL

1. As you many know, the Bush administration has been wiretapping telephone conversations between United States citizens living in the United States and suspected terrorists living in other countries without getting a court order allowing it to do so. Do you think the Bush administration is right or wrong in wiretapping these conversations without obtaining a court order?[a]

	REPUBLICANS	INDEPENDENTS	DEMOCRATS	ALL
Right	86	50	33	55
Wrong	13	47	63	42
Depends/don't know	1	3	4	3

2. When the CIA questions suspects whom they believe to have information about possible terror plots against the United States, do you think they should have to abide by the same Geneva Convention standards that apply to the United States military, or should they be able to use more forceful interrogation techniques?[a]

	REPUBLICANS	INDEPENDENTS	DEMOCRATS	ALL
Abide by Geneva Convention	49	60	61	57
Use more forceful techniques	44	35	35	38
Depends/don't know	7	5	4	5

3. As you may know, in the United States legal system the government is required to show defendants the evidence it has against them. In some terrorism trials, the government believes that showing defendants certain evidence may put American lives in danger. In your view, which would be worse, convicting defendants of terrorism based on evidence they are never shown, or having some terrorism suspects go free because the government chooses to withhold evidence rather than show it to the defendants?[a]

	REPUBLICANS	INDEPENDENTS	DEMOCRATS	ALL
Convict on evidence not shown	46	45	51	48
Letting some terrorists go free	44	41	38	41
Don't know	10	14	11	11

4. When it comes to dealing with people suspected of involvement in terrorist attacks against the United States, which would you prefer: (1) trying them in open criminal court with a jury, unanimous verdict, and a civilian judge, or (2) trying them in a closed military court with a military judge and without a unanimous verdict?[b]

	REPUBLICANS	INDEPENDENTS	DEMOCRATS	ALL
Criminal court	37	46	63	49
Military court	59	46	33	46
Don't know	4	8	4	5

(continued)

TABLE 8.2 *(continued)*

	REPUBLICANS	INDEPENDENTS	DEMOCRATS	ALL
5. Do you think it is sometimes justified to use torture to get information from a suspected terrorist, or is torture never justified?[b]				
Sometimes justified	50	32	25	35
Never justified	38	59	67	56
Depends (volunteered)	6	4	5	5
Don't know	6	5	3	4

[a] *USA Today*/Gallup Poll, September 15–17, 2006.
[b] CBS News/*New York Times* Poll, September 15–19, 2006.

THE DEMOCRATS' RESPONSE

Democrats were, not surprisingly, outraged by the Republicans' efforts to label them appeasers and terrorist sympathizers, and partisan acrimony intensified. The reactions of the two surviving former Democratic presidents were emblematic. Asked by television host Larry King about his reaction to "Vice President Cheney's assertion that the criticism of Iraq, the Iraq War, emboldens United States enemies and makes allies doubt American resolve," Jimmy Carter replied, "Well, the vice president unfortunately has been consistently very careless with the truth. . . . [H]e's had a policy in my opinion of deliberately trying to mislead the American people by making untrue statements and there's no reason to give any credence to his ridiculous claims. . . ."[77] When a television docudrama implied that his administration had wasted opportunities to get bin Laden, Bill Clinton lashed back with "I tried and I failed to get bin Laden. I regret it, [but] they had eight months to try. They did not try. I tried." Clinton later said that his administration had left warnings about al Qaeda and a plan for taking out bin Laden that the Bush administration ignored, a claim Secretary of State Condoleezza Rice hotly denied, calling his assertion of inactivity "just flatly false."[78] That the spectacle of America's most eminent senior leaders denouncing one

---

[77] Interview on *Larry King Live*, September 13, 2006, transcript at http://transcripts.cnn.com/TRANSCRIPTS/0609/13/lkl.01.html.
[78] "Rice: Clinton Claims 'Flatly False,'" CBS/AP, September 26, 2006, at http://www.cbsnews.com/stories/2006/09/26/politics/main2039404.shtml?source=RSSattr=HOME_2039404.

another as liars excited so little comment was a sign of how polarized national politics had become by Bush's sixth year in office.

Clinton's counterattack had taken a page from Karl Rove's playbook, taking on the administration at its presumed strong point. And with some apparent success: Responding to a Gallup poll taken shortly after the controversy erupted that asked which president was more to blame for the failure to capture bin Laden, 53 percent said Bush, and 36 percent, Clinton. Partisans were, of course, strongly at odds on this question, but independents blamed Bush by a 58 to 31 percent margin.[79]

Bush's defenders could and did denounce Clinton's claims as partisan politics, but conclusions in a National Intelligence Estimate assessing the terrorist threat, issued in April but leaked to the press in early September and then, under pressure, released in excerpts by the administration on September 27, were harder to dismiss. The classified report, summarizing the consensus of sixteen United States intelligence-gathering agencies, implied that the war on terrorism was not going well. It concluded that "activists identifying themselves as jihadists . . . are increasing in both number and geographic dispersion. . . . If this trend continues, threats to US interests at home and abroad will become more diverse, leading to increasing attacks worldwide." Among the reasons: "The Iraq conflict has become the 'cause celebre' for jihadists, breeding a deep resentment of US involvement in the Muslim world and cultivating supporters for the global jihadist movement." These conclusions directly contradicted the Bush administration's view that the Iraq War had made the United States safer from terrorist attacks and were quickly taken by the administration's Democratic critics as evidence that the invasion of Iraq was not only a distraction from the war on terrorism but was in itself counterproductive. But the report's next sentence could be read to support the administration's case for staying and winning in Iraq: "Should jihadists leaving Iraq perceive themselves, and be perceived, to have failed, we judge fewer fighters will be inspired to carry on the fight."[80] The public tended to accept both of these arguments (Table 8.3). Prior to the report's publication and Bush's impassioned denial of its conclusions

---

[79] The partisan breakdown: Republicans—71 percent Clinton, 18 percent Bush; Democrats—83 percent Bush, 7 percent Clinton. See Lynda Saad, "Bush Blamed More Than Clinton for Failure to Capture Bin Laden," Gallup Poll, September 27, 2006, at http://www.gallup.com/poll/24733/bush-blamed-more-than-clinton-failure-capture-bin-laden.aspx (accessed September 27, 2006).

[80] "Declassified Key Judgments of the National Intelligence Estimate "Trends in Global Terrorism: Implications for the United States Dated April 2006," at http://media.washingtonpost.com/wp-srv/nation/documents/Declassified_NIE_Key_Judgments_092606.pdf (accessed September 29, 2006).

TABLE 8.3
Public Opinion on Issues in the National Intelligence Estimate (Percentages)

	REPUBLICANS	INDEPENDENTS	DEMOCRATS	ALL

1. Right now, is the United States involvement in Iraq and Afghanistan creating more terrorists who are planning to attack the United States, or is the United States eliminating terrorists who were planning to attack the United States, or is the United States involvement in Iraq and Afghanistan not affecting the number of terrorists planning to attack the United States?

	REPUBLICANS	INDEPENDENTS	DEMOCRATS	ALL
Creating more terrorists	34	57	68	54
Eliminating terrorists	29	12	5	15
Not affecting the number	29	23	20	24
Don't know	8	8	7	7

2. If the United States withdrew its troops from Iraq now, do you think the threat of terrorism against the United States would increase, decrease, or stay about the same?

	REPUBLICANS	INDEPENDENTS	DEMOCRATS	ALL
Increase	65	42	19	42
Decrease	3	5	17	8
Stay about the same	31	48	63	48
Don't know	1	5	1	2

SOURCE: CBS News/*New York Times* Poll, September 15–19, 2006, at http://www.cbsnews.com/htdocs/pdf/poll_president_092006.pdf.

about the spread of terrorism, a plurality of Republicans were inclined to think that the war was creating rather than eliminating terrorists, and Democrats and independents were decisively of this opinion. However, people were also far more likely to think that immediate withdrawal of United States troops would increase rather than decrease the terrorist threat to the United States, although the plurality thought it would make little difference.

The National Intelligence Estimate, then, raised in an indirect but unmistakable way the conundrum that had bedeviled the war's critics almost from the beginning: Even if the United States should never have gone into Iraq in the first place, might it not compound the damage to leave before the Iraqis have established a government capable of imposing order and preventing their country from becoming exactly what the war's proponents claimed it had become under Saddam Hussein: a prime staging and training ground for anti-American Islamic terrorists? The difficulty Democratic leaders continued to find in moving beyond criticism of the original decision to articulating an alternative strategy for dealing with its consequences reflected this quandary. Hence, although a large majority of Americans continued to doubt that the Bush administration had a clear plan for winning the war, an even larger majority doubted that the Democrats had one.[81]

The quandary was also reflected in the public's views on the war. Support for staying in Iraq until conditions stabilized (as opposed to leaving as soon as possible regardless of conditions there) remained higher than support for having invaded the country in the first place. On average, support for staying the course ran about 6 percentage points higher than retrospective support for the invasion. Moreover, the gap was greatest among Democrats. Over the first two years of Bush's second term, Democrats' opposition to immediate withdrawal ran an average of about 14 points higher than their retrospective support of the war (and more than 20 points higher than their rating of Bush's job performance). Among independents, the gap averaged 11 points. Among Republicans, in contrast, support for staying the course actually averaged 5 points *lower* than retrospective support for the war.

The difficulty of formulating an alternative strategy to Bush's for coping with the violent legacy of the Iraq invasion may have helped keep popular support for continuing the United States effort from collapsing, but it did not make people who thought the war had been a mistake any more favorable to the president who initiated it; thus, for example, Bush's approval rating in the January 2006 Gallup poll among those who said the war had been a mistake stood at 9 percent, regardless of whether they preferred to stay the course or set a timetable for withdrawal. Indeed, people who thought that the war had been a mistake but that the United States now had little choice but to bear the heavy costs of trying to redeem it might be especially angry with the person chiefly responsible, particularly if they believed that he had not only made the wrong decision in attacking Iraq but had deliberately deceived the country into following his lead.

---

[81] In a *USA Today*/Gallup poll taken September 15–17, 2006, 61 percent of respondents said that the Bush administration lacked "a clear plan for handling the situation in Iraq," while 67 percent said the Democrats lacked such a plan; at http://pollingreport.com/iraq.htm (accessed October 2, 2006).

INTENTIONAL POLARIZATION

The Bush administration's campaign to revive support for the Iraq War by linking it to the war on terrorism, paint Democrats as appeasers and defeatists, and thereby secure Republican retention of Congress was, in a way, deliberately polarizing. The president and his spokespersons did everything they could to suggest that there were only two starkly opposed alternatives, supporting Bush's vision and policies or giving up on Iraq and surrendering to terrorists. The use of straw men—attributing to unnamed Democrats views none of them had ever expressed and then offering the administration's position as the only reasonable alternative—embodied this strategy rhetorically and had by then become so routine as to inspire a "straw man watch" among anti-Bush bloggers. An example comes from Bush's address to the nation on the 2006 anniversary of 9/11: "Whatever mistakes have been made in Iraq, the worst mistake would be to think that if we pulled out, the terrorists would leave us alone." Of course, no Democratic critic of the war had ever said that they would.[82]

Aside from its tactical uses, defining the options in black and white was also consistent with Bush's theory of leadership and, by all accounts, his own sincere beliefs. In a widely reported meeting with conservative journalists in the Oval Office on September 13, his first words after "hello" were "Let me just first tell you that I've never been more convinced that the decisions I made are the right decisions," and he went on to reiterate his conception of leadership: "If you believe in a strategy . . . you've got to stick to that strategy, see. . . . It's tactics that shift, but the strategic vision has not, and will not, shift. If you don't have a set of principles to fall back on, you flounder, and it matters. It creates waves, and the waves rock the decision-making process."[83] Nothing, according to a

---

[82] Another example: "There's a group in the opposition party who are willing to retreat before the mission is done. They're willing to wave the white flag of surrender"; see "Remarks by the President at Talent for Senate Dinner," June 28, 2006, at http://findarticles.com/p/articles/mi_m2889/is_26_42/ai_n25453475/ (accessed March 23, 2010). When a Bush aide was later asked for names, he could provide none. For examples of the straw man watch, see Brendan Nyhan, "Straw Man Watch," September 30, 2006, at http://www.brendan-nyhan.com/blog/2006/09/bush_straw_man_.html (accessed October 2, 2006), and Dan Froomkin, "Bush's Imaginary Foes," September 27, 2006, at www.washingtonpost.com/wp-dyn/content/linkset/2005/10/11/LI2005101100925.html.

[83] Rich Lowry, "The 'W' Is Not for 'Wobble,'" *National Review Online*, September 13, 2006, at http://article.nationalreview.com/?q=NDdiZGNlMjgxMzUxYTI1OTdmMWFiMTE4ZmZiMzc2ZDM=(accessed October 2, 2006).

statement reported by Bob Woodward, would induce Bush to change course in Iraq: "I will not withdraw, even if Laura and Barney [a family dog] are the only ones supporting me."[84] In addition to Bush's political and psychological motives for holding firm, Rumsfeld and Cheney had by then been joined by Henry Kissinger in warning him that to do otherwise would result in a debacle worse than Vietnam. With the perceived stakes so high, it was no time for scruples in the effort to discredit and defeat Democratic critics of the war. If doing so exacerbated partisan divisions, so be it.

Democrats, eager to seize the opportunity they saw to retake control of Congress, were no more inclined to restraint. Public unhappiness with the war and the president were their main electoral assets, and Democratic leaders went all out to exploit them. Senator Mary Landrieu's statement on the Senate floor in mid-September serves as an example:

> America is tired of the wrongheaded and boneheaded leadership of the Republican Party that has sent six-and-a-half billion dollars a month to Iraq when the front line was Afghanistan and Saudi Arabia. That led this country to attack Saddam Hussein, when we were attacked by Osama bin Laden. Who captured a man that did not attack the country and left loose a man that did. Americans are tired of boneheaded Republican leadership that alienates our allies when we need them the most. And Americans are most certainly tired of leadership that—despite documented mistakes after mistake after mistake, even of their own party admitting mistakes—never admit that they ever do anything wrong."[85]

The Iraq War thus continued to be the nexus of the extraordinarily intense partisan divisions among national leaders regarding the president and his policies, and these differences continued to be echoed in the views of ordinary Republicans and Democrats. Any leader who crossed this partisan divide did so at considerable electoral risk. Senator Joseph Lieberman, Al Gore's running mate in 2000 but a staunch Bush ally in the Iraq War, lost the Connecticut Democratic primary to an antiwar candidate and had to depend on Republican votes to win reelection as an independent.

---

[84] Bob Woodward, *State of Denial* (New York: Simon and Schuster, 2006), 430.
[85] Quoted in Dan Froomkin, "Off Message," September 15, 2006, at http://busharchive.froomkin.com/BL2006091500608_pf.htm (accessed March 23, 2010).

THE 2006 MIDTERM ELECTIONS

Just as in 2002 and 2004, President Bush and his policies on national
security and the war in Iraq were central issues in the 2006 midterm congressional elections. But this time the administration's efforts to use these
issues to advantage failed. Instead, public disillusionment with the Iraq
War and the president responsible for it, reinforced by financial and personal scandals besetting some congressional Republicans, produced a
classic, negative midterm referendum on the party in power. Democrats
picked up thirty seats in the House, winning a majority one seat larger
than that held by the Republicans in the 109th Congress. Democrats also
gained six Senate seats, all taken from Republican incumbents, to win a
one-seat majority in the upper house. Remarkably, Democrats lost not a
single seat in either body, the first election in United States history in
which a party retained all of its congressional seats.

Unhappiness with the course of the Iraq venture, the president's low
approval ratings—in the 30s, lower than those of any president at
midterm since Harry Truman in 1950—and congressional malfeasance
had handed the Democrats their main campaign strategies: Attack
Republicans for loyally supporting the president and his misconceived
war and for sharing a "culture of corruption" in Congress, emphasizing the latter especially in states and districts where the incumbent's
personal record gave the charge local resonance. And frame the choice
in national terms, urging voters to use their franchise to express their
unhappiness with the Republican regime and, most particularly, its
leader.

Republican candidates faced a more complicated set of options.
One, standard for the circumstances, was to try to distance themselves
from their party and president (for example, by criticizing aspects of
the war or calling for Rumsfeld's resignation), emphasizing instead
their independence, devotion to local interests, and record of delivering
valued projects and services to constituents. But the public mood, as
well as Democratic opponents, worked against such an insulation strategy, and it was no more successful than it had been for Democratic
incumbents facing a similarly disgruntled public in 1994.[86] Bush didn't
help Republican candidates who were trying to change the subject

---

[86] Jacobson, *Politics of Congressional Elections*, 176–182.

when, just before the election, he praised Rumsfeld and Cheney for "doing fantastic jobs" and said they would remain in place until the end of his presidency.[87]

Another Republican tactic, taking a hard-line stance on immigration through an enforcement-only policy and voting to build a 700-mile fence along the 2,000-mile Mexican border, also put them at odds with the president, but it proved ineffective in attracting voters beyond the party's conservative base. Republican candidates also revived their customary charges that Democrats in power would raise taxes, over-spend, and stunt economic growth, but tax and spending issues were not high on the list of public concerns in 2006. The war in Iraq was, however, and to the end, Bush sought to turn the tide for Republican candidates by continuing to insist that victory in the war was vital to American security—"If we give up the fight in the streets of Baghdad, we will face terrorists in the streets of our own cities."[88]—which would be at risk if Democrats were to win control of Congress: "However they put it, the Democrat approach in Iraq comes down to this: The terrorists win and America loses."[89] From the September terror-ism agenda onward, the idea was to use the specter of jihadist terror-ism in the United States to frighten enough of the ambivalent into vot-ing Republican to keep the party's majorities in Congress, replicating at the congressional level Bush's successful strategy against John Kerry in 2004 (see Chapter 7).

It did not work in 2006. Neither did Republican attempts to redirect voters' attention to local concerns or to the Democrats' tax-and-spend reputation. The Democrats' efforts to nationalize the election and turn it into a referendum on President Bush, the war, and the Republican Con-gress largely succeeded. As Figure 8.10 shows, more than a third of the electorate said that their vote for Congress was a vote against Bush, a noticeably larger proportion than for any of his three predecessors at midterm, including Bill Clinton in 1994. The reversal since 2002, when an unusually high proportion of voters said their vote would be an expression of *support* for President Bush, is especially striking. The

---

[87] Terrance Hunt, "Bush Says Rumsfeld, Cheney Should Stay," at http://www.msnbc.msn.com/id/15516265/ (accessed March 23, 2010).

[88] Anne E. Kornblut and Sheryl Gay Stolberg, "In Latest Push, Bush Cites Risk in Quitting Iraq," *New York Times*, September 1, 2006, A6.

[89] "Remarks by the President at Georgia Victory 2006 Rally," October 30, 2006, at http://www.washingtonpost.com/wp-dyn/content/article/2006/10/30/AR2006103000530.html (accessed March 23, 2010).

FIGURE 8.10
Is Your Vote for Congress a Vote for or Against the President?

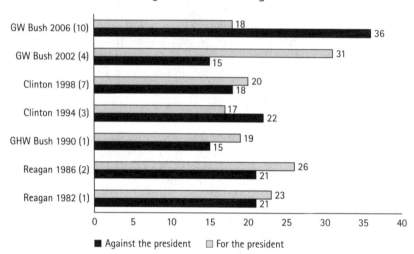

Note: Number of surveys averaged is in parentheses.

Source: Pew Research Center for the People and the Press, "October 2006 Survey on Electoral Competition: Final Topline," October 17-22, 2006, at http://people-press.org/reports/questionnaires/293.pdf.

proportion of voters who said control of Congress would be a factor in their vote was also higher than usual.[90] Democrats were especially inclined to say their vote would express opposition to Bush and a desire for Democratic control of Congress (more than 70 percent did so); they were also more enthusiastic about voting than were Republicans.[91] Negative opinions of presidential performance tend to motivate voters more strongly than positive opinions do,[92] and among Democrats, strongly negative views of Bush were the norm in 2006.

[90] An average of 58 percent compared with averages of 43 percent to 46 percent in the previous four lelections; see Gary C. Jacobson, "Referendum: National Politics in the 2006 Midterm Congressional Elections," Political Science Quarterly 122 (Spring 2007).

[91] "Republicans Cut Democratic Lead in Campaign's Final Days," research report, Pew Research Center for the People and the Press, November 6, 2006, at http://people-press.org/reports/display.php3?ReportID=295 (accessed November 27, 2006).

[92] Samuel Kernell, "Presidential Popularity and Negative Voting: An Alternative Explanation of the Midterm Congressional Decline of the President's Party," American Political Science Review 71 (1977): 44–66.

THE VOTE

The electorate was as sharply divided along party lines as it had been in any of the other elections of the Bush years—exit polls found 93 percent of Democrats and 91 percent of Republicans voting for their party's House candidate—but whereas in 2002 and 2004, Republicans were a couple of percentage points more loyal than Democrats, the opposite was true in 2006. Moreover, according to the exit polls, the partisan composition of the electorate was a point or two more favorable to the Democrats in 2006 than it had been in 2002 or 2004. However, the largest single contribution to the Democrats' gains evidently came from independents. Voters classifying themselves as independents had favored Republican candidates in 2002 and had given the Democrats a modest 54 percent to 46 percent edge in 2004; in 2006, they broke decisively for the Democrats, 57 percent to 39 percent. Independent voters were also the key to Democratic victories over Republican Senate incumbents in several of the "red" states: Montana, Missouri, and Virginia.[93]

A compelling explanation for the Democrats' advantage among independents in 2006 is provided by the data in Figures 1.2, 6.2, 6.13, 6.14, 8.4, and 8.8, which show that independents' opinions on Bush's performance and the Iraq War had grown much closer to those of Democrats than to those of Republicans. In surveys taken during the month before the 2006 election, for example, Bush's average approval rating among independents (29 percent) was 50 points below his average rating among Republicans (79 percent) and only 20 points above his rating among Democrats (9 percent). Similarly, independents' average level of support for the Iraq War during this period, at 36 percent, was more than twice as far below that of Republicans (73 percent) as it was above that of Democrats (19 percent).

The relationship between these opinions and voters' preferences in 2006 is illustrated in Figure 8.11. Views on Bush and the Iraq War affected the House vote of people in all three categories but made a much larger difference for independents than for partisans. Those independents who approved of Bush and the war voted Republican at rates 71 points higher than the rates of those who rejected both, so it was greatly to the Republicans' disadvantage that independents were more

---

[93] Jacobson, "Referendum: National Politics in the 2006 Midterm Congressional Elections."

FIGURE 8.11
Opinions on Bush and the Iraq War and Voting in the 2006 House Elections

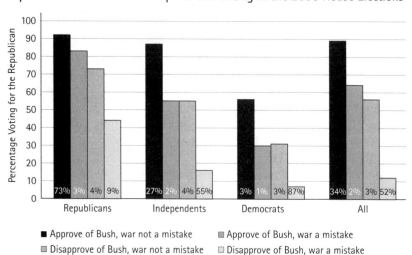

Note: Percentage of respondents in the category is listed at the bottom of each column; respondents with no opinion on one or both questions (about 8%) are excluded.

Source: 2006 Cooperative Congressional Election Survey.

than twice as common in the latter category than in the former. Seventy-three percent of Republican respondents to the 2006 Cooperative Congressional Election Study (CCES) supported the war and approved of Bush's performance, and of this group, 92 percent voted for the Republican House candidate. Among the small fraction (9 percent) of Republicans unhappy with both Bush and the war, more than half defected to the Democratic candidate in these elections. Democrats were even more united, with 87 percent rejecting Bush and the war; among this group, only 7 percent voted for the Republican House candidate. In contrast, more than half of the tiny fraction (3 percent) of Democratic voters who supported the president and the war voted for the Republican. The voting patterns of respondents with mixed views fell in between, but notice how rare they had become by 2006; only about 5 percent reported inconsistent opinions on the president and the war.

In the broad perspective, it is ordinary Republicans who stand out in both the opinion and the election data for 2006. Their approval of and trust in Bush, support for his war, and loyalty to Republican candidates declined during the first half of the president's second term, to be sure, but the decline was surprisingly modest considering all that had gone wrong for the administration, from the mishandling of Katrina to the bloody stalemate in Iraq. Similarly beset by increasingly problematic wars, Harry Truman and Lyndon Johnson saw their approval ratings among their own partisans drop by 20 and 26 percentage points, respectively, between their elections and the following midterms. The comparable falloff for Bush was only about 10 points, and his ratings remained substantially higher among his fellow partisans than those of his predecessors (averaging 79 percent, compared with 57 percent for Truman and 59 percent for Johnson) as the midterm election neared. As before, the more religiously devout Republicans remained Bush's staunchest supporters. Figure 8.11 suggests how important Republican loyalty to Bush and the war was in keeping the 2006 election from turning into an even greater Republican rout.

Although every preelection indicator pointed to a major Democratic victory in 2006, to the very end Bush and his immediate advisors, most prominently Karl Rove, insisted that Republicans would retain control of Congress. The administration's public optimism was reminiscent of its upbeat assertions of progress in Iraq and appeared to be yet another expression of Bush's belief that effective leadership requires a show of confidence and faith in success regardless of ominous signs to the contrary. In this case, the election resolved any ambiguity and delivered an unmistakable message: Change course in Iraq.

CHAPTER 9

A New Way Forward

The day after the Democrats' midterm victory, President Bush spoke in conciliatory terms, reiterating his old aspiration to be a uniter:

> When I first came to Washington nearly six years ago, I was hopeful I could help change the tone here in the capital. As governor of Texas, I had successfully worked with both Democrats and Republicans to find common-sense solutions to the problems facing our state. While we made some progress on changing the tone, I'm disappointed we haven't made more. I'm confident that we can work together. I'm confident we can overcome the temptation to divide this country between red and blue. . . . By putting this election and partisanship behind us, we can launch a new era of cooperation and make these next two years productive ones for the American people.[1]

Aside from the dubious notion that progress had been made in "changing the tone," these were appropriate sentiments for the circumstances. But they were not grounded in any reality. The election had only intensified partisan conflict, and the president's agenda—most importantly regarding the Iraq War—remained as contentious as ever. In the end, partisanship not only prevailed, but according to Poole and Rosenthal's roll-call based

---

[1] "Press Conference by the President," White House press release, November 8, 2006, at http://www.cnn.com/2006/POLITICS/11/08/bush.transcript/index.html (accessed March 25, 2010).

measures of ideology, the congressional parties ended up further apart in the 110th Congress (2007–2008) than in any Congress since the end of Reconstruction (see Figure 2.2).

In his postelection speech, Bush immediately recanted some of his anti-Democratic campaign rhetoric and his vow to keep Donald Rumsfeld through his second term. Of the soon-to-be Democratic leaders of Congress, he said, "I truly believe that Congresswoman Pelosi and Harry Reid care just as much—they care about the security of the country like I do." He also felt it necessary to warn the terrorists that they had *not*, in fact, won: "To our enemies: Do not be joyful. Do not confuse the workings of our democracy with a lack of will."[2] Bush also announced Rumsfeld's resignation and then immediately nominated his replacement, Robert Gates, conceding that the change had been in the works even as he was telling the country that Rumsfeld was in for the duration. The quick about-face revealed the basic disingenuousness of the administration's midterm campaign; it also raised the question of what other reversals might be coming, specifically regarding Iraq.

Pressure to change course in Iraq had been building well before the election. Back in March 2006, Congress, with the reluctant consent of the administration,[3] had established the Iraq Study Group, a bipartisan body of ten eminent, highly experienced and presumably wise national leaders, charged with exploring alternative strategies for achieving an acceptable outcome in Iraq. The commission was headed by a Republican, James Baker, secretary of state in the senior Bush's administration and G. W. Bush's point man in the Florida recount battle, and a Democrat, Lee Hamilton, a former congressman who had cochaired the 9/11 Commission. To keep its deliberations free of campaign politics, the group was to report in December, after the election.

The implicit premise underlying the Iraq Study Group's formation was that the administration's current policies were not working and no longer seemed likely to achieve their stated ends, so new approaches had to be considered. Until the election, Bush continued to reject this premise, at least in public, but he did find it necessary to show that he was not, as Bob Woodward had suggested, in denial about Iraq. While

---

[2] Ibid.
[3] Robert Dreyfuss, "A Higher Power: James Baker Puts Bush's Iraq Policy into Rehab," *Washington Monthly*, September 2006, at http://www.washingtonmonthly.com/features/2006/0609.dreyfuss.html (accessed December 6, 2006).

insisting that the goal of "victory" was not up for discussion, Bush said he was open to ideas for tactical changes to pursue the goal more effectively.[4] The need to appear at once steadfast and flexible led to a bizarre attempt at historical revisionism. In a televised interview on October 22, 2006, Bush surprised everyone by saying that his Iraq policy "has never been stay the course." Questioned on this, Bush's press secretary, Tony Snow, told Fox News that his staff "could find only eight times where [Bush] ever used the phrase stay the course."[5] Googling bloggers soon posted dozens of instances since the war's onset when Bush had used the phrase to characterize his Iraq policy; it had served, after all, as pithy rhetorical antithesis to the Democrats' alleged desire to "cut and run."

The administration's disavowal of "stay the course" reflected the reality that even those who retained faith in the ultimate success of United States policy in Iraq had to concede that victory was nowhere in sight. During a July 14, 2006, briefing of congressional staffers on the war, the Army Chief of Staff, General Peter J. Schoomaker, was asked: "Is the United States winning?" After reportedly mulling over the question for more than 10 seconds, he replied, "I think I would answer that by telling you I don't think we're losing" and went on to say that "I think that we're closer to the beginning than to the end of all this."[6] His sobering assessment matched the news coming out of Iraq as well as the confidential National Intelligence Estimate's assessment that "insurgents and terrorists retain the resources and capabilities to sustain and even increase current level of violence through the next year [2007]."[7] The growing sense that victory, even if possible, was not on the horizon was shared by the public; by the end of 2006, as many Americans believed the insurgents were winning as believed the United States was winning, although a majority (63 percent in December) saw it as a standoff (Figure 9.1).[8]

The growth of sectarian violence in Iraq during 2006 led to another effort by the administration to shape public opinion by controlling the

---

[4] See the quote in Chapter 8 on pages 185–186, for example.
[5] "Snow Falsely Claims Bush Said 'Stay the Course' Only 8 Times (Actually, It's at Least 30)," Think Progress, October 24, 2006, at http://thinkprogress.org/2006/10/24/snow-stay-the-course/ (accessed December 8, 2006).
[6] Peter Spiegel, "Is United States Winning: Army Chief at a Loss," Los Angeles Times, July 15, 2006, A11.
[7] Bob Woodward, "Secret Report Disputes White House Optimism," Washington Post, October 1, 2006, A1.
[8] Very few Republicans thought the insurgents were winning, but they were split on whether it was the United States or neither side winning; two-thirds of Democrats and independents thought neither side was winning. CBS News/New York Times Poll, July 21–25, 2006; CNN Poll, August 30–September 2, 2006; Los Angeles Times/Bloomberg Poll, September 16–19, 2006.

FIGURE 9.1
Who Is Winning the War in Iraq?

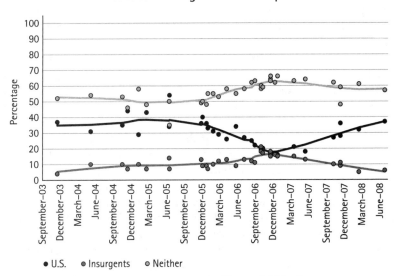

Source: CBS News/New York Times, Gallup, Los Angeless Times, and CNN polls.

definition of reality. The tit-for-tat cycle of mass murder, kidnapping, torture, and execution perpetrated by Sunni and Shiite factions, more widespread and deadlier than the continuing skirmishes between the coalition forces and the insurgents, naturally led to speculation that Iraqis were now engaged in a civil war. Mainstream news organizations had generally avoided the term until after the election, when several—including NBC, the *Los Angeles Times,* and *Newsweek*—evidently decided that the label had become appropriate for what was happening on the ground in Iraq. It certainly fit by any standard academic criteria.[9] The Bush administration objected strongly, arguing that because the conflict did not involve rival armies competing for territory and was concentrated in

---

[9] Monica Duffy Toft, "Is This a Civil War, or Isn't It?" *Neiman Watchdog,* July 28, 2006, at http://www.niemanwatchdog.org/index.cfm?fuseaction=ask_this.view&askthisid=220 (accessed December 7, 2006); Edward Wong, "A Matter of Definition: What Makes a Civil War, and Who Declares It So?" *New York Times,* November 26, 2006, at http://www.nytimes.com/2006/11/26/world/middleeast/26war.html?ex=1322197200&en=916272a5feb0f926&ei=5090&partner=rssuserland&emc=rss (accessed December 7, 2006).

Baghdad, it was not a civil war at all. Assumed to be at stake was continued public support for the United States involvement; the worry was that if the public came to see the conflict as a battle between equally unsympathetic religious and tribal factions, support for American involvement would collapse.

This worry was probably overblown. By early 2006, most Americans had already come to believe a civil war was either already in progress or soon would be. Asked in March if "there is a civil war going on in Iraq among different groups of Iraqis right now," 71 percent of respondents to the CBS News/*New York Times* Poll said "yes." In their April survey, that figure was up to 78 percent, and in their June survey, 82 percent.[10] The August ABC News/*Washington Post* Poll asked a more nuanced question and got a more nuanced distribution of responses; 34 percent said Iraqis were in a civil war, while 51 percent said they were "not in a civil war but close to one."[11] The growing belief that Iraqis were engaged in or verging on civil war did not, however, lead to a significant decline in public support for keeping the United States troops in the country during this period. But nothing guaranteed that a crystallized consensus that civil war had become the main event in Iraq would not eventually intensify popular demands for a United States withdrawal; at best, conceding the reality of civil war would put the Bush administration at a rhetorical disadvantage in countering Democrats' proposals for a systematic pull-back of American forces.

In fact, the question of whether the violence in Iraq constituted civil war had probably become moot by the time the administration and news organizations were dueling over it. Whatever it was called, the situation in Iraq in the fall of 2006 was plainly getting worse for Iraqis and United States interests alike, and leaders of both political parties were increasingly open in expressing their doubts that current United States policies could turn things around. A signal moment arrived when, during the early December Senate hearings on his nomination as secretary of defense, Robert Gates replied to a senator's question asking if the United States was winning the war in Iraq with "No, sir." His predecessor Rumsfeld's parting memo, leaked to the press, implied the same conclusion:

---

[10] CBS News/*New York Times* polls, March 9–12, April 6–9, and June 10–11, 2006. Partisan differences on this question were comparatively small; for the June survey, for example, 92 percent of Democrats, 81 percent of independents, and 71 percent of Republicans said yes.
[11] ABC News/*Washington Post* Poll, August 3–6, 2006. Four September 2006 surveys (CNN, *Los Angeles Times*/Bloomberg, Gallup, and NBC/*Wall Street Journal* polls) that asked whether Iraq was in a civil war found an average of 64 percent saying yes and 28 percent, no.

"It is time for a major adjustment. Clearly, what United States forces are currently doing in Iraq is not working well enough or fast enough."[12] Rumsfeld then presented a range of policy options, not a few of which had been scornfully dismissed by administration officials when Democrats had proposed them.

Prior to his nomination, Gates had been a member of the Iraq Study Group, and its report, delivered on December 6, provided the basis for his pessimistic assessment of the war. The report described the situation in Iraq in the bleakest terms: increasing insurgent and criminal violence, an ineffective government, and the prospect of "a slide toward chaos . . . [that] could trigger the collapse of Iraq's government and a humanitarian catastrophe" if trends did not change.[13] The Iraq Study Group left no doubt that, in its judgment, the administration's current approach was failing and had no prospect of ever succeeding. "We do not recommend a 'stay the course' solution," Baker said at the news conference announcing delivery of the report. "In our opinion, that approach is no longer viable."[14]

The report recommended seventy-nine specific changes, the most important of which was to initiate a comprehensive "diplomatic offensive" to bring all of Iraq's neighbors, including Syria and Iran, plus the U.N. Security Council and the European Union, into a process for stabilizing Iraq and addressing broader Middle Eastern issues, particularly the Israel-Palestine conflict. The report also recommended shifting the role of United States troops from combat to training Iraqi forces, with the goal of gradual disengagement, although, importantly, it did not call for setting a firm timetable for withdrawal of United States forces. And it proposed threatening to withhold military, economic, and diplomatic help if necessary to induce the Iraqi government to improve its poor performance.

Beyond advocating specific policy changes, the Study Group also wanted its bipartisan work to provide a blueprint for building a national consensus on moving forward that would bridge the partisan divisions the war had provoked. In a letter from the cochairpersons accompanying the report, Baker and Hamilton wrote,

Many Americans are dissatisfied, not just with the situation in Iraq but with the state of our political debate regarding Iraq. Our political

---

[12] Michael R. Gordon and David S. Cloud, "Rumsfeld Memo Proposes 'Major Adjustment' in Iraq," *New York Times,* December 3, 2006, A1.
[13] *The Iraq Study Group Report,* December 6, 2006, 6, at http://www.usip.org/isg/iraq_study_group_report/report/1206/index.html (accessed December 7, 2006).
[14] Paul Richter, "Iraq Policy 'No Longer Viable,'" *Los Angeles Times,* December 7, 2006, A12.

leaders must build a bipartisan approach to bring a responsible con-clusion to what is now a lengthy and costly war. Our country deserves a debate that prizes substance over rhetoric, and a policy that is ade-quately funded and sustainable. The president and Congress must work together. Our leaders must be candid and forthright with the American people in order to win their support. . . .

What we recommend in this report demands a tremendous amount of political will and cooperation by the executive and legislative branches of the United States government. It demands skillful implementation. It demands unity of effort by governmental agencies. And its success depends on the unity of the American people in a time of political polar-ization. Americans can and must enjoy the right of robust debate within a democracy. Yet United States foreign policy is doomed to failure—as is any course of action in Iraq—if it is not supported by a broad consensus. The aim of our report is to move the country toward such a consensus.[15]

Baker and Hamilton were calling for changes on the home front per-haps as difficult to achieve as redirecting Iraq policy toward a more promising path: substance over rhetoric, candor, realistic funding, coop-eration across parties and institutions, skillful implementation, unity of effort, and a broad public consensus. In effect, the study group thus issued an emphatic call for the president not only to change course in Iraq, but also to change the entire political tenor of his administration, at least in the realm of foreign policy. And not just the president: The Democratic opposition, about to control Congress, was also being urged to stifle its well-honed partisan reflexes in the interest of national unity—and was pointedly warned of the dire consequences if the United States was simply to withdraw from Iraq.

THE PRESIDENT'S RESPONSE

Bush's initial reaction was noncommittal; he welcomed "some really very interesting proposals" in the report but declined to respond in detail until three internal reports he had ordered from the Pentagon, State Department, and National Security Council reviewing the options in Iraq had been completed.[16] These reports would keep the Iraq Study Group's

---

[15] "'There Is No Magic Formula,'" *Los Angeles Times*, December 7, 2006, A13.
[16] "'An Opportunity to Come Together,'" *Los Angeles Times*, December 6, 2006, A13.

ideas from being the only options on the table and would counter the image of an administration that had stumbled into a morass from which only older and wiser outsiders could rescue it. Moreover, Bush clearly maintained aspirations for the war that the Iraq Study Group's report had, by omission, implicitly abandoned. In a joint press conference with Tony Blair the day after the report was submitted, Bush reiterated his belief that "the only way to secure a lasting peace for our children and grandchildren is to defeat the extremist ideologies and help the ideology of hope, democracy, prevail"; he later vowed, "We will stand firm again in this first war of the 21st century. We will defeat the extremists and the radicals. We will help a young democracy prevail in Iraq."[17] Responding to a pointed question asking if he was not still in denial about the situation, he answered,

> I understand how tough it is. And I've been telling the American people how tough it is. And they know how tough it is. . . . I also believe we're going to succeed. I believe we'll prevail. . . . I understand how hard it is to prevail. But I also want the American people to understand that if we were to fail—and one way to assure failure is just to quit, is not to adjust, and say it's just not worth it—if we were to fail, that failed policy will come to hurt generations of Americans in the future.[18]

And for good measure, he capped his answer with cautionary references to nuclear blackmail and 9/11. In short, Bush did not sound at all like someone ready to change objectives or to adopt any policy that was inconsistent with his past vows to persevere until victory as he defined it was achieved.

The Iraq Study Group report was highly critical of the United States' management of the war, but it also emphasized the danger of failing to contain the conflict. Most members of Congress from both parties said they welcomed the report, albeit often selectively and with reservations. They were at least generally united on the need for a new direction. Democrats believed the report vindicated their own criticisms of the war, and many viewed it as a plan to begin extricating the United States from Iraq. Republicans, burned by the Iraq issue in 2006, also sought a

---

[17] "President Bush Meets with British Prime Minister Tony Blair," White House transcript, December 7, 2006, at http://archives.cnn.com/TRANSCRIPTS/0609/11/se.01.html (accessed March 25, 2010).
[18] Ibid.

TABLE 9.1

Public Opinion on What to Do in Iraq (Percentages)

Which comes closest to your view: (1) The United States should continue fighting the war in Iraq using the same military strategy and tactics it is using now; or (2) the United States should continue fighting the war in Iraq but needs to change its strategy and tactics; or (3) the United States should remove all its troops from Iraq?

	Republicans	Democrats	Independents	All
Continue, same strategy	6	1	2	3
Continue, change strategy	64	28	40	43
Remove all troops	28	69	53	52
Don't know	2	2	5	2

SOURCE: CBS News/*New York Times* polls, October 27–31, 2006, and January 1–3, 2007, at http://www.cbsnews.com/htdocs/pdf/poll_midterms_110106.pdf.

change of course to keep it from dragging them down again in 2008. However, the new direction advocated by a few prominent Republicans, notably Senator John McCain, was escalation, sending in United States combat troops rather than shifting the United States military role to training. Conservative pundits were also quick to attack the report, especially for its recommendation to engage Syria and Iran, its silence on promoting democracy in the Islamic world, and its lack of a plan for winning the kind of victory envisioned by the president and the neoconservatives who had been the war's most fervent promoters.[19] Thus, if he followed the report's advice, Bush risked splitting his own party, losing Republican support without necessarily gaining the backing of long-estranged Democrats and independents.

Regardless of what path Bush chose in response to this report or any of the others he would be getting, the approach had to look like something other than "stay the course" to be politically sustainable. Although there was no popular consensus on what to do next in Iraq, there was a strong consensus on what *not* to do: continue current policy. Table 9.1 lists responses to a question about the direction of Iraq policy, which was posed by the CBS News/*New York Times* survey taken in January 2007. The option to "continue fighting the war . . . using the same military

---

[19] Greg Miller, "Return Fire from the Right," *Los Angeles Times*, December 8, 2006, A1.

strategy and tactics it is using now" was rejected overwhelmingly regardless of party. A majority wanted to remove all troops rather than try a new strategy. Partisan differences were substantial, but the percentage of Republicans ready to pull all the troops out was 19 points higher than it had been when the same question was asked two months earlier in a pre-election survey.

THE "NEW WAY FORWARD"

On January 10, 2007, Bush told the nation that he would pursue victory in Iraq by adding 21,500 American troops to the 132,000 already in Iraq and assigning most of them to help clear and hold Baghdad neighborhoods; persuading the Iraqi government to attack all sources of sectarian violence, including Shiite militias; and expanding economic development aid. By largely rejecting the Iraq Study Group's assessment of American prospects in Iraq and its recommendations for revamping United States policy, Bush also effectively rejected its call for bipartisan cooperation and other changes in the political management of the war. To his mostly Democratic critics in Congress, the proposed "surge," as it was dubbed, was simply more of the same, and with the same dismal prospects of success. The public's response reiterated the stark partisan differences that had become the norm for opinions on the Iraq War; in nineteen surveys taken during the first quarter of 2007, the surge drew support from an average of 65 percent of Republicans but only 11 percent of Democrats, 32 percent of independents, and 34 percent overall.

Having won majority status in an election that was largely a negative referendum on Bush and the war, congressional Democrats naturally opposed the surge, preferring the Iraq Study Group's approach aimed at winding down the American involvement. But with only a 51 to 49 majority in the Senate and with the president wielding the veto, they lacked the votes to prevail without support from at least some Republicans. The most important showdown came in May 2007, when House and Senate Democrats adopted a rider to the emergency war appropriations bill that set a calendar for withdrawal of United States troops. The bill passed only because, as a budget measure, it could not be filibustered in the Senate. When Bush vetoed the bill as promised, the House failed to override by a wide margin when all but two Republicans sided with the president. This exemplified the pattern throughout

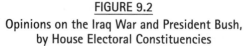

FIGURE 9.2

Opinions on the Iraq War and President Bush, by House Electoral Constituencies

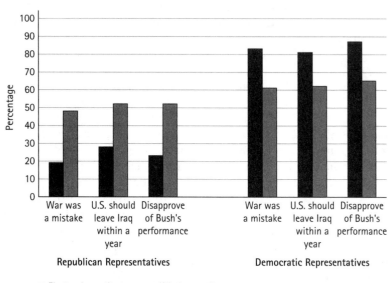

■ Electoral constituency   ■ Whole constituency

Source: 2006 Cooperative Congressional Election Survey.

2007: The Democrats' repeated efforts to alter Iraq policy failed repeatedly because they could persuade no more than a handful of Republicans to join them.

Both Democratic persistence and Republican resistance were grounded in electoral realities. Figure 9.2 displays data from the 2006 CCES, comparing four sets of respondents: those who voted for the winning House Republicans and winning House Democrats—that is, the two respective electoral constituencies—and those who comprised all voters in each of those districts. More than 80 percent of the Democrats' electoral constituents disapproved of Bush, opposed the war, and wanted out of Iraq within a year; and more than 60 percent of all of their constituents took these positions. Fewer than 20 percent of Republicans' electoral constituents believed the war was a mistake, and fewer than 30 percent favored a quick exit from Iraq or disapproved of Bush's performance, although about half of their full constituencies did so.

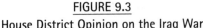

FIGURE 9.3
House District Opinion on the Iraq War

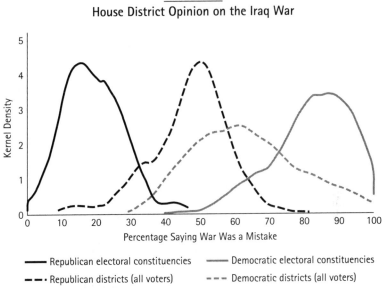

Source: 2006 Cooperative Congressional Election Survey.

The CCES sample was large enough to provide rough estimates of opinion in each district,[20] and even at this disaggregated level, very few members appeared to owe their election to voters opposed to the dominant position of the members' party on these questions. Consider, for example, the distribution of opinions across electoral constituencies and across whole Republican and Democratic districts (including all voters) on whether the war was a mistake (Figure 9.3). Only two Democrats represented districts in which a majority of the people who voted for them did not think the war was a mistake; no Republicans represented districts in which a majority of their supporters did not think it was the right decision.[21] The full constituencies represented by Democrats and

---

[20] The survey provides a weighted average of 33 electoral constituents (standard deviation, 13) and an average of 51 total constituents (standard deviation, 21) per district. It includes all 435 House districts.

[21] A similar pattern appears in responses to the other two questions. Only one Democrat had an electoral constituency with a majority opposed to withdrawing from Iraq within a year, and only one had an electoral constituency in which the majority approved of Bush's performance; only three Republicans were elected by majorities of supporters favoring swift withdrawal from Iraq, and only one had an electoral constituency in which a majority disapproved of Bush's performance.

Republicans were not sharply polarized, but their electoral constituencies certainly were. The wide partisan division among House members on war policy thus accurately mirrored the wide partisan division among the voters responsible for their election. It is obvious why Democratic congressional majorities continued throughout 2007 to try to force a change in the president's Iraq policies, and why they continually failed to win enough Republican support to succeed.

Democratic strategists had expected that as the 2008 elections approached, Republicans would come under increasing pressure to distance themselves from the unpopular president and war. But by late summer 2007, the president's New Way Forward, under the leadership of General David Petraeus, was showing enough evidence of success to begin easing the pressure. Petraeus's military strategy aimed to secure the Iraqi population by clearing and holding areas in joint operations with Iraqi and local security forces. The initiative's timing was fortunate. In the north, Sunni tribal leaders, alienated by the extreme brutality and fanaticism of the foreign-led al Qaeda in Iraq, were ready to ally with United States forces to drive them out. Elsewhere, sectarian killings declined after years of violent sorting had consolidated separate factional enclaves. Shiite leader Moqtada al-Sadr, for reasons not yet clear, ordered his Mahdi Army to refrain from attacking United States troops. The surge's political goals remained largely unmet, but the level of violence declined noticeably, and a semblance of normal life began returning to many parts of Iraq. More important to most Americans, United States casualties, which had initially spiked with the augmented troop levels and more aggressive strategy, fell sharply in the last quarter of 2007 and remained comparatively low thereafter (Figure 9.4).

The public responded to these developments with growing optimism about the war's progress. The proportion saying the war was going well doubled, from about 30 percent in mid-2007 to about 60 percent by the end of 2008 (see Figure 8.3), with partisans in every category displaying the same upward trajectory (see Figure 8.4). Belief that the surge was helping (rather than hurting or making no difference) grew (Figure 9.5), as did the belief that the United States was winning the war and was likely to achieve its goals in Iraq.[22]

---

[22] In CNN surveys, the proportion saying the United States was winning grew from 32 percent in August 2007 to 50 percent in February 2009 (at http://www.pollingreport.com/iraq.htm, accessed June 12, 2009); in Pew surveys, the proportion saying the United States was certain or likely to achieve its goals in Iraq rose from 42 percent in September 2007 to 61 percent in January 2009 (at http://people-press.org/reports/questionnaires/483.pdf, accessed June 12, 2009). See also Figure 9.1.

FIGURE 9.4
Monthly United States Deaths in Iraq, 2003–2008

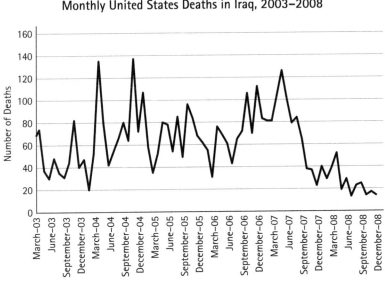

Source: Data from http://www.icasualties.org.

Yet greater optimism regarding Iraq did little to revive popular support for the war (see Figures 6.1 and 6.2), and it did not make Americans any less eager to get the United States troops out (see Figures 8.5 and 8.6). Support for the war rose only a couple of points, and the small increase was confined to Republicans and independents; Democrats were completely unmoved. Substantial improvements in conditions on the ground, casualty rates, and prospects for success thus did little to shake up what had by then become settled opinions on whether going to war was a good or bad idea in the first place, confirming John Mueller's conclusion that, once lost, popular support for a war does not return.[23]

---

[23] John E. Mueller, "The Iraq Syndrome," *Foreign Affairs* 84 (November/December 2005): 44–54. As Mueller noted presciently in late 2005, "But should good news start coming in from Iraq—including, in particular, a decline in American casualty rates—it would more likely cause the erosion in public support to slow or even cease rather than trigger a large upsurge in support. For support to rise notably, many of those now disaffected by the war would need to reverse their position, and that seems rather unlikely. . . . If you purchase a car for twice what it is worth, you will still consider the deal to have been a mistake even if you come to like the car" (p. 49).

FIGURE 9.5
Is the Surge Helping?

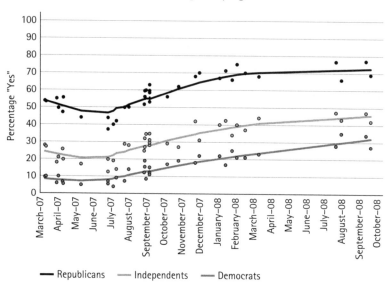

Source: CBS News/New York Times, Pew Center for the People and the Press, NBC/Wall Street Journal, and Gallup polls.

FAULTY MEMORIES

Approval of George Bush's handling of the war rose about 5 points as prospects brightened in Iraq, but Republicans were largely responsible for the improvement (see Figure 1.7). Their approval ratings rose 15 points, to about 75 percent, while those of Democrats remained mired in single digits, where they had languished since the end of 2006. While not impervious to good news in their assessments of progress in Iraq, Democrats never revised their negative opinions on the war or the president. Indeed, opposition to the war had become so entrenched that a remarkable proportion of Democrats no longer remembered that they had once believed in the war's premises and supported the venture. The evidence is from four surveys of my design, two conducted in conjunction with the 2006 and 2008 elections, two taken in November 2007 and January 2008 in

FIGURE 9.6
Initial, Remembered, and Current Beliefs About the Iraq War

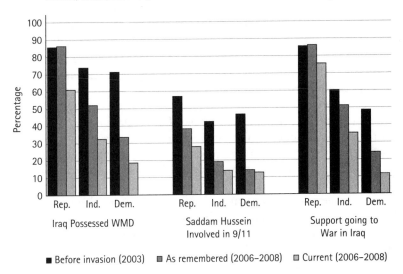

Sources: See footnotes 24–27.

between the elections.[24] All four surveys asked whether, at the time the war began, respondents believed Iraq possessed WMD and supported the decision to go to war. Three also asked whether they remembered believing that Saddam Hussein was involved in the terrorist attacks of 9/11. A large majority of respondents—from 89 percent to 95 percent in these surveys—said they did remember and were willing to answer the question. Their responses can be instructively compared with the results of surveys taken in late 2002 and early 2003, before the war began.

Figure 9.6 displays the distribution of responses to the questions tapping memory of belief in the war's central premises and support for the

[24] Gary C. Jacobson, Cooperative Congressional Election Study, 2006: UCSD Content (computer file), release 2 (UCSD, 2007), at http://dvn.iq.harvard.edu/dvn/dv/cces/faces/StudyListingPage.xhtml?mode=1&collectionId=1650; Stephen Ansolabehere, Cooperative Congressional Election Study, 2007: Common Content (computer file), release 1 (Cambridge, MA: MIT, February 13, 2008), at http://web.mit.edu/polisci/portl/cces/commoncontent.html; Gary C. Jacobson, Cooperative Congressional Election Study, 2008: UCSD Content (computer file), release1 (UCSD, February 2009), at http://dvn.iq.harvard.edu/dvn/dv/cces/faces/StudyListingPage.xhtml?mode=1&collectionId=1650; Gary C. Jacobson, "Question Order Effects on Reported Memories and Perceptions Regarding the Iraq War," TESS research report, 2008.

invasion. The distribution of responses was largely consistent across surveys so I display only the averages of the four. The results of this analysis are striking. A rather large proportion of Democrats and independents evidently reconstructed their memories to match their current beliefs. In eight surveys taken prior to the war, between 57 percent and 83 percent of Democrats said they thought Iraq possessed WMD; the average was 71 percent.[25] But in the four 2006–2008 surveys, less than half this proportion remembered believing in WMD; the average difference between Democrats' remembered views on WMD and those expressed in surveys taken before the war is thus a remarkable 38 percentage points. The pattern among independents is similar although less dramatic, with a difference of about 22 points between remembered opinions and those measured in the earlier surveys. Republican memories, in contrast, matched opinions expressed in the months leading up to the war exactly.

On the question of Saddam Hussein's personal involvement in 9/11, the gap between remembered beliefs of Democrats and independents and those expressed in the months leading up to the war is also very wide.[26] Only about 16 percent of Democrats remembered having believed Saddam was involved, whereas in five polls taken before the war, between 38 percent and 50 percent of Democrats (an average of 46 percent) expressed this view. The difference is nearly as large for independents; respondents in both categories produced memories that were far closer to their current views than to those expressed during the run-up to the war.

Democrats and, to a lesser extent, independents also, not at all coincidentally, tended to forget that they had once supported the war. In twenty-seven surveys taken between February 1, 2003, and the beginning of the war, an average of nearly half of Democrats and 60 percent of independents said they favored going to war.[27] But only about 28 percent of Democrats and 51 percent of independents remembered supporting the war at that time. Republican memories again matched the 2003 survey averages closely.

---

[25] Data are from CBS News/*New York Times* (5), ABC News/*Washington Post* (1), and Gallup (2) surveys taken between September 2002 and February 2003.

[26] Data are from CBS News/*New York Times* (3) and Gallup (2) surveys taken between August 2002 and March 2003.

[27] Data are from ABC News/*Washington Post*, CBS News/*New York Times*, Gallup, *Time*/CNN, *Newsweek*, *Los Angeles Times*, Pew, and NBC News/*Wall Street Journal* surveys taken between February 1 and March 18, 2003.

MOTIVATED REASONING AND PARTISAN POLARIZATION

These survey results invite a closer look at the psychological processes, some alluded to in earlier chapters, that have contributed to extreme partisan differences in the distribution of responses to survey questions about George Bush and the Iraq War. The tendency of Democrats to forget they once believed in the war's premises and supported it, like the tendency of Republicans to continue to believe that Iraq possessed WMD at the time of the invasion (an average of 61 percent in these surveys), are classic manifestations of *motivated reasoning*. The theory of motivated reasoning, an intellectual descendent of cognitive dissonance theory and related approaches,[28] rests on the idea that a "tension between drives for accuracy and belief perseverance underlies all human reasoning."[29] Specifically, "in motivated reasoning, . . . it is important not just to get the right outcome, but also to get a certain preferred outcome, regardless of correctness."[30] Insofar as prior attitudes and beliefs are at stake, people will engage in motivated reasoning, and new information will therefore be absorbed in a biased fashion.

The principal mechanisms producing biased information processing include these:

- *Selective judgment, also called motivated skepticism.* People invest more time and cognitive resources in picking apart arguments or questioning information that challenges their current opinions than in evaluating arguments and information confirming them; the former tend to receive skeptical scrutiny, but the latter, uncritical acceptance. Skepticism, then, is asymmetrical.
- *Selective perception.* People are more likely to get the message right when it is consistent with prior beliefs and more likely to miss it when it is not.
- *Selective memory.* People are more likely to remember things that are consistent with current attitudes and to forget or misremember things that are inconsistent with them.

---

[28] Leon Festinger, *A Theory of Cognitive Dissonance* (Stanford, CA: Stanford University Press, 1957); Ziva Kunda, "The Case for Motivated Reasoning," *Psychological Bulletin* 108, no. 3 (1990): 636–647.

[29] Milton Lodge and Charles S. Taber, "Three Steps Toward a Theory of Motivated Political Reasoning," in Arthur Lupia, Mathew D. McCubbins, and Samuel L. Popkin, eds., *Elements of Reason: Cognition, Choice, and the Bounds of Rationality* (Cambridge: Cambridge University Press, 2000).

[30] Matthew J. Lebo and Daniel Cassino, "The Aggregated Consequences of Motivated Reasoning and the Dynamics of Partisan Presidential Approval," *Political Psychology* 28 (2007): 722

■ *Selective exposure.* People tend to seek out and attend to information from sources likely to confirm prior opinions and beliefs and to
avoid information from sources likely to challenge them.

People can thus defend current beliefs and attitudes against discordant
information by some combination of avoiding, disbelieving, misperceiv-
ing, forgetting, or misremembering it. The theory does not claim that
current views are immune to new information, for it assumes that people
also prefer their knowledge of the world to be accurate. The balance
"hinges . . . on the relative weight that people assign to reality itself
against their desire to arrive at convenient conclusions."[31]

The extent to which these psychological mechanisms are mobilized to
defend current attitudes against discordant information thus depends on
several variables. First, the more strongly held the prior attitude is, the
more it will be defended by one or more of these psychological devices;
that is, the stronger the motive, the more biased the reasoning. Second, the
more complex or ambiguous the situation is, the more priors will hold
sway; in contrast, the more readily available unambiguously "objective"
information is, the more likely "reality" will prevail. Third, greater knowledge and sophistication do not necessarily produce greater objectivity in
processing information because they also enable more effective exercises in
motivated skepticism; when partisanship induces motivated skepticism,
the informed may be more biased and thus more polarized along party
lines than the uninformed.[32]

Several modes of motivated reasoning can be detected in Republicans'
continuing belief that Iraq possessed WMD. Those who believe WMD
have actually been found (15 percent to 31 percent in the four surveys
analyzed for the previous section) certainly managed to miss the well-
publicized fact that, to its profound embarrassment, the Bush administration never turned up any. Those who believe WMD probably existed
but have not been found have either misread or consciously rejected official reports to the contrary. There is evidence for both responses. As
noted in Chapter 7, a survey taken in September–October 2004 found

---

[31] Danielle Shani, "Know Your Colors: Can Knowledge Correct Partisan Bias in Political Perceptions?"
Paper delivered at the Annual Meeting of the Midwest Political Science Association, Chicago, April
20–23, 2006, 4.
[32] Lodge and Taber, "Motivated Reasoning"; Charles S. Taber and Milton Lodge, "Motivated Skepticism
in the Evaluation of Political Beliefs," *American Journal of Political Science* 50 (July 2006): 755–769;
Shani, "Know Your Colors"; on the last point, see also John Zaller, *The Nature and Origin of Mass
Opinion* (Cambridge: Cambridge University Press, 1992).

that 57 percent of Bush supporters got the Duelfer Report, commissioned and accepted by the administration, exactly backwards, believing incorrectly that it concluded that Iraq possessed WMD or had a major program to build them (see Table 7.1). Another 18 percent got the report right but disbelieved it—an exercise in motivated skepticism. Any inclination toward skepticism could have been reinforced by stories still circulating in the conservative media as late as 2006 that WMD had actually been found.[33] Even if aware that no WMD had been found, Republicans could have taken comfort in Rumsfeld's maxim that "the absence of evidence is not evidence of absence,"[34] resolving the irreducible residual uncertainty in favor of their prior beliefs.

Belief in the war's second unconfirmed premise, that Saddam Hussein was personally involved in 9/11, was less widespread but also more common among Republicans than among other respondents. In the three CCES surveys that asked about his involvement, an average of about 18 percent of respondents reported believing that he was involved, while 65 percent said he was not.[35] Among Republicans, it was 29 percent believing in his involvement, compared with 14 percent among independents and 12 percent among Democrats.[36]

The theory of motivated reasoning holds that people with more strongly held attitudes are more likely to resist discordant information than are people with more weakly held attitudes. Consistent with this hypothesis, in three of the four surveys, self-identified strong Republicans were the most likely to continue to think Iraq had WMD.[37] Strong Republicans were also the most likely to believe Saddam Hussein was personally involved in 9/11. But the Republicans most strongly motivated to support the president and his decision to go to war were those who believed Bush had been chosen by God to lead a global war on terrorism, and they were, as we saw in Chapter 6 (see Figure 6.17), the most resistant to discordant information regarding the missing WMD.

---

[33] "Report: Hundreds of WMDs Found in Iraq," Fox News, June 22, 2006, at http://www.foxnews.com/politics/2006/06/22/report-hundreds-wmds-iraq/ (accessed July 10, 2009). The claim was based on the discovery of pre-1991 ordnance contaminated with degraded chemical nerve agents.

[34] United States Department of Defense, news transcript, June 2, 2002, at http://www.defenselink.mil/transcripts/ transcript.aspx?transcriptid=3490 (accessed January 15, 2006).

[35] The ranges were from 15 percent to 21 percent and 63 percent to 67 percent across the three CCES; there was no evidence of any trend over the 2006–2008 time period.

[36] The ranges were from 26 percent to 32 percent for Republicans, 11 percent to 17 percent for independents, and 11 percent to 14 percent for Democrats.

[37] The exception was the 2008 CCES, in which, curiously, independents who leaned Republican were most likely to believe Iraq possessed WMD.

They were also nearly twice as likely as other Republicans to believe that Saddam Hussein had been personally involved in 9/11 (40 percent to 21 percent). Thus, the subset of Republicans with compelling incentives to engage in selective judgment and misperception were most likely to do so.

Democrats, of course, were much less likely to have strong prior opinions to defend against the official reports discrediting the war's premises; if anything, their biases would incline them readily to accept such information. As noted earlier, nearly half the Democrats and about 60 percent of independents had backed the invasion just prior to its onset, and almost all who did so thought that Iraq possessed WMD.[38] When neither WMD nor a 9/11 connection could be confirmed, and with rising sectarian and criminal violence in Iraq and a growing list of American casualties, many Democrats (and not a few independents) who had initially backed the war and the president no longer had any reason to do so. Disillusionment was sufficiently profound to induce many of them to forget, or at least not to acknowledge, that they had once believed in the war's justifications and had supported the venture.

Once disillusioned, and having developed strongly negative opinions of Bush,[39] Democrats also exhibited strongly biased information processing. Regarding the war's origins, for example, about 95 percent of Democrats in the 2006 and 2008 CCES samples who thought the war was a mistake believed that, in making the case for war, the Bush administration had deliberately misled the public; two other national surveys from 2007 and 2008 put that figure at 87 percent.[40] No one knows for sure how confident the president and his advisors were in their judgment that Iraq was making and hiding WMD, but their reactions suggest that they were as surprised as anyone else when they could not find at least some hidden caches or manufacturing facilities. But primed to think the worst of the president, Democrats who had turned against the war resolved the uncertainties about Bush's candor in his disfavor.

---

[38] In the three CBS News/*New York Times* surveys taken in January and February 2003, 87 percent to 90 percent of Democrats and 87 percent to 97 percent of independents who supported going to war believed Iraq possessed WMD; the February survey also asked about Saddam Hussein's involvement in 9/11, and in that survey, 94 percent of both Democrats and independents who supported the war believed either that Saddam was involved in 9/11 or that Iraq was hiding WMD.

[39] Eighty-four percent of Democrats in the 2006 and 2008 CCES studies and 82 percent in the 2007 CCES study said they disapproved of Bush "strongly."

[40] CNN/Opinion Research Corporation Poll, March 9–11, 2007; Gallup Poll, February 21–24, 2008.

SELECTIVE EXPOSURE

Finally, selective exposure also contributed to partisan divisions on the war and the president. Americans are now able to draw on ideologically diverse sources of news and information, and there is plenty of evidence they tend to choose sources more likely to confirm than challenge their political opinions.[41] Specifically regarding Iraq, Kull, Ramsey, and Lewis found strong variation across users of different news sources in acceptance of the Bush administration's version of Iraqi realities and users' perceptions of established facts about the war, with the Fox News audience showing the highest levels of support for the war and misperception of facts that might have undermined it.[42] The CCES surveys also asked a subset of respondents where they got most of their national news and found even more striking differences between the viewers of Fox News and other news programs than had Kull and his colleagues. Differences across television news sources in beliefs about the war's premises and support for it and Bush are displayed in Figure 9.7.

The Fox audience is, to put it mildly, distinctive; the remaining news audiences fall roughly into two subcategories based on the distributions of their responses to the questions: viewers of the three national broadcast networks' programs plus CNN and viewers of PBS and MSNBC. Fox News watchers were far more likely than others to continue to believe the original justifications for the Iraq War and to support the war and Bush. PBS and MSNBC audiences were overwhelmingly skeptical about the war's premises and critical of the war and the president. Viewers of the broadcast networks and CNN fell in between but took positions much more similar to those of the PBS and MSNBC audiences than to those of the Fox audiences.

The differences in Figure 9.7 are largely, perhaps entirely, the product of viewers' selectively exposing themselves to news sources in line with

---

[41] Pew Research Center for the People and the Press, "News Audiences Increasingly Polarized," news release, June 8, 2004, 14–15, at http://people-press.org/reports/display.php3?ReportID=215 (accessed July 7, 2005); National Annenberg Election Study, "Fahrenheit 9/11 Viewers and Limbaugh Listeners About Equal in Size Even Though They Perceive Two Different Nations, Annenberg Data Show," news release, August 3, 2004, at http://www.annenbergpublicpolicycenter.org/naes2004_03_fahrenheit_08-03_pt.pdf (accessed August 10, 2004).

[42] Steven Kull, Clay Ramsay, and Evan Lewis, "Misperceptions, the Media, and the Iraq War," *Political Science Quarterly* 118 (Winter 2003–2004): 589–590.

FIGURE 9.7

Television News Sources and Opinions on G. W. Bush and the Iraq War

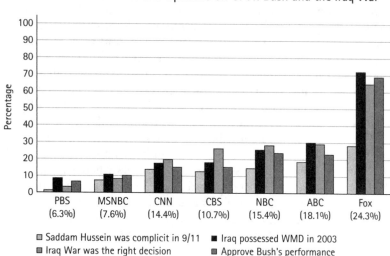

☐ Saddam Hussein was complicit in 9/11   ■ Iraq possessed WMD in 2003
☐ Iraq War was the right decision   ■ Approve Bush's performance

Note: The percentage of respondents naming each news outlet as their primary source is in parentheses.
Source: 2006 Cooperative Congressional Election Survey.

their partisan and ideological predispositions (Table 9.2).[43] For example, 54 percent of Republicans and 59 percent of conservatives said they got their TV news from Fox, compared with 10 percent of Democrats and 8 percent of liberals. Only 4 percent of Republicans or conservatives said they watched PBS or MSNBC, whose comparatively small audiences are disproportionately Democratic and liberal. Viewing the data from the perspective of the networks, 57 percent of the Fox audience is made up of Republicans, and 64 percent, of conservatives, compared with 10 percent each of the PBS and MSNBC audiences. These patterns of usage are broadly consistent with the reputed political leanings of these various outlets and readily account for the results in Figure 9.7.

These data stand as clear evidence of widespread selective exposure and are consistent with other findings in the literature on party differences in the choice of news media. They do not, however, tell us if the news source itself has an independent effect on viewers' beliefs and opinions. Kull and his

---

[43] For this table, I draw on the full 2006 CCES survey to take advantage of the much larger number of cases it provides.

TABLE 9.2
Party, Ideology, and Choice of Television News Source

	PBS, MSNBC		ABC, CBS, NBC, CNN		FOX	
	Percentage Viewing Program	Percentage of Audience	Percentage Viewing Program	Percentage of Audience	Percentage Viewing Program	Percentage of Audience
Republicans	4	10	43	21	54	57
Independents	14	36	61	28	25	24
Democrats	13	47	76	48	10	14
Conservatives	4	10	38	20	59	64
Moderates	12	51	69	52	19	29
Liberals	18	39	73	28	8	7

NOTE: Total percentages viewing program read across; total percentages of audiences read down.

SOURCE: Full 2006 CCES (party ID N = 12,808; ideology N = 11,875).

colleagues offer evidence that it does, at least for Fox audiences, and Della Vigna and Kaplan have detected a "Fox effect" that they contend has raised Republican vote totals significantly in recent years.[44] The data in Figure 9.7 are certainly consistent with a substantial Fox effect and perhaps other news source effects on attitudes toward Bush and the war, but we cannot rule out the possibility that the results are entirely a consequence of people choosing information sources compatible with their existing beliefs and preconceptions. What does seem clear is that the availability of ideologically diverse news outlets—not just on television, but in newspapers and magazines and on the radio and the Internet—gives people ample opportunity to select information sources likely to confirm their preconceptions and to avoid political information that might bring them into question. Many evidently take advantage of this opportunity, and thus selective exposure contributes to biased information acquisition and hence to partisan polarization.

How did the biased information processing produced by the various modes of motivated reasoning contribute to the wide partisan divisions on the Iraq War? To address this question, I estimated an ordered logit model with support for the war as the dependent variable and party identification, ideology, beliefs about Bush's divine selection, current and remembered beliefs about Iraq's WMD, and Saddam Hussein's complicity in 9/11 as independent variables.[45] The latter three variables were, as we have seen, to an important degree the product of motivated reasoning. Table 9.3 lists the results. Other things equal, beliefs and memories about the war's premises were strongly and significantly related to support for the war; only one of the nine relevant coefficients fails to meet the $p < .001$ level of statistical significance (Saddam's involvement, 2008, $p = .11$). Table 9.4 displays the change in the probability of supporting the war associated with these variables, individually and collectively. Each has an appreciable effect; collectively, they make a huge difference in the probability of supporting the war.

As the coefficients on party identification indicate, support for the war is strongly related to partisanship, but partisan divisions are much wider if respondents displayed evidence of motivated reasoning as measured by the three relevant variables. For example, on average, the estimated difference in the probability of supporting the war between a weak Republican who believed that Iraq possessed WMD and that Saddam was complicit in 9/11

[44] Kull, Ramsay, and Lewis, "Misperceptions," 589–590; Stefano Della Vigna and Ethan Kaplan, "The Fox News Effect: Media Bias and Voting," manuscript, Berkeley, CA, March 30, 2003, at http://elsa.berkeley.edu/~sdellavi/wp/foxvote06-03-30.pdf (accessed March 28, 2007).

[45] Memory of belief in Saddam's complicity in 9/11 had no independent effect in any of the equations and thus was dropped from this part of the analysis.

TABLE 9.3
Beliefs About and Support for the Iraq War

| | CCES STUDY | | |
	2006	2007	2008
Party identification	.430 (.083)***	.337 (.046)***	.412 (.062)***
Ideology	.261 (.205)	.315 (.102)**	.276 (.192)
Bush was chosen	1.312 (.392)***	1.234 (.290)***	1.093 (.351)**
Not sure Bush was chosen	.946 (.292)***	.318 (.198)	.573 (.353)
Iraq had WMD	.857 (.160)***	.564 (.102)***	.597 (.153)***
Remember believing Iraq had WMD	1.042 (.191)***	.378 (.102)***	.935 (.195)***
Saddam involved in 9/11	.628 (.195)***	.378 (.106)***	.278 (.176)
Cut 1	.530 (.257)	2.300 (.280)	2.871 (.655)
Cut 2	1.295 (.268)	3.523 (.285)	3.673 (.684)
Wald Chi squared	193.23	467.8	186.40
Pseudo R^2	.52	.32	.41
Number of cases	760	1625	710

NOTE: The dependent variable is 1 if respondent thought the Iraq War was the right thing to do, 0 if unsure, −1 if it was a mistake or the wrong thing to do; party identification is a 7-point scale ranging from strong Democrat (−3) to strong Republican (3); ideology is a 5-point scale ranging from very liberal (−2) to very conservative (2); belief about Bush's divine selection takes the value of 1 if respondent expressed the view indicated, or 0 otherwise; the final three variables take values of 1 if the respondent responded yes, −1 if no, and 0 if unsure; robust standard errors are in parentheses.

**p < .01
***p < .001

and a weak Democrat who did not believe these things and who claimed never to have believed in the WMD is .78; the difference in the same probability between a weak Republican who no longer believed these rationales for the war and a weak Democrat who remembered having once believed Iraq had WMD is .35—thus shrinking the partisan gap by .44.[46] For

---

[46] Estimated using Clarify with the other variables set at their means for the respondent's party; see Michael Tomz, Jason Wittenbert, and Gary King, "Clarify: Software for Interpreting and Presenting Statistical Results," manuscript, January 5, 2003, at http://www.stanford.edu/~tomz/software/clarify.pdf (accessed November 10, 2008).

TABLE 9.4
Estimated Effects of Beliefs on Support for the Iraq War

BELIEFS AND MEMORIES	2006	2007	2008
Iraq had WMD	.42	.36	.42
Iraq did not have WMD	.12	.16	.18
Difference	.30	.20	.24
Iraq had WMD (memory)	.40	.33	.42
Iraq did not have WMD (memory)	.08	.13	.10
Difference	.32	.20	.32
Saddam was involved in 9/11	.42	.34	.35
Saddam was not involved in 9/11	.17	.19	.24
Difference	.25	.15	.11
Yes to all three	.82	.61	.68
No to all three	.03	.07	.06
Difference	.79	.54	.62

NOTE: Entries are the probability of supporting the war with the other variables set at their means, estimated by Clarify from the ordered logit equations in Table 9.3.

strong partisans, the gap between these two hypothetical matchups shrinks by .39, and for independents leaning toward a party, by .50.

The same pattern appears in simple bivariate analyses; for example, Republicans who still believed that Iraq possessed WMD supported the war an average of 84 percent of the time across the four surveys (the TESS data can be used here), compared with only 3 percent of Democrats who said they had not thought that Iraq was hiding WMD at the time of the invasion, producing a partisan gap of 81 percentage points. By comparison, an average of 54 percent of Republicans who did not then believe Iraq had possessed WMD supported the war, as did 26 percent of Democrats who remembered once believing in the WMD, a gap of only 28 points.

The equations also show that beliefs about Bush's divine selection were strongly related to support for the war over and above their effect on beliefs about the war's premises. In simple terms, between 78 percent and 88 percent of respondents in the surveys who thought Bush had been chosen by God supported the war, compared with 27 percent to 31 percent of those who did not think that.[47] Belief in Bush's divine mission was, of course, far more prevalent among Republicans than among Democrats (see Chapter 6). Not surprisingly, it was most prevalent among the party's conservative Christians. About 80 percent of those who believed in Bush's divine mission described themselves as born-again Christians; about three-quarters classified themselves as conservatives, and 70 percent, as Republicans. The highly skewed partisan distribution of theological views therefore also contributed to the extraordinarily wide partisan differences on the war.

In sum, partisan differences on the war and the president grew extraordinarily wide in part because circumstances both permitted and strongly motivated so many Americans to engage in biased modes of information processing. Bush's identity as an evangelical Christian and his response to the trauma of September 11 gave him a deep reservoir of support among ordinary Republicans, most of whom subsequently resolved ambiguous or dissonant information about the premises and execution of the Iraq War in his favor. Democrats, not inclined to support any conservative Republican president and doubting Bush's legitimacy, backed the war only insofar as they were persuaded that Saddam Hussein was a threat to American security. Once the war's premises turned out to be faulty, many of its former Democratic supporters grew so disaffected that they repressed or denied their earlier views. Together with the Democrats who had opposed the war despite believing that Iraq possessed WMD, they came to believe that Bush had deliberately misled the country into an unnecessary war and evaluated him accordingly. The availability of ideologically diverse news outlets also facilitated the development and maintenance of what emerged from these myriad processes as the most highly polarized distributions of partisan opinion measured for any president or war.

THE FINAL YEAR

Although President Bush was able to stave off Democrats' efforts to shape his policies toward Iraq after they had taken control of Congress, his domestic agenda was largely moribund. Proposals to overhaul the tax

---

[47] The 2008 CCES included questions on beliefs about evolution and creationism; 75 percent of those who said that God had chosen Bush also said they believed that God had created the world in six days. Barker, Hurwitz, and Nelson (2008) find biblical literalists to be prone to what they term "'messianic' militarism," an attitude that would strengthen commitment to the Iraq War and thus to biased information processing.

code, reform immigration laws, make his signature tax cuts permanent, and limit medical malpractice damages got nowhere. He did win from Congress additional money for fighting AIDS in Africa and ratification of a nuclear-cooperation deal with India, but most of his victories were negative: stopping Congress from enacting policies he opposed, such as eliminating tax breaks for oil and gas companies. As his term neared its end, however, a final crisis pushed Bush and the Democratic Congress into a true exercise in bipartisan compromise and cooperation for the first time. Americans were also in agreement in their opinions of the action: Partisans of all persuasions panned it, and Bush's ratings sank to the lowest point of his presidency.

THE ECONOMIC CRISIS

Whatever benefit Bush might have reaped from the drop in violence and American casualties in Iraq—limited as it might have been by long-settled attitudes toward the war and the president—was more than offset by what was happening in the economy. The housing bubble began deflating in late 2006, leaving many subprime mortgages worthless, eventually wiping out financial institutions that had invested heavily in mortgage-backed bonds, and freezing the credit markets. By early 2008, just when public optimism about Iraq began rising, the faltering economy eclipsed the war as the most salient national problem.[48] By the summer, the fallout was hammering the stock market, driving share prices down more than 30 percent for the year, and sharply reducing the wealth and retirement funds of millions of Americans. In mid-September, the banking crisis hit full force, prompting a huge government bailout aimed at preventing a total implosion of the financial system. By the end of the year, economists were virtually unanimous in predicting a deep recession with massive job losses, perhaps the worst since the Great Depression of the 1930s.

The threat of recession created a bipartisan consensus of sorts in early 2008: Virtually every politician in Washington proposed some

---

[48] Jeffrey M. Jones, "Economy Surpasses Iraq as Most Important Problem," Gallup report, February 20, 2008, at http://www.gallup.com/poll/104464/Economy-Surpasses-Iraq-Most-Important-Problem.aspx (accessed June 28, 2009); Jeffrey M. Jones, "Economy Runaway Winner as Most Important Problem," Gallup report, November 21, 2008, at http://www.gallup.com/poll/112093/Economy-Runaway-Winner-Most-Important-Problem.aspx (accessed June 28, 2009).

government action to stimulate the economy. The Bush administration and the Democratic leaders in Congress agreed sufficiently on specifics to cut a deal that provided tax rebates to middle- and low-income Americans, including people who paid little or no income tax (the Democrats' priority), and business tax breaks (the Republicans' priority). The final bill, a true compromise, passed the Senate 81 to 16 and the House 380 to 34. All of the Senate opponents and 26 of the House opponents were Republicans who objected to its costs. Both key elements of the package enjoyed bipartisan public support as well, although partisans were somewhat more favorable toward their party's component than to the opposing party's.[49] But there was also a broad bipartisan consensus that the bill did not do enough and would not prevent a recession.[50]

The consensus was on target, and the economic news kept getting worse. The financial crisis came to a head in mid-September, when the prospect of massive bank failures and collapsing stock markets worldwide had sober experts calculating the odds of another Great Depression. In response, on the advice of Federal Reserve Chairman Ben Bernanke and Treasury Secretary Hank Paulson, Bush proposed a $700 billion rescue package for the beleaguered financial sector that also gave the government unprecedented authority over it. The proposal split both parties badly; many congressional Democrats objected to what they viewed as a bailout of greedy and irresponsible Wall Street speculators, while many Republicans saw it as a betrayal of their party's free market principles. An initial version of the bill was defeated in the House, 205 to 228, with 95 of 235 Democrats and 133 of 198 Republicans voting against it. That action sparked a record 777-point drop in the Dow, signaling the potentially calamitous cost of doing nothing. A revised version of the bill then passed with bipartisan majorities in the Senate but with a majority of House Republicans still opposed.[51] The failure of the White

---

[49] In the January 30–February 2 Gallup Poll, 89 percent of Democrats, 82 percent of independents, and 78 percent of Republicans supported the targeted tax rebates; the respective figures for the business tax breaks were 68 percent, 69 percent, and 83 percent.

[50] In an early February CNN poll, 70 percent said the bill did not do enough; three months later, that figure had risen to 83 percent in the April 28–30 CNN Poll; in both surveys, majorities of all political persuasions took this position. In the April 10–13 ABC News/*Washington Post* Poll, 79 percent believed (accurately as it turned out) that the stimulus package would not prevent a recession, including 88 percent of Democrats, 80 percent of independents, and 68 percent of Republicans.

[51] The Senate vote was 74 to 25 (Democrats, 39 to 9, and Republicans, 34 to 15); the House vote was 263 to 171 (Democrats, 172 to 63, and Republicans, 91 to 108); Benton Ives and Alan K. Ota, "Financial Rescue Becomes Law," *CQ Weekly*, October 6, 2008, 2692–2699.

House's intensive lobbying effort to swing more House Republicans behind the bill underlined Bush's loss of influence, at least on domestic issues, over what had once been his strongest congressional backers, conservative Republicans.

Congressional resistance to the bailout was rooted in practical politics as well as ideology, for the action was not at all popular with the public. The idea of providing money to rescue financial institutions never won majority approval and became less popular after the rescue bill passed.[52] Partisan differences on the issue were small, averaging in the low single digits, with Republicans only slightly more supportive. In October polls taken after the bill passed, less than a third approved of the action, while slightly more than half disapproved; every partisan subgroup contained more disapprovers than approvers, with independents expressing the most opposition. The polls also identified the source of opposition: Twice as many people believed the infusion of cash would mostly benefit Wall Street investors as believed it would also help ordinary Americans.[53] Americans are supposed to like it when the president and Congress cooperate on a bipartisan strategy to meet a dire national crisis; in this case they did not, and approval ratings of both institutions fell.[54]

The public spread blame for the financial crisis among the banks and their executives, investment firms, imprudent borrowers, government regulators, Congress, and the president, but the administration was always prominent on the list of culprits. More generally, and regardless of culpability, the public holds presidents responsible for the performance of the national economy.[55] Thus, as Americans' views of the economy turned decisively negative (Figure 9.8) and the huge and unprecedented partisan differences in evaluation of the Bush administration's performance diminished, Bush's already-dismal job ratings fell

---

[52] In the CBS News/*New York Times* polls completed September 24, September 30, October 5, and October 10, approval of "the federal government's plan to provide money to financial institutions to help them get out of their financial crisis" went from 42 percent, to 43 percent, to 36 percent, and finally, to 32 percent.

[53] CBS News/*New York Times* polls of October 3–5 and October 19–22, 2008.

[54] Gary C. Jacobson, "The 2008 Presidential and Congressional Elections: Anti-Bush Referendum and Prospects for the Democratic Majority," *Political Science Quarterly* 124 (Spring 2009): 6.

[55] Cf. Robert S. Erikson, Michael MacKuen, James A. Stimson, *The Macro Economy* (Cambridge: Cambridge University Press, 2002); Nathaniel Beck, "The Economy and Presidential Approval: An Information Theoretical Approach," in Helmut Norpoth and Jean-Dominic Lafay, eds., *Economics and Politics* (Ann Arbor: University of Michigan Press, 1991).

FIGURE 9.8
Rating of the Economy, 2001–2008

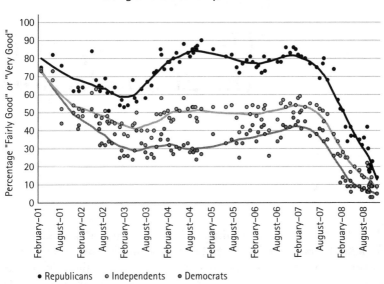

• Republicans ○ Independents ◦ Democrats

Source: 101 CBS News/New York Times polls.

even lower. His average approval rating for October 2008 dropped to 24 percent, falling to 53 percent among Republicans, 19 percent among independents, and 5 percent among Democrats, all record lows for his presidency (see Figures 1.1 and 1.2). For the first time, less than a majority of Republicans gave him a positive grade on managing the economy (see Figure 1.5). Thus, although approval of his handling of the Iraq War did rise modestly between the 2006 and 2008 elections, from an average of 27 percent to an average of 33 percent, the rise was more than offset by the drop in approval of his handling of the economy, from 42 percent to 18 percent, over the same period. Obviously, this did not bode well for the Republican Party in the upcoming 2008 elections. But it was by no means the only debilitating legacy Bush passed on to his party; indeed, the cumulative effect of his presidency had left the Republicans in their weakest electoral position in more than two decades.

CHAPTER **10**

■ ■ ■ ■ ■

The Bush Legacy in the 2008 Elections

"Hello, I'm Jim Greer, chairman of the Republican Party of Florida. As the party of Abraham Lincoln, Teddy Roosevelt and Ronald Reagan prepares to choose its nominee for president of the United States, Florida is honored to host tonight's Republican president debate."[1] The seven Republican candidates invited to Orlando for the October 2007 event also seemed to have forgotten about their current leader, George W. Bush; he was mentioned only twice, once critically and once neutrally, while Reagan's name was invoked reverently a dozen times, a pattern repeated throughout the Republican preprimary debate season.[2] The party's lineup of speakers at the Republican convention in August was equally reluctant to acknowledge the man who had led the party to victory in 2000 and 2004, referring to Bush by name only six times over four days—with Laura Bush accounting for five of the mentions.[3]

---

[1] The transcript for the debate is at http://www.cfr.org/publication/14580/republican_debate_transcript_florida.html (accessed December 10, 2007).

[2] Dan Froomkin, "White House Watch," December 14, 2007, at http://www.washingtonpost.com/wp-dyn/content/blog/2007/12/14/BL2007121401204_5.html?hpid=topnews.

[3] Johanna Neuman, "John McCain Gives President Bush One Last Nod," at http://latimesblogs.latimes.com/presidentbush/2008/09/mccain-gives-bu.html; in his acceptance speech, John McCain briefly praised "the president" but did not mention Bush by name. Determined to avoid a repeat of the Katrina fiasco, Bush cancelled his scheduled speaking engagement in Minneapolis to keep an eye on Hurricane Gustav, addressing the convention instead from the White House via satellite. The McCain camp was not displeased; see Adam Nagourney, "Response to Storm Shows Changes in McCain Campaign," *New York Times*, September 1, 2008.

The party could not, however, expect voters to forget about its leading figure, even in the unlikely event that its rivals had let it happen (the Democrats' speakers mentioned Bush's name more than 140 times at their convention[4]). A president's party cannot escape the shadow he casts. Like it or not, the president's words and actions largely define his party's current principles and objectives. Judgments about his competence in managing domestic and foreign affairs inform assessments of his party's competence in such matters. The components of a president's supporting coalition, and the interests he favors while governing, help to define the party's constituent social basis and thus appeal as an object of individual identification. In short, every administration inevitably shapes public perceptions about whom and what the president's party stands for and how well it governs when in office.

All of this was arguably even truer of George W. Bush than of any recent predecessor. With a few notable exceptions, his administration pursued a partisan agenda using partisan tactics while receiving extraordinarily high levels of support from Republican leaders in Congress and elsewhere. Even as Bush's approval ratings drifted well south of 50 percent after the start of his second term, congressional Republicans remained largely supportive, notably in sticking with him on the Iraq War, if only because their own core Republican constituents continued to give the president high approval ratings until near the very end of his presidency (see Figure 1.2). Bush also devoted more energy than any other modern president to party building, fundraising, and campaigning for his partisan team.[5] Finally, there was little ambiguity about the coalition he represented and served: social and religious conservatives, the corporate sector, antitax enthusiasts, and foreign policy hawks.

PARTY IMAGE

Defined largely by Bush, the Republican Party suffered unavoidable collateral damage as the president and his Iraq War became increasingly unpopular during his second term. The damage showed up in the party's image, in changes in popular partisanship, and ultimately in the 2008

---

[4] Ibid.
[5] Sidney M. Milkis and Jesse H. Rhodes, "George W. Bush, the Republican Party, and the 'New' American Party System," *Perspectives on Politics* 5 (September 2007): 461–488.

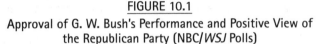

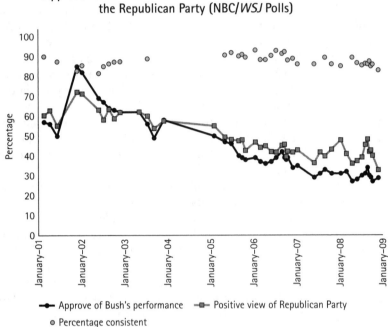

elections. The president's harm to the Republican Party's image was evident in responses to survey questions about the parties asked at irregular
intervals during his presidency. The NBC News/*Wall Street Journal* poll
asked respondents to evaluate various leaders and institutions, including
the Republican and Democratic parties, as very positive, somewhat positive, neutral, somewhat negative, or very negative. Figure 10.1 displays
the trends in Bush's approval rating and the proportion of respondents
who rated the Republican Party positively rather than negatively (with
the neutral category, typically about 15 percent of respondents, omitted).
The Gallup poll asked respondents whether they viewed each party
favorably or unfavorably; Figure 10.2 displays the trends in Bush's
approval and the proportion with favorable views of his party. Both
charts also show the percentage of respondents offering consistent
views—approving of Bush and holding positive or favorable views of
the Republican Party or disapproving of Bush and holding negative or

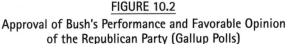

FIGURE 10.2

Approval of Bush's Performance and Favorable Opinion
of the Republican Party (Gallup Polls)

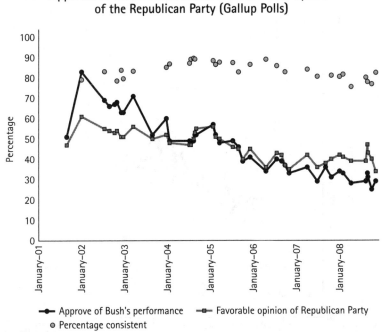

   ━●━ Approve of Bush's performance   ━■━ Favorable opinion of Republican Party
   ◉ Percentage consistent

unfavorable views of the party—for those surveys available for secondary analysis.

These figures show that evaluations of Bush and his party moved together over time and that, as both declined after peaking in the wake of the terrorist attacks of September 11, 2001, the cross-sectional correspondence between the two remained tight.[6] Figure 10.3 provides another perspective on this relationship by plotting positive and favorable views of the Republican Party against Bush approval (with additional data from CBS News/*New York Times*, Pew, CNN, ABC News/*Washington Post*, Fox News, and GW Battleground polls, which also occasionally asked the party favorability question).[7] The figure depicts a strong linear

---

[6] An average of 86 percent of respondents offered consistent evaluations of Bush and the Republican Party—both favorable or both unfavorable—in the data for these two figures.
[7] These data were gathered from the *i*POLL facility at the Roper Center archive at http://www.ropercenter.uconn.edu and from http://www.pollingreport.com.

FIGURE 10.3

Approval of Bush's Performance and Opinion of the Republican Party

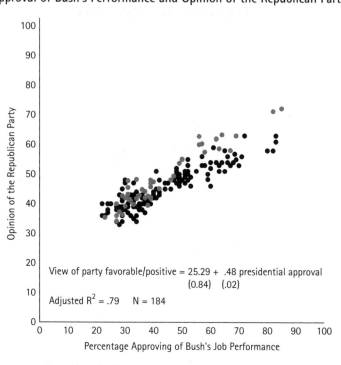

View of party favorable/positive = 25.29 + .48 presidential approval
(0.84)   (.02)

Adjusted R^2 = .79   N = 184

y-axis: Opinion of the Republican Party

x-axis: Percentage Approving of Bush's Job Performance

● Favorable ● Positive

relationship between opinions of the president and his party; according to the regression coefficient, a 10-point movement in presidential approval is estimated to produce a 4.8-point movement in Republican Party evaluations.

Of course, individual partisanship is the most powerful determinant of attitudes toward the parties, but evaluations of Bush's performance had a significant effect on the judgments offered by partisans of all persuasions, as Figure 10.4 demonstrates. The differences among partisans were very large (on average in these data, 88 percent of Republicans rated their party favorably, compared with 40 percent of independents and 16 percent of Democrats), but regardless of the respondent's partisanship, there is a strong linear relationship between approval of Bush and favorability toward the Republican Party. The estimated slopes are .39

FIGURE 10.4

Approval of G. W. Bush's Performance and Favorable Opinion of the Republican Party, by Party Identification

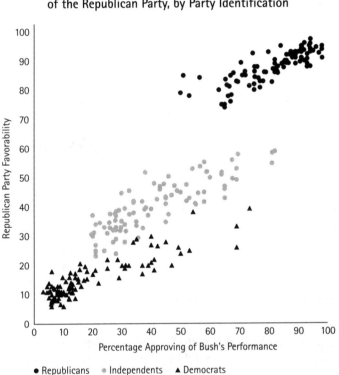

● Republicans   ● Independents   ▲ Democrats

for Republicans, .46 for independents, and .37 for Democrats. For all three groups, the linear fit is very good.[8]

Bush's approval ratings thus strongly affected evaluations of the Republican Party. Did they also affect evaluations of the Democratic Party? It is easy to imagine that aggregate opinion on Bush and the Democratic Party would move in opposite directions: The better (or worse) people think of a president, the worse (or better) they might think of the opposition party. This was, in fact, not the pattern observed.

---

[8] Republicans: party approval = 56.1 (2.3) + .39 (.03) presidential approval, adjusted R^2 = .67, N = 95; independents: party approval = 21.2 (1.3) + .46 (.03) presidential approval, adjusted R^2 = .72, N = 95; Democrats: party approval = 8.3 (0.6) + .37 (.02) presidential pproval, adjusted R^2 = .76, N = 95. Standard errors are in parentheses.

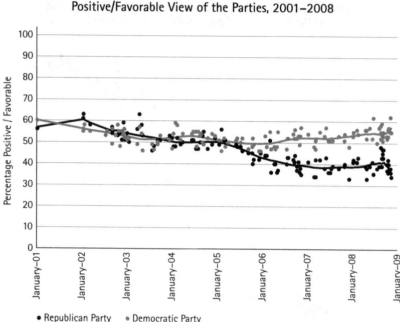

FIGURE 10.5

Positive/Favorable View of the Parties, 2001–2008

• Republican Party   • Democratic Party

Aggregate opinion on Bush and the Democratic Party were nearly orthogonal. Insofar as a relationship did exist, it was positive, not negative, but only because approval of every national institution, including both parties, rose in the post 9/11 rally (see Chapter 4).[9] If the two Bush terms are treated separately, estimates indicate a significant positive relationship between aggregate opinion on Bush and the Democratic Party during the first term, but a larger, negative relationship during the second term, when Bush's falling popularity was accompanied by increasingly favorable views of the Democrats.[10] Democrats enjoyed a substantial advantage in party favorability during Bush's final two years in office (Figure 10.5), averaging 18 points in the final quarter of 2008, but it was more the

---

[9] Democratic Party approval = 51.7 (1.0) + .026 (.021) presidential approval, adjusted R^2 = .003, N = 184.
[10] First term: Democratic Party approval = 46.7 (3.0) + .12 (.05) presidential approval, adjusted R^2 = .07, N = 67; second term: Democratic Party approval = 61.5 (1.7) − .26 (.05) presidential approval, adjusted R^2 = .20, N = 117. Standard errors are in parentheses.

result of the Republicans' deteriorating image than of the much more modest increase in favorable views of the Democratic Party.[11]

INDIVIDUAL PARTY IDENTIFICATION

Bush's second-term slide certainly hurt the Republican Party's public image, although it did not give the Democrats a fully proportionate boost. However, nothing in these data would suggest that Bush did his party any harm that could not be repaired once he was no longer its public face. If Bush's standing with the public did have more than transient and reversible consequences for either party, they are most likely to appear as changes in the distribution of partisan identities in the general public. The rival social-psychological and economic (or Bayesian) conceptions of party identification both acknowledge that, although always the most stable of political attitudes, individual partisanship is subject to change in response to short-term political conditions, including the president's approval level.[12] Even Donald Green and his colleagues, the most insistent defenders of the idea that partisan identities are "enduring features of citizens' self-conceptions," akin to and as stable as religious identities, concede that "presidential approval represents a . . . proximal cause of partisan change," although they also contend that "at the individual level, voters quickly return to their long-term attachments" as the effect of the "shocks" produced by presidents or other ephemeral political phenomena wear off.[13] The issue, then, is not whether assessments of presidents can move party identification at both the individual and the mass levels, but how durable these changes are.

There is no question that reactions to Bush's presidency altered the distribution of partisans in the electorate, at least in the short

---

[11] Based on ten Gallup, NBC News/*Wall Street Journal*, CBS News/*New York Times*, Quinnipiac College, Fox News, CNN, and the Pew Research Center for the People and the Press surveys.

[12] Morris P. Fiorina, "Economic Retrospective Voting in American National Elections: A Micro Analysis," *American Journal of Political Science* 22 (1978): 426–443; Michael MacKuen, Robert S. Erikson, and James A. Stimson, "Macropartisanship," *American Political Science Review* 83 (1989): 1125–1142; Robert S. Erikson, Michael MacKuen, and James A. Stimson, "What Moves Macropartisanship? A Response to Green, Palmquist, and Schickler," *American Political Science Review* 92 (1998): 901–921; Donald Green, Bradley Palmquist, and Eric Schickler, "Macropartisanship: A Replication and Critique," *American Political Science Review* 92 (1998): 883–899; Donald Green, Bradley Palmquist, and Eric Schickler, *Partisan Hearts and Minds: Political Parties and the Social Identities of Voters* (New Haven, CT: Yale University Press, 2002).

[13] Green, Palmquist, and Schickler, *Partisan Hearts and Minds*, 6, 99, 59.

run.[14] Data from the American National Election Studies panels covering the 2002–2004 and 2004–2006 periods demonstrate the effects at the individual level. Table 10.1 shows how respondents' positions on the standard 7-point ANES party identification scale moved in conjunction with their assessments of Bush's job performance between each pair of elections.[15] For each of the four possible combinations of presidential evaluations—approving both years; approving, then disapproving; disapproving, then approving; and disapproving in both years—the table lists the percentage of respondents who changed party identification categories between elections.

The patterns were consistent across both panel studies. Changes in presidential approval had a substantial effect on the party balance; there was a substantial net movement away from the Republican Party among respondents who switched from approval to disapproval, and a substantial net movement toward the party among respondents who switched from disapproval to approval. These differences remain if the analysis is confined to movements of two or more steps on the 7-point scale. The aggregate consequences were clearly detrimental to the Republican Party, because only a handful of respondents moved from disapproval to approval of Bush's performance between either pair of elections (3% and 1%, respectively), far fewer than grew disillusioned from one election to the next (15% and 17%). Republicans also gained a bit among respondents who approved of Bush's performance in both waves, while two consecutive negative responses produced a substantial net Democratic advantage in partisan shifts. Similar effects appear in analyses of panel studies from the Ford, G. H. W. Bush, and Clinton administrations, but they are noticeably greater for G. W. Bush than for his predecessors.[16]

MACROPARTISANSHIP

Individuals, then, tended to change their locations on the party identification scale in response to their evaluations of Bush's performance. Net changes in individual partisanship summed up to changes in macropartisanship—the

---

[14] Gary C. Jacobson, "Effects of Bush Presidency on Partisan Attitudes," *Presidential Studies Quarterly* 39 (June 2009): 184–195.
[15] In this scale, 0 = strong Democrat, 1 = weak Democrat, 2 = independent leaning Democratic, 3 = pure independent, 4 = independent leaning Republican, 5 = weak Republican, and 6 = strong Republican.
[16] For details and additional analyses, see Jacobson, "Effects of Bush Presidency on Partisan Attitudes," 184–190.

TABLE 10.1

Presidential Approval and Changes in Party Identification Between Elections

	Toward President's Party	Toward Opposition Party	Difference	No Change
	CHANGE IN SELF-PLACEMENT ON THE PARTY IDENTIFICATION SCALE (PERCENTAGES)			
2002–2004 (N = 771)				
Approve, 2002 and 2004 (56%)				
Moved at least one step on the 7-point scale	24	13	11	63
Moved two or more steps	8	4	4	88
Approve in 2002, disapprove in 2004 (15%)				
Moved at least one step on the 7-point scale	7	31	−24	62
Moved two or more steps	1	10	−11	89
Disapprove in 2002, approve in 2004 (3%)				
Moved at least one step on the 7-point scale	50	10	40	40
Moved two or more steps	0	0	0	100
Disapprove, 2002 and 2004 (26%)				
Moved at least one step on the 7-point scale	9	28	−19	63
Moved two or more steps	3	5	−2	92
2004–2006 (N = 543)				
Approve, 2004 and 2006 (32%)				
Moved at least one step on the 7-point scale	22	16	6	62
Moved two or more steps	7	8	−1	85
Approve in 2004, disapprove in 2006 (17%)				
Moved at least one step on the 7-point scale	14	44	−30	41
Moved two or more steps	3	27	−24	70

(continued)

TABLE 10.1 *(continued)*

	Toward President's Party	Toward Opposition Party	Difference	No Change
Disapprove in 2004, approve in 2006 (1%)				
Moved at least one step on the 7-point scale	33	17	16	50
Moved two or more steps	33	0	33	67
Disapprove, 2004 and 2006 (50%)				
Moved at least one step on the 7-point scale	10	34	−24	56
Moved two or more steps	5	15	−10	80

SOURCE: National Election Studies.

aggregate distribution of partisanship across the citizenry—which thus varied with Bush's public standing over the course of his administration. The broad shape of the relationship is depicted in Figure 10.6, which plots for the Gallup series the monthly average of the Republicans' share of partisans (including partisan leaners—those who initially call themselves independents but then admit to leaning toward one of the parties) against Bush's average monthly approval ratings and displays the regression equation estimating the relationship. The strong, nearly linear relationship between the two is obvious.[17] If partisan leaners are excluded, the regression slope is shallower (.13), and the fit is less precise (adjusted $R^2 = .50$), but the coefficient remains highly significant ($t = 9.71$, $p < .001$).[18] More elaborate models of these relationships, akin to those found in the macropartisanship literature, generally reiterate these findings, and the estimated effects of presidential approval on macropartisanship during the Bush administration are in line with previous results reported in this literature.[19]

---

[17] Nonlinear models allowing for diminishing returns (logarithmic or quadratic) provide a slightly better fit, with an adjusted R^2 of .73 compared with .69 for the linear model shown in the figure.

[18] I also performed the equivalent analysis using the CBS News/*New York Times* party identifications series, also excluding leaners, and the slope was even shallower (.10) and less precisely estimated, although the coefficient remained statistically significant ($p < .001$); the equation is % Republican = 40.74 (0.73) + .10 (.01) approval, $R^2 = .34$, months = 87 (standard errors are in parentheses; data are missing for eight months).

[19] Jacobson, "Effects of Bush Presidency on Partisan Attitudes," 190–192.

FIGURE 10.6
Approval of Bush and Republican Share of Partisan Identifiers
(Monthly Averages)

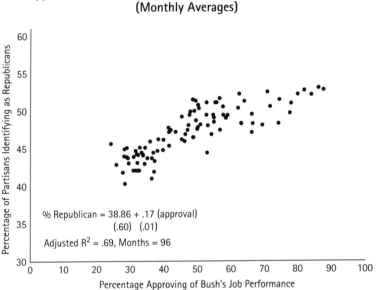

Because macropartisanship responds to changes in presidential approval, the cumulative effect of four years of negative net evaluations of Bush reduced the proportion of Republican identifiers substantially. The trend is most visible in the Gallup series when leaners are included as partisans (Figure 10.7). Republicans moved ahead in mass partisanship in the months after 9/11, when Bush was at his peak of popularity, and stayed basically even with the Democrats through 2003; Democrats pulled ahead in early 2004, but the parties were tied again by the time Bush won reelection. However, from early in Bush's second term onward, Republican identification shrank while Democratic identification grew. In the thirty surveys taken during 2008, the Democrats' advantage averaged 12 percentage points.

The picture is not quite so positive for Democrats if the analysis excludes partisan leaners, for the Gallup data suggest that Democratic gains were mainly from respondents who initially identified themselves as independents but then said they leaned toward the Democrats. From the fourth quarter of 2004 to the fourth quarter of 2008, the proportion of Republican identifiers (excluding leaners) dropped 7.8 percentage points, while the proportion of Democratic identifiers (excluding leaners)

FIGURE 10.7

Party Identification During the Bush Administration (Leaners Included)

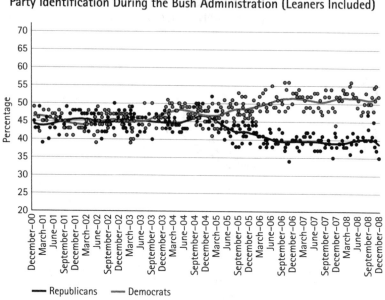

— Republicans   — Democrats

Source: 252 Gallup polls.

grew by only about 1.5 percentage points. Meanwhile, the share of independents (including the independent leaners) increased by about 5.1 percentage points. Just as with party evaluations, Bush's low approval ratings weakened the Republican Party more than they strengthened the Democratic Party.

Still, the net effect was to increase the Democrats' partisan advantage, a trend confirmed by party identification data from additional surveys. Figure 10.8 offers a broader picture of changes in macropartisanship during the G. W. Bush administration by comparing them to changes during previous presidencies going back to the first Reagan administration. The figure displays the annual averages for the share of Republicans among all party identifiers (excluding leaners), as indicated in surveys taken by five national polling organizations active during all or most of this period.[20]

---

[20] The Pew series began only in 1990; the Gallup series began in 1988, when Gallup switched to telephone interviews, which tend to produce more Republican respondents, making results incomparable to earlier Gallup surveys.

FIGURE 10.8

Republicans' Share of Major Party Identifiers, 1981–2008 (Annual Averages)

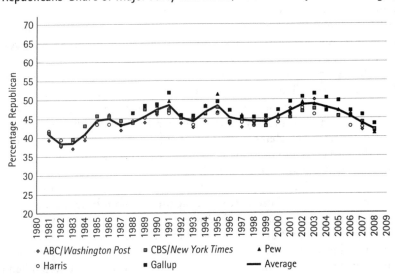

All five series move together nicely, sharing a common pattern of trends that are readily interpretable from the political history of this period. During the Reagan administration, the Democrats' advantage in partisanship diminished significantly and has never fully recovered.[21] Since then, party strength has varied with political conditions, including the popular standing of the president.[22] Republican identification grew during the first part of the G. W. Bush administration but then lost all of that gain and more as Bush's ratings fell deeper into negative territory after 2004. Averaged across surveys, the Democrats' advantage in mass partisanship grew from 51 to 49 in 2003 to 58 to 42 in 2008, its widest margin since Reagan's first term.

---

[21] Herbert F. Weisberg and Charles E. Smith, "The Influence of the Economy on Party Identification in the Reagan Years," *Journal of Politics* 53 (1991): 1077–1092; Warren E. Miller and J. Merrill Shanks, *The New American Voter* (Cambridge, MA: Harvard University Press, 1996).

[22] The high points for Republicans (low points for Democrats) came in 1991 (G. H. W. Bush riding high in the wake of the first Gulf War), 1995 (a Clinton low point after the Republican takeover of Congress), and 2002–2003 (when G. W. Bush was at his most popular). Their low points occurred in early 1992–1993 (the collapse of G. H. W. Bush's support and Clinton's election), the late 1990s (as Clinton's popularity soared on a strong economy and the Republicans' failed effort to impeach and remove him from office), and in 2006–2007 (with an unpopular Republican president presiding over an unpopular war).

NEW VOTERS

Republicans, observing the cyclical pattern in Figure 10.8, might have anticipated that their fortunes would improve again once Bush was out of the picture. But one partisan trend portends a more enduring problem for the Republican Party: Young people entering the electorate for the first time during the Bush administration favored the Democrats over the Republicans by a wide margin. According to the social-psychological conception of party identification, partisan identities are adopted in early adulthood, stabilize quickly, and thereafter become highly resistant to more than transient change. Political events and personalities therefore have their greatest and most lasting influence during the stage in life when partisan identities are being formed. In the words of Green and his colleagues, "The influences of the political environment are most noticeable among new voters, whose partisan attachments often bear the stamp of the political Zeitgeist that prevailed when they reached voting age."[23]

Data from the set of Pew surveys taken between January and October 2006 provide a striking demonstration of this point. Figure 10.9 displays partisanship by age cohort—specifically, the percentage of Republican and Democratic identifiers among respondents who turned twenty during the year indicated. Table 10.2 lists the average partisan balance among respondents who came of age during each of the last twelve administrations. The "stamp of the political Zeitgeist" is unmistakable. Popular presidencies attract young voters to the president's party; unpopular presidencies tend to drive them away. The most Republican cohorts emerge from the Eisenhower and Reagan–G. H. W. Bush years; the most Democratic cohorts—until the G. W. Bush administration— came of age during the Roosevelt and Truman years and the Nixon–Ford administrations. Presidents whose ratings dropped at the end of their terms—Truman, Carter, G. H. W. Bush—presaged shifts in the partisan balance toward the opposing party during the next administration.

According to the Pew data, Americans who turned twenty during the Bush administration form the most Democratic cohort in the electorate, giving the party a 15-point advantage in popular identification. If generational imprinting works as it has in the past, the Bush administration could thus prove more detrimental to the Republican Party in the long run than even the Nixon administration. But also note that the pro-Democratic trend

---

[23] Green, Palmquist, and Schickler, *Partisan Hearts and Minds,* 108; see also Miller and Shanks, *New American Voter,* 166–178.

FIGURE 10.9
Party Identification, by Age Cohort, 2006

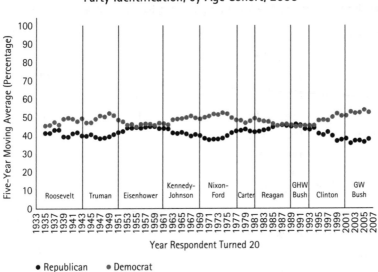

Year Respondent Turned 20

● Republican   ● Democrat

Source: Pew Research Center for the People and the Press surveys from January through October 2006, compiled by Michael Dimock; N = 17,599.

began with Clinton, suggesting that Republican problems with younger voters did not begin with Bush, although he evidently made them worse.

Certainly, younger voters did have a problem with Bush. As Figure 10.10 shows, respondents under the age of thirty gave the president his lowest job approval rating of any age group. From the beginning of 2006 onward, their average rating was 7.6 percentage points lower than that offered by the thirty- to forty-nine-year-olds, the cohort most favorably disposed toward the president, and 4.7 points lower than that of the fifty-and-older cohort.[24] The downward trend in favorable opinions of the Republican Party has also been more pronounced among younger respondents, while their views of the Democratic Party have grown increasingly positive (Figure 10.11). In 2008, the Democratic Party on average enjoyed a 29-point favorability advantage over the Republican Party among respondents younger than thirty, compared with a 10-point advantage among older respondents.

---

[24] The slightly greater propensity of younger respondents to offer no opinion at all accounts for only about 20 percent of these differences.

TABLE 10.2

Party Identification at Age 20 of Respondents, by Administration (Percentages)

President		Republican	Democrat	Democratic Advantage
Roosevelt	1932–1945	41	48	7
Truman	1945–1952	39	50	11
Eisenhower	1953–1960	45	45	1
Kennedy	1961–1963	42	47	6
Johnson	1964–1968	41	50	9
Nixon	1969–1974	38	51	13
Ford	1974–1976	40	51	11
Carter	1977–1980	44	47	3
Reagan	1981–1988	43	47	4
G. H. W Bush	1989–1992	46	45	−1
Clinton	1993–2000	40	49	9
G. W. Bush	2001–2006	37	52	15

NOTE: Percentages include leaners as partisans.

SOURCE: Pew Research Center for the People and the Press surveys from January through October 2006, compiled by Michael Dimock; N = 17,599.

Why did younger people sour on Bush and his party even more than older Americans? Perhaps surprisingly, the Iraq War does not seem to be the answer. According to Gallup data from twenty-two surveys taken in 2007 and 2008, the under-thirty cohort was actually more supportive of the war than were its elders (Table 10.3). Moreover, the difference was largely accounted for by Democratic identifiers; younger Democrats were 10 points more likely than older Democrats to say the war was not a mistake. The under-thirty group was also less inclined to offer consistent opinions of the war and the president, a consequence of the larger proportion of younger respondents who supported the war but still disapproved of Bush's performance (17 percent, compared with 10 percent among older respondents).

If the Iraq War is not the explanation, what is? The most likely answer lies in party differences on social and other domestic issues, on which younger Americans typically take more liberal positions than their elders. For example, a Pew study from late 2006 found that

FIGURE 10.10
Approval of G. W. Bush's Job Performance, by Age Group

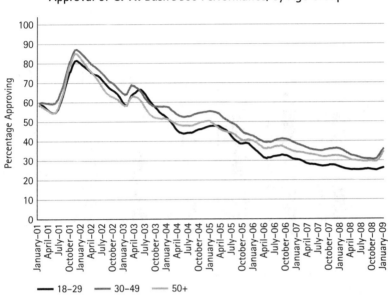

Legend: —— 18–29   —— 30–49   —— 50+

Source: Lowess-smoothed data from 283 Gallup polls.

eighteen- to twenty-five-year-olds had a more positive view of government and were more accepting of homosexuality, more favorable toward immigrants, and less hawkish than older respondents. These younger voters were also more inclined to believe in evolution rather than in creationism.[25] A compilation of the Pew studies conducted in 2006 found these young adults to be notably less religious, with 20 percent classified as having no religion or being atheist/agnostic, as compared with 11 percent of their elders. The younger adults were also the most likely of any age cohort to call themselves liberals and the least likely to call themselves conservatives.[26] Other studies reported

[25] In the eighteen to twenty-five age group, 63 percent said they believed in evolution, compared to 57 percent of the twenty-six to forty group, 47 percent of the forty-one to sixty group, and 42 percent of the sixty-plus group.

[26] The Pew figures for the eighteen to twenty-five group were 26 percent liberal, 29 percent conservative; the respective figures for the twenty-six to forty group were 22 percent and 33 percent; for the forty-one to sixty group, 19 percent and 37 percent; and for the sixty-one-plus group, 14 percent and 42 percent; see Pew Research Center for the People and the Press, "A Portrait of 'Generation Next,'" Survey Report, January 9, 2007, at http://people-press.org/report/300/a-portrait-of-generation-next (accessed September 10, 2007).

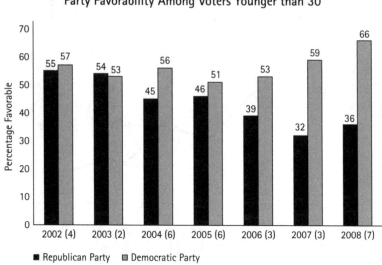

FIGURE 10.11
Party Favorability Among Voters Younger than 30

■ Republican Party   ▣ Democratic Party

Note: The number of polls averaged is in parentheses.
Source: Gallup polls.

similar findings. For example, a May 2007 Gallup survey found that 75 percent of eighteen- to thirty-four-year-olds thought homosexuality was "acceptable as an alternative lifestyle," compared with 58 percent of the thirty-five to fifty-four cohort and 45 percent of the fifty-five

TABLE 10.3
Opinions on the Iraq War, by Age Cohort (Percentages)

	18–29	30 AND OLDER
Believe Iraq War was not a mistake:		
All respondents	42	40
Democrats	25	15
Independents	38	36
Republicans	77	73
Opinions of Bush and Iraq War are consistent	79	86
Support Iraq War, disapprove of Bush	17	10

Source: Averages from twenty-two Gallup polls taken between January and November 2008.

and older cohort.[27] On average, in the twenty-one Gallup polls analyzed for Table 10.3, the eighteen to twenty-nine cohort contained more self-identified liberals (29 percent) than conservatives (28 percent), whereas among older respondents conservatives outnumbered liberals nearly two to one (39 percent to 21 percent).

In light of such attitudinal differences, it is no mystery why younger Americans tend to favor the Democrats over the Republicans more lopsidedly than do their elders. Green and his colleagues argue that people develop stereotypes about which groups belong in each party and come to identify with the party whose social composition seems most like them. Moreover, "the matching process by which people examine the fit between their self-conceptions and what they take to be the social bases of the parties tends to evolve rapidly in young adulthood and slowly thereafter."[28] Thus, as social and religious conservatives have become increasingly prominent within the ranks and leadership of the Republican Party, those younger voters with moderate or liberal attitudes would have a harder time seeing themselves as fitting into it.

The growing presence of religious conservatives in the Republican coalition, and the party image thereby projected, predated Bush—the Republican congressional leaders behind Clinton's impeachment, as well as that action itself, put this faction front and center, for example—but Bush's own very public profession of evangelical Christian beliefs as well as his administration's policies and his 2004 reelection campaign no doubt solidified it. Younger Americans with comparatively liberal social views were unlikely to see themselves in a party in which large and vocal segments favored constitutional bans on abortion and same-sex marriage, rejected evolution, and denied the reality of human-induced global warming.[29] It is hard to imagine many in this age group accepting "abstinence only" as practical or effective advice on sex. The antigay themes Karl Rove employed to rally conservative Christians behind Bush's candidacy in 2004 may have paid off in the short run,[30] but the message

---

[27] Lynda Saad, "Tolerance for Gay Rights at High-Water Mark," Gallup News Service, May 29, 2007, at http://www.gallup.com/poll/27694/tolerance-gay-rights-highwater-mark.aspx (accessed July 8, 2007).

[28] Green, Palmquist, and Schickler, *Partisan Hearts and Minds*, 10.

[29] See http://www.gallup.com/poll/10585/Americans-Evenly-Divided-Constitutional-Marriage-Amendment.aspx; also, http://www.gallup.com/poll/27847/Majority-Republicans-Doubt-Theory-Evolution.aspx.

[30] David E. Campbell and Quin Monson, "The Case of Bush's Re-Election: Did Gay Marriage Do It?" in David E. Campbell, ed., *A Matter of Faith: Religion in the 2004 Presidential Election* (Washington, DC: Brookings Institution Press, 2007).

those themes conveyed would have weakened the appeal of the Republican Party to a generation familiar with and largely unfazed by gays and lesbians. More generally, as Michael O'Hanlon of the Brookings Institution put it, "It cannot help your party if you're a Republican to have had many people come of age in an administration that has so botched so many enterprises."[31] It also cannot help that more of them have gotten their spin on the administration's doings from Jon Stewart than from Bill O'Reilly.[32] If voting habits are established in young adulthood, the generation coming of age during the Bush administration will be offsetting the Reagan-era cohort for decades to come.

These partisan trends contributed significantly to the Democrats' successes in 2006 and 2008, for both elections featured the high levels of party-line voting that have become the norm over the past decade or so. According to the national exit polls, the Republicans held a 3-point advantage in party identifiers in the 2002 House electorate, and the parties were at parity in 2004; the Democrats took a 2-point lead in 2006, which grew to 7 points in 2008.[33] Party-line voting in the 2008 presidential election was second only to 2004's all-time high in the ANES series going back to 1952. According to calculations based on ANES data, had the distribution of partisans in the electorate been the same in 2008 as in 2004 and had partisans voted as they did in 2008, Obama's vote share would have been 3.8 percentage points lower. The shift in distribution of partisan identifiers in the electorate thus made a crucial contribution to Obama's presidential victory in 2008.[34] So did the influx of young voters into the Democratic ranks. Voters under thirty, who, according to the exit polls, had given Al Gore 48 percent of their votes in 2000 and John Kerry 54 percent in 2004, gave Obama 66 percent in 2008. The effect was not limited to the presidential

---

[31] Catherine Dodge, "Bush Stirs Young Voters' Enthusiasm for Democrats, Ballot Box," Bloomberg, December 11, 2007, at http://www.bloomberg.com/apps/news?pid=20601070&sid=alh.XF5j16kI (accessed July 5, 2009).

[32] Pew Research Center for the People and the Press, "Cable and Internet Loom Large in Fragmented Political News Universe," Survey Report, January 11, 2004, at http://www.pewinternet.org/Reports/2004/Cable-and-Internet-Loom-Large-in-Fragmented-Political-News-Universe.aspx (accessed September 7, 2007).

[33] The Democrats' advantage was estimated to be 9 points in the 2008 CCES.

[34] In the 2004 ANES data, Democrats held a slight advantage among voters, 47.5 percent to 47.0 percent (with independent leaners treated as partisans); in 2008, the respective figures were 51.0 percent Democrats and 42.4 percent Republicans. These differences do not appear to be the result of changes in partisan turnout rates, but we cannot be sure; reported turnout in ANES studies is of doubtful reliability because of misreporting. Obama won 53.7 percent of the major-party national vote; ANES respondents gave him a 54.9 percent share.

election; voters in this age group gave Democratic House candidates 48 percent of their votes in 2002, 55 percent in 2004, 62 percent in 2006, and 63 percent in 2008.[35]

THE PRESIDENT, THE WAR, AND THE 2008 NOMINATIONS

Considering the cumulative damage suffered by the Republican Party during his second term, Bush's main influence on the 2008 elections may have already registered well before the first January caucuses in Iowa. But his presidency also shaped the election in other important ways. For one, it played a central role in both parties' nominations. If progress in Iraq did little to revive support for the war or the president, it certainly helped Arizona Senator John McCain win the Republican nomination. McCain had been a vocal proponent of sending additional troops to Iraq long before Bush ordered the surge; had the stalemate continued and American casualties remained at the levels of 2006 and early 2007, it seems doubtful that McCain could have prevailed over his Republican rivals. It was also McCain's good fortune to have sewn up the nomination by early February, just as polls showed the economy replacing Iraq as the most important national problem. His comparative advantage lay in foreign and military policy: "The issue of economics is not something I've understood as well as I should," he conceded at a December 2007 New Hampshire town hall meeting.[36] Had the economy been as dominant a concern as it later became, Mitt Romney, a successful business entrepreneur, might have gained more traction. On the other hand, McCain might well have won by default anyway, for neither Romney's nor McCain's other rivals succeeded in exciting more than a fraction of the Republican electorate. In any case, McCain's early advocacy of the surge strategy turned out to be an asset rather than a liability during the 2008 primaries.

Albeit in a different way, the Iraq War was even more central to Obama's nomination than to McCain's. A young first-term African American senator with a foreign-sounding name, Obama began the campaign unfamiliar to most voters. He trailed the vastly more experienced

---

[35] In the 2008 CCES, 63 percent of the eighteen to thirty-four age cohort voted Democratic for United States Representative, and 65 percent voted Democratic for Senator.
[36] Sasha Issenberg, "McCain Tested on the Economy," *Boston Globe,* January 26, 2008.

and better known Hillary Clinton in national surveys of Democratic voters throughout 2007. But after winning the Iowa primary in January, Obama passed Clinton in the horse-race polls and took an early lead in the delegate count that Clinton managed to erode with victories in later primaries but ultimately could not overcome.[37] Obama's victory in the drawn-out, hotly contested battle for delegates was a product of superior strategy, organization, fundraising, and rhetorical skills, but he was also helped immeasurably by George Bush and the Iraq War. It is unlikely that Obama would have attracted so much support had disaffection with Bush and the war not been so deep and widespread among ordinary Democrats. Clinton had voted to authorize the war; Obama had opposed it from the start. More generally, Clinton represented experience and continuity with the Democratic past, while Obama, as his campaign never tired of telling us, embodied change. And after eight years of Bush, whose approval rating among ordinary Democrats had reached the astonishing record low of 3 percent in several preelection Gallup polls, the desire for something fundamentally new prevailed. Obama's prodigious Internet fundraising, a key component of his successful campaign for the nomination, reflected these sentiments.[38]

The 2008 CCES data allow an empirical test of the effect of Democrats' views of the Iraq War on the nominating process. The Common Content segment of the study, which included the questions examined here, surveyed 32,800 respondents, providing a large sample of participants in primaries and caucuses.[39] The CCES question measuring support for the Iraq War offered a more nuanced set of options than the standard war-support questions:

Which comes closest to your opinion on United States decisions regarding Iraq:

> 1. *The Iraq War was a mistake from the beginning; it never should have been started, and the United States should withdraw now;*

---

[37] Gary C. Jacobson, "The 2008 Presidential and Congressional Elections: Anti-Bush Referendum and the Prospects for the Democratic Majority," *Political Science Quarterly* 124 (Spring 2009): 12.

[38] Michael Malbin, "Large Donors, Small Donors, and the Internet: The Case for Public Financing After Obama," Campaign Finance Institute working paper, April 2009, at http://www.cfinst.org/president/pdf/PresidentialWorkingPaper_April09.pdf (accessed June 10, 2009).

[39] The 2008 Cooperative Congressional Election Study involved thirty teams, yielding the Common Content sample of 32,800 cases. All cases were selected through the Internet, and YouGov/Polimetrix constructed matched random samples for this study. See Ansolabehere, "Guide to the 2008 Cooperative Congressional Election Survey," at http://web.mit.edu/polisci/portl/cces/material/CCES_Guide_2008_Rough_Draft_v2.pdf. (accessed March 24, 2010) for a full description of the methodology.

2. *The Iraq War was a mistake, but since the United States did invade Iraq, it has been worth the cost in American lives and money to avoid a failure there that would be even worse for United States;*
3. *The United States was right in going to war in Iraq, but mistakes made following the invasion have made the results too costly in American lives and money to be worth it;*
4. *The United States was right in going to war in Iraq, and despite mistakes made following the invasion, the results have been worth the cost in American lives and money;*
5. *The United States was right in going to war in Iraq and made no serious mistakes following the invasion; the difficulties the United States has faced were unavoidable, and the war's results have been worth the cost in American lives and money.*

The distribution of responses, shown in Figure 10.12, replicated the familiar pattern of sharp partisan differences of opinion on the war. Three-quarters of the Democrats deemed the war a mistake from the start and favored immediate withdrawal. Two-thirds of Republicans thought the war

FIGURE 10.12
Opinions on the Iraq War

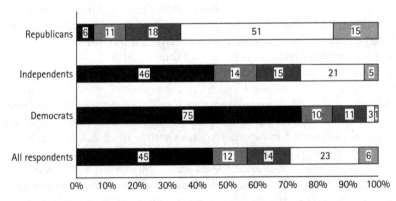

■ War was a mistake from the beginning
▣ War was a mistake, but avoiding failure is worth the cost of fighting it
■ U.S. was the right in going to war, but mistakes have made it too costly to be worth it
□ War was the right decision and worth it despite mistakes
▣ War was the right decision, worth the cost, no serious mistakes

Source: 2008 CCES.

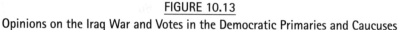

FIGURE 10.13

Opinions on the Iraq War and Votes in the Democratic Primaries and Caucuses

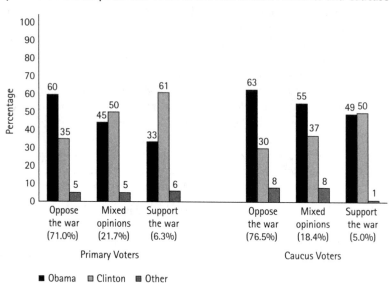

Source: 2008 CCES.

was the right thing to do and has been worth the cost. About a quarter of all respondents had mixed views on the war; among independents, it was 29 percent. I examined the relationships between responses to this question and to a variety of related questions and found that it divides respondents into three basic categories: firm opponents of the war (option 1), firm supporters of the war (options 4 and 5), and people with mixed assessments (options 3 and 4). Differences within each of the latter two pairs on other relevant questions were small and generally insignificant. Accordingly, for analytical purposes, I collapsed responses into a three-category index of opinion on the war: firm support, mixed views, or firm opposition.

The CCES also asked respondents whom they voted for in primaries or caucuses. Among those who participated in the Democratic nomination process, candidate preferences were strongly related to views on the Iraq War (Figure 10.13).[40] Among primary voters, 60 percent of firm opponents of the war preferred Obama, while 61 percent of firm supporters

---

[40] Figure 10.13 is based on data from 11,211 primary voters and 987 caucus participants.

preferred Clinton. Those with mixed views of the war gave Clinton a slight edge. Because 71 percent of participants in Democratic primaries opposed the war and only 6 percent firmly supported it, Obama obviously benefited from the issue. Caucus participants were even more inclined to oppose the war, and Obama drew more support from them than from primary participants across all categories of war opinion, evidence, presumably, of his campaign's superior capacity to identify and mobilize supporters in the caucus states.

Attitudes toward the war remain strongly related to the Democratic primary vote under various controls. Multivariate analyses confirm that, consistent with informal observation as well as findings from the media polls taken during the primary season, Obama drew disproportional support from voters who were younger, better educated, and African American; Clinton attracted voters who were older, more conservative, female, and Latino. But taking these factors into account, Obama still did much better among opponents than among supporters of the Iraq War; the results suggest that attitudes toward the war were second only to race in differentiating Obama from Clinton voters.[41] By this evidence, then, the lopsided Democratic rejection of the war worked strongly to Obama's advantage in his pursuit of the nomination. Clinton also won a solid majority (63 percent) of those who approved of Bush's performance, but they comprised only 6 percent of Democratic primary voters; Obama won the votes of 59 percent of the much larger population (93 percent) of disapprovers.

THE GENERAL ELECTION

Although his stance on Iraq helped McCain win the nomination, it did him little good in the general election, not only because the economy had swamped all other issues, but also because the success of the surge did not make voters, at least those outside the Republican base, any more enthusiastic about the war or less eager to put it behind them. Indeed, the decline in United States casualties led to something of a convergence on Iraq policy between the Bush administration and its critics. Progress against the

---

[41] For details see Gary C. Jacobson, "George W. Bush, the Iraq War, and the Election of Barack Obama," *Presidential Studies Quarterly* 40 (June, 2010): 207–224. Opinions on the war did little to distinguish voter preferences in Republican primaries, except that the tiny fraction of Republicans who thought the war had been a mistake from the start gave antiwar libertarian Ron Paul nearly half their votes, and McCain did a bit better among those who had mixed assessments of the war than among those who firmly favored it, although he remained the top choice of both groups.

insurgents emboldened the Iraqi government to demand a timetable for the withdrawal of United States troops, which became part of the Status of Forces agreement negotiated with the administration during the summer and fall of 2008 (although not signed until after the election); the agreement had all United States troops leaving Iraqi cities by the summer of 2009 and the country entirely by the end of 2011. A step that Democrats had been advocating and Bush steadfastly rejecting for the past five years as a recipe for defeat —scheduling an American withdrawal from Iraq—thus became administration policy.[42] The dispute was no longer over whether the United States should withdraw on a schedule, but only over whether the schedule should be accelerated or retarded by a few months. Although he promised to remain in Iraq until victory had been won no matter how long it took, McCain could not effectively pit "stay the course" against "cut and run," as Bush had in 2004, because these catchphrases no longer defined the range of options.

Still, McCain was the best hope Republicans had of retaining the White House. As something of a party maverick and the first nominee of the sitting president's party since 1952 to have had no role in the current administration (either as president or vice president), he could, and did, run against it. McCain's campaign ran television ads declaring that "we're worse off than we were four years ago" and "we can't afford four more years of the same." It was McCain, not Obama, who rallied the crowd at a Missouri campaign stop with "I promise you, if you're sick and tired of the way Washington operates, you only need be patient for a couple of more months. Change is coming! Change is coming! Change is coming."[43] His most memorable zinger in the presidential debates was "Senator Obama, I am not President Bush. If you wanted to run against President Bush, you should have run four years ago."[44] For obvious reasons, McCain did not ask Bush to campaign for him, and Bush was savvy enough to recognize that any hope of vindication through a McCain victory depended on minimizing their association. Thus, the president's voice was conspicuously absent from the 2008 campaigns, a stark departure from the previous four national elections.

---

[42] The administration sought to retain flexibility by calling the deadline "aspirational," but Iraq prime minister Maliki spoke of it as final; see Karen deYoung, "Lacking an Accord on Troops, United States and Iraq Seek a Plan B," *Washington Post*, October 14, 2008, at http://www.washingtonpost.com/wp-dyn/content/article/2008/10/13/AR2008101302846.html?sid=ST2008101302913 (accessed July 12, 2009).

[43] Peter Baker, "Party in Power, Running As If It Weren't," *New York Times*, September 5, 2008, at http://www.nytimes.com/2008/09/05/us/politics/05assess.html (accessed December 3, 2008).

[44] Jim Rutenberg, "Candidates Clash over Character and Policy," *New York Times*, October 16, 2008, at http://www.nytimes.com/2008/10/16/us/politics/16debate.html (accessed December 5, 2008).

Although treating Americans to the unique spectacle of a contest in which both parties' candidates ran against the incumbent administration, McCain ultimately could not persuade most voters that he was a better vehicle for change than was Obama. He came closest at the Republican convention in late August, which produced a brief upsurge in Republican Party favorability (from an average of 41 percent in the two months before the convention to 46 percent in three polls immediately after the convention, temporarily narrowing the Democrats' favorability advantage from 14 to 8 points), suggesting that for a week or two at least, McCain (and, perhaps more notably, Sarah Palin) had begun to give the Republican Party a new face. This was also the only period in which McCain edged ahead of Obama in some horse-race polls.

In the end, though, the economic meltdown after mid-September finally tilted the field decisively in favor of Obama. Campaigns always compete to frame the choice in a way that favors their side. Obama's campaign wanted voters to view the economy and the Bush administration's record as the deciding issues; McCain wanted the electorate's attention focused on national security and terrorism. The economic crisis brought Obama's frame dramatically to the forefront, and it put Bush back on the front page, depressing his approval ratings further (see Figure 1.1), raising public dissatisfaction with the direction of the country to as high as 90 percent in some surveys, and driving Republican Party favorability ratings back down to an average of 38 percent for the remainder of the campaign. McCain's response to the economic crisis was erratic and unfocused, while Obama stuck to his disciplined script, appearing more the seasoned pro than McCain. By mid-September Obama had reassumed a lead in the polls that he never relinquished.

THE VOTE

With the economic concerns so dominant and Iraq policy no longer as salient or contentious as it had once been, the electoral effect of the war might have been exhausted by its contribution to the political environment in which the economic meltdown took place. Survey evidence indicates that it was not. The simple relationship between opinions on the war and the 2008 presidential vote, displayed in Figure 10.14, was very strong and remains so when respondents are separated by party. The same

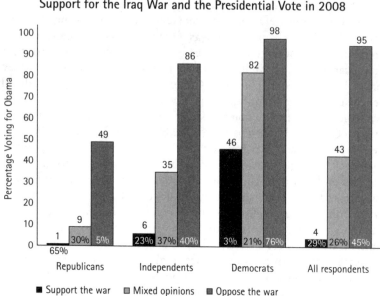

FIGURE 10.14

Support for the Iraq War and the Presidential Vote in 2008

Note: The share of respondents in each category is listed at the bottom of the column; total N = 22,468.
Source: 2008 CCES.

results appear in analyses of the 2008 ANES data.[45] The relationship between evaluations of Bush's performance and the presidential vote was also very tight, even within partisan categories (Figure 10.15).

Opinions on the Iraq War and the president remain strongly related to the presidential vote when opinions on the economy and other relevant variables are taken into account. The CCES asked respondents if they thought that over the past year the economy had gotten much better, better, worse, much worse, or stayed the same. Only a few oblivious (or perverse) souls said it had gotten better (1 percent), and only a handful thought it was unchanged (5 percent). The main distinction was between those who said "much worse" (59 percent) rather than just "worse" (34 percent). Thus, for analytical purposes, I transformed the responses into a simple dichotomous variable distinguishing those who thought it

[45] Jacobson, "Election of Barack Obama," Figure 7.

FIGURE 10.15
Presidential Approval and the Vote in 2008

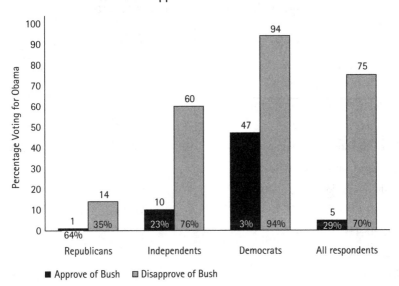

Note: The share of respondents in each category is listed at the bottom of the column; total N = 22,832.
Source: 2008 CCES.

was much worse from the rest. The survey also asked respondents to name the most important national problem, and I created a variable distinguishing those who mentioned the economy (63 percent, including those who mentioned high prices) from the rest on the assumption that voters who accepted Obama's frame should have, other things equal, favored his candidacy. These variables—along with the Iraq War support index, Bush approval, and other pertinent control variables—appear in the logit equation that estimates the 2008 presidential vote and is shown in Table 10.4

Unlike regression coefficients, logit coefficients cannot be interpreted directly, so the right-hand column of the table estimates the relative effect of each variable, measured as the expected change in the probability of voting for Obama between the highest and lowest values of the variables, with the other variables set at their mean values. The economic variables both work as expected, with respondents expressing the most negative opinions of the economy and viewing it as the most important problem having a significantly higher probability of reporting a vote for Obama.

TABLE 10.4
Logit Model of the 2008 Presidential Vote

	Coefficient	Robust Standard Error	Effect
War support (3-point scale)	−1.71***	.06	−.69
Economy most important problem	.56***	.07	} .23
Economy much worse	.45***	.08	
Party identification (7-point scale)	.66***	.02	.76
Ideology (5-point scale)	−.76***	.05	−.64
Bush job approval (5-point scale)	−.52***	.04	−.46
Age 18–29	1.33***	.14	
Age 30–49	.53***	.09	} .32
Age 50–64	.31***	.09	
Woman	−.13	.07	−.03
African American	2.49***	.17	.47
Latino	.02	.13	.01
Constant	2.86***	.19	
Wald chi square	3992.8		
Percentage correctly predicted (null = 55.1)	93.9		
Pseudo R^2	.76		
Number of cases	21,634		

NOTE: Effect (third column) is the estimated change in probability of voting for Obama between the lowest and highest settings of the variable, with the other variables set at their mean values; the dependent variable takes the value of 1 if respondent voted for Obama, 0 if for McCain; war support is scored 1 if respondent is firm supporter, 0 if mixed, and −1 if a firm opponent; ideology is scored from most liberal to most conservative, party from strong Republican to strong Democratic.

SOURCE: 2008 CCES.

***$p < .001$

But notice that taking into account the economic variables plus partisanship, ideology, and some voter demographics,[46] opinions on the Iraq War shaped the voting decision as strongly as did party identification and ideology. Notice also that opinions of Bush's performance (which incorporate reactions to both the war and the dismal economy) continued to have a strong effect on the 2008 vote after controlling for the other factors. Obama's special appeal to younger voters and to African Americans is evident; however, gender and status as a Latino made no significant difference in this equation (although in simple cross-sectional comparisons, Obama did run significantly better among both women and Latinos).

McCain's attempt to dissociate himself from Bush and to rebrand the Republican Party was a long shot, its failure not surprising. On the question of who was the better prospective agent of change, late October and early November polls gave Obama an advantage ranging from 17 to 27 percentage points.[47] In the national exit poll, voters split 48 to 48 on the question of whether McCain would continue Bush's policies. Those who said he would went for Obama, 90 to 8; those who said he would not went for McCain, 85 to 13. That is, not only did voters who thought a McCain administration would constitute a third Bush administration vote overwhelmingly for Obama, but about 90 percent of those who voted for McCain did so in the belief that his administration would *not* be a continuation of Bush's.[48] In the end, Barack Obama won the largest share of votes cast for any Democrat since Lyndon Johnson in 1964, defeating McCain by 52.9 percent to 45.7 percent. Obama took all nineteen states Kerry had won in 2004 plus another nine, winding up with a 365 to 173 electoral vote margin.

THE CONGRESSIONAL ELECTIONS

The anti-Republican tide swept over the Congress as well; Democrats picked up 21 seats in the House and 8 in the Senate. The House victories, added to the 31 seats they gained in 2006 and some pickups in subsequent special elections, left them holding 257 seats to the Republicans'

---

[46] Income was unrelated to the vote in this model and has been omitted.
[47] See http://www.pollingreport.com/wh08.htm.
[48] Calculated from the national exit poll, reported at http://www.cnn.com/ELECTION/2008/results/polls/#USP00p1 (accessed December 5, 2008).

178, a gain of 55 seats over the two elections. In the Senate, where for the second election running, the Democrats held onto every seat they defended, their total grew to 59 and then to 60 when Pennsylvania Senator Arlen Specter switched sides after the election, 15 more than they had held after the 2004 election. The cumulative results of the 2006 and 2008 congressional elections effectively overturned the verdict of 1994, thereby reducing Republican representation to what it had been before the party's historic rise to majority status fourteen years earlier.

Public dissatisfaction with the Bush administration and, consequently, the Republican Party, which had contributed to Republican losses in 2006 and continued to grow afterward, laid the groundwork for further House and Senate losses in 2008. The prevalence of these sentiments in 2007, along with the Republicans' loss of control of Congress, worked to the Democrats' advantage in 2008 in part by shaping potential candidates' always-consequential decisions about whether to run for office. The Democrats' takeover of the House and Senate in 2006 immediately made service in Congress less satisfying to Republicans. Just as the Republicans' victory in 1994 prompted an abnormally large Democratic exodus from Congress in 1996, the insults of minority status made retirement more attractive to Republicans in 2008. The attraction was all the greater because conditions that had made 2006 such a tough year for Republicans had continued to deteriorate, making reelection less certain and a quick recapture of majority status most unlikely. The loss of three additional Republican seats in special elections held in early 2008—including the seat vacated by former Speaker Dennis Hastert in Illinois—signaled how bad conditions were for the party. As a result, five Republican senators and twenty-six Republican representatives chose not to seek reelection. Of the latter group, only three left to pursue higher office (none succeeded); the remaining twenty-three retired from electoral politics.

Among Democrats, in contrast, not a single senator and only six House members retired, and three of the six left to run for the Senate (two succeeded). After primary defeats and a death further culled the ranks of reelection-seeking incumbents, Republicans were left defending twenty-nine open House seats to the Democrats' seven, and five open Senate seats to the Democrats' none. By anticipating a bad year for their party, departing Republican incumbents helped to bring it about. Democrats won twelve of the twenty-nine open Republican seats (41 percent) but only fourteen of 170 (8 percent) of the seats defended by Republican incumbents. Democrats also picked up three of the five open Senate seats, compared with four of the eighteen defended by Republican incumbents. The imbalance of open seats between the parties—the most lopsided of the entire post–World War II era—thus both reflected and contributed to the Republicans' woes in 2008.

The same conditions that inspired Republican incumbents to retire helped Democrats attract capable candidates and finance their campaigns. Looking forward to 2008, Democratic leaders, potential candidates, and associated activists had reason to believe that conditions were as conducive to success as they had been in 2006, and they acted accordingly. Just as in 2006, the Democrats fielded high-quality candidates for most of the potentially vulnerable Republican House and Senate seats and generously funded almost all of their campaigns. And again as in 2006, despite an expanding field of Republican targets as the election approached (attributable to the financial crisis), Democratic committees had sufficient resources to provide major financial assistance to every promising candidacy that came to their attention, and very few were overlooked.

As in the presidential race, evaluations of the Iraq War and President Bush had direct as well as indirect effects on House and Senate voting. Figures 10.16 and 10.17 replicate Figures 10.14 and 10.15 for the House

FIGURE 10.16
Support for the Iraq War and the House Vote in 2008

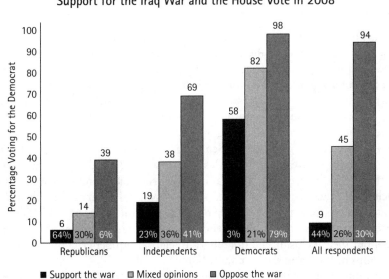

■ Support the war   ▨ Mixed opinions   ▤ Oppose the war

Note: The share of respondents in each category is listed at the bottom of the column; total N = 19,356.
Source: 2008 CCES.

FIGURE 10.17

Presidential Approval and the House Vote in 2008

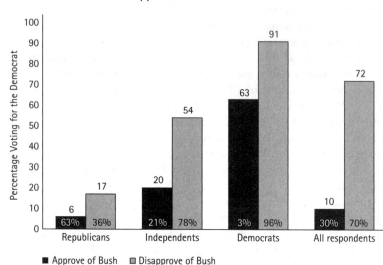

Note: The share of respondents in each category is listed at the bottom of the column; total N = 22,832.
Source: 2008 CCES.

vote. The differences in voting between war supporters and opponents are not quite as large as in the presidential contest (typically, they are about one-third lower), but they are still very wide. (The equivalent analysis for Senate voters replicate the House results very closely and thus is not displayed). Multivariate analyses akin to those reported in Table 10.4 estimate the effect of war support on the probabilities of voting for the Democrat (equivalent to the entries in the right-hand column of the table) as $-.39$ and $-.47$, respectively, in House and Senate races (compared with $-.69$ in Table 10.4); the respective effects of Bush approval are $-.20$ and $-.22$ (compared with $-.46$ in the presidential equation). Controls for incumbency were also included in these equations, which showed its usual potent effect (the estimated difference in probability of voting Democratic varies by .33 in House races and .23 in Senate races, depending on the candidates' incumbency status), but their inclusion did not alter the relationship between the vote and opinions of Bush and the war appreciably.

In sum, popular responses to the Bush administration had both direct and indirect electoral consequences in the 2008 elections. The powerful effect of partisanship underlines the importance of the shift in mass party identification in the Democrats' favor during Bush's second term. Obama's special appeal to younger voters reflected not only his personal qualities, but also the disdain for the president and his party that had become prevalent among voters under thirty well before Obama's arrival on the scene. Disaffection with Bush was a major force behind the widespread enthusiasm for the Obama candidacy among other ordinary Democrats as well, stoking his campaign's record-setting fundraising—at $745 million, twice as much as that for any previous candidate.[49] The continuing value of incumbency in the congressional contests points to the price Republicans paid for the imbalance of open House and Senate seats left by their incumbents' retirement decisions. Beyond these indirect effects, opinions of Bush's performance and the Iraq War continued to have very large direct effects on the presidential vote and substantial effects on individual House and Senate vote choices as well, which, with approval of both at a low ebb, only added to the Democrats' vote totals. Barack Obama's historic victory and solid Democratic majorities in the House and Senate were the most conspicuous political legacies of George W. Bush. The longer-term implications of his presidency for the shape of American public opinion and politics more generally are the subject of the next, and final, chapter.

---

[49] "Obama Amassed $745M for Campaign," CBS News, December 5, 2008, at http://www.cbsnews.com/stories/2008/12/05/politics/main4649880.shtml?source=related_story (accessed September 22, 2009).

CHAPTER **11**

■ ■ ■ ■ ■

Conclusions and Speculations

George W. Bush chose the Texas House of Representatives as the venue for his December 13, 2000, victory address because, he said on the occasion, "it had been home to bipartisan cooperation. The spirit of cooperation we have seen in this hall is what is needed in Washington, D.C."[1] No doubt the president sincerely wanted to be a "uniter, not a divider," as he had been in Texas. The question was, on whose terms? The answer turned out to be, on his terms. Bipartisan cooperation emerged on issues where Democrats' preferences were basically compatible with Bush's preferences: the education bill, the prescription drug benefit, legislative responses to 9/11, the bank rescue bill. When they were not compatible, Bush pursued a conservative Republican agenda that could have won bipartisan support only via the abject capitulation of congressional Democrats.

Between 2003 and 2007, with both chambers of Congress and the federal regulatory apparatus in Republican hands, and with the wartime conditions created by 9/11 to augment presidential power, Bush did not need significant Democratic support to achieve a number of notable changes in public policy that were welcomed by his conservative Republican base. And mobilizing that base rather than reaching out to

---

[1] Quoted in Fred I. Greenstein, "The Leadership Style of George W. Bush," in Fred I. Greenstein, ed., *The George W. Bush Presidency: An Early Assessment* (Baltimore: Johns Hopkins University Press, 2003), 6.

Democrats or the dwindling ranks of the uncommitted was a successful electoral strategy in both 2002 and 2004. In contrast to his experience in Texas, where Democrats had controlled one or both houses of the legislature during his term as governor, Bush as president did not need to be a uniter to achieve many of his main goals, and the goals were obviously more important to him than the unity. Bipartisanship was a means to win legislative battles, not an end in itself, and was dispensable if unneeded or unduly confining. Even after Democrats took control of Congress in 2007, Bush avoided any compromise on his Iraq policies by wielding the veto, sustained by Republican loyalists in Congress. And by then, he was far too unpopular among ordinary Democrats and independents for Democratic leaders to feel any pressure to work with him on domestic matters. Only the national emergency brought on by the looming collapse of the global financial system compelled real bipartisan action, but by then it was far too late to alter the dynamic.

Combined with the historical currents he inherited, his peculiar road to the White House, and the problematic nature of the Iraq War, Bush's style, agenda, and tactics ultimately provoked the most polarized public assessments of any president since the advent of regular polling on the president's job performance. Did it matter to Bush that Americans became so deeply divided along party lines over his presidency? It assuredly beat having a bipartisan consensus on a *negative* view of his performance; the wide partisan gap meant that, unlike some of his predecessors (see Johnson, Nixon, and Carter in Figure 1.3), Bush retained the support of at least his own partisans. Even in his worst month, October 2008, more than half the Republicans approved of his job performance. Did it matter that Democrats grew to condemn it with near unanimity? No doubt it mattered pragmatically, as, for example, when the overwhelming opposition of ordinary Democrats to Social Security reforms labeled as the president's denied congressional Republicans the bipartisan cover they would need to risk touching the "third rail." But there is no reason to believe it otherwise mattered to this president. In his own words, "I really don't care what polls and focus groups say. What I care about is doing what I think is right."[2] Not that he and his political advisors, notably Karl Rove, were other than avid consumers of data from polls and focus groups; administration pollsters conducted extensive

---

[2] Kathryn Dunn Tenpas, "Words vs. Deeds: President George W. Bush and Polling," *The Brookings Review* (Summer 2003): 32.

public opinion research, although, to maintain the fiction that Bush was a leader who disdained polling, largely out of sight of the press or public.[3] But the research was aimed at finding out how best to market policies, not to discover what the public wanted (or at least thought it wanted). Mass opinion was something to be molded and led, not respected or followed.

The Bush administration was of course not at all unique in this regard. Every administration seeks to shape public opinion to further its policy goals; if it does not, it risks abandoning the field to opponents mobilizing the public against them. The "permanent campaign," extending the rhetorical and sometimes organizational tactics used in election campaigns to win public support for a president's proposals, goes back decades.[4] But the Bush administration was unusual in its desire to initiate major policy changes for which there was little popular demand and in its routine reliance on deceptive rhetoric to rally enough public support to get its way in Congress.[5] In his memoir, a penitent Scott McClellan, Bush's press secretary from July 2003 to April 2006, describes the permanent campaign as "a game of endless politicking based on manipulated shades of truth, partial truth, twisting of truth, and spin" and judges that "the Bush White House . . . embraced and institutionalized the permanent campaign even more deeply than its predecessors."[6] The campaign to rally the public behind the Iraq War is only McClellan's most egregious example. The objective was always to win the battle for public (and hence political) support, and if winning required mangling the truth, so be it.

Bush's evident comfort with what McClellan calls a "strategy of deception" was consistent with his conception of himself and his role. For a president who liked to present himself as something of a populist, Bush's conception of leadership was decidedly elitist: He knew what was best for the American people and insisted on pushing for it even if most of them might prefer otherwise. Popular or not, his policies were still the

---

[3] Ibid.; also, Joshua Green, "The Other War Room," *Washington Monthly* (April 2002), at http://www.washingtonmonthly.com/features/2001/0204.green.html (accessed August 12, 2004).

[4] The term was first mentioned in 1976 by Patrick Caddell, Jimmy Carter's pollster, but the phenomenon is even older; see Joe Klein, "The Perils of the Permanent Campaign," *Time*, October 30, 2005, at http://www.time.com/time/columnist/klein/article/0,9565,1124237,00.htm (accessed September 10, 2009).

[5] See, for example, George C. Edwards III, *Governing by Campaigning: The Politics of the Bush Presidency,* 2007 ed. (New York: Pearson Longman, 2008).

[6] Scott McClellan, *What Happened: Inside the Bush White House and Washington's Culture of Deception* (New York: PublicAffairs, 2008), xiii and 65.

right ones, and history would ultimately vindicate him. This was of course his response to criticisms of his handling of Iraq, and, conveniently, Bush pushed the judgment of history far enough into the future to put the claim beyond disproof during his lifetime. As he told journalist Robert Draper in 2007, echoing what he had said to Bob Woodward back in 2003,[7] "You can't possibly figure out the history of the Bush presidency—until I'm dead."[8] He need never, then, be disturbed by any evidence that he might have made the wrong decision.

Bush's policies were often elitist in a more material sense as well, delivering major benefits to wealthy individuals and corporations with scant regard to their effects on less affluent or less well-connected Americans. I do not assume cynicism here; Bush appeared to believe sincerely in the current Republican orthodoxy that ensuring the prosperity of the wealthy while weakening the social safety net is the road to betterment for all. It not only provides more capital for capitalists to invest in productive enterprises (old-fashioned trickle-down economics), but it also compels people to take greater responsibility for assuring their own economic well-being, thereby strengthening their moral character. Help for the needy who remain is best delivered by private, faith-based charities, which, unlike government agencies, can insist on conformity to traditional social norms as a condition of assistance.

That Bush achieved as much as he did on the domestic side is testimony to the skill with which he and his strategists managed to feed and exploit what Larry Bartels has identified as the public's "unenlightened self-interest."[9] For example, the mystery of why popular majorities favored repealing an estate tax that only about 2 percent of families will ever pay becomes less mysterious when we find nearly half the public believing that "most families have to pay" and only one-third knowing that "only a few families have to pay." Among the 57 percent who said they favored repeal, 69 percent said one reason was "It might affect YOU some day."[10] The administration's rhetoric about saving the family farm or small business from the "death tax," regardless of how misleading,

---

[7] "History. . . . We won't know. We'll all be dead." Quoted in Bob Woodward, *Plan of Attack* (New York: Simon and Schuster, 2004), 443.
[8] Robert Draper, *Dead Certain: The Presidency of George W. Bush* (New York: Free Press, 2007), ix.
[9] Larry Bartels, "Homer Gets a Tax Cut: Inequality and Public Policy in the American Mind," *Perspectives on Politics* 3 (March 2005): 21
[10] NPR/Kaiser Family Foundation/ John F. Kennedy School of Government Poll, August 2003, quoted in Bartels, "Homer Gets a Tax Cut."

faced little skepticism among people so grossly misinformed.[11] Widespread public ignorance of basic political facts has long been a staple finding of survey research[12]; the work by Bartels and others also reveals a widespread inability to make connections between policies and desired outcomes. Under such circumstances, careful manipulation of language to frame the debate and to define relevant "facts" can be a potent tactic.

Its potency, however, depends strongly on the existing beliefs and attitudes of the audience and the exclusion of alternative frames and facts. Bush was least successful when trying to shape public opinion on matters about which people had firm prior beliefs or some personal familiarity with the issue at hand. Social Security is a prime example. Hurricane Katrina is another; the administration's upbeat assertions of progress in its immediate aftermath made no headway against the scenes of destruction and desperation Americans could see on their television screens. The public's response to the Schiavo affair also suggests that opinions on deeply personal, directly experienced, or readily imaginable matters remain resistant to political manipulation. The Bush administration was most successful when it was able to define reality in ways consistent with people's prior beliefs in domains where a rationally ignorant public normally defers to supposedly better-informed opinion leaders, as in the lead-up to the Iraq invasion. Most of the time, however, Bush succeeded spectacularly in persuading Republicans, especially the party's conservative Christian faction, to accept his vision and leadership but failed to sway more than a small proportion of Democrats and a somewhat larger minority of independents to see reality his way.

COMPETING REALITIES

I use the term *reality* here advisedly; one of the intriguing features of the Bush administration was its implicit premise that, for all practical political purposes, perceptions *are* reality, and that reality could therefore be shaped to its convenience. There is a certain irony in discovering that a

---

[11] The American Farm Bureau Federation, lobbying for the estate tax repeal, could not cite a single instance of a family farm lost because of the estate tax; see David Clay Johnston, "Talk of Lost Farms Reflects Muddle of Estate Tax Debate," *New York Times,* April 8, 2001.

[12] Cf. Philip E. Converse, "The Nature of Belief Systems in Mass Publics," in David E. Apter, ed., *Ideology and Discontent* (Glencoe, IL: Free Press, 1964); Michael X. Delli Carpini and Scott Keeter, *What Americans Know About Politics and Why It Matters* (New Haven, CT: Yale University Press, 1996).

president and administration that professed firm belief in divinely ordained absolutes were, operationally, postmodern social constructionists. And not only of perceptions; *New York Times* reporter David Suskind reported the following dialogue with a "senior advisor to Bush" (commonly assumed to be Karl Rove) in 2004:

> *The aide said that guys like me were "in what we call the reality-based community," which he defined as people who "believe solutions emerge from judicious study of discernable reality." I nodded and murmured something about enlightenment principles and empiricism. He cut me off. "That's not the way the world really works anymore," he continued. "We're an empire now, and when we act, we create our own reality. And while you're studying reality—judiciously, as you will—we'll act again, creating other new realities, which you can study too, and that's how things will sort out. We're history's actors . . . and you, all of you, will be left to just study what we do."*[13]

The Bush administration's policies certainly created their own reality in Iraq, but obviously not the one intended: An imagined terrorist hotbed with links to al Qaeda was turned into a real one. The task of realizing a democratic, stable, peaceful Middle Eastern nation that respects the human rights of its citizens proved far more difficult than the war's advocates anticipated. Rival realities arising from Iraqi history, religion, and culture kept getting in the way. The "reality-based community" reasserted itself, and its "judicious study of discernable reality" in Iraq led to widespread criticism of the decision to go to war and a loss of trust in George W. Bush's leadership in that community and among citizens who shared its perspectives. Bush's support remained firm, however, among those whose notions of reality derived from a priori beliefs that were simply not open to empirical refutation. Certainly, there were "reality-based" defenders of the president and his invasion of Iraq, but it is hard to imagine that Bush would have retained as much support as he did, especially among Republicans, without the tenacious loyalty of religious conservatives for whom faith in the president was largely impervious to changing events or new information.

In addition to Iraq, implacable natural and economic realities (Hurricane Katrina, the financial crisis) also proved impervious to rhetoric or

---

[13] Ron Suskind, "Without a Doubt," *New York Times*, October 17, 2004, section 6, 44.

FIGURE 11.1

Presidential Approval in the Final Gallup Poll of the Administration,
Truman to G. W. Bush

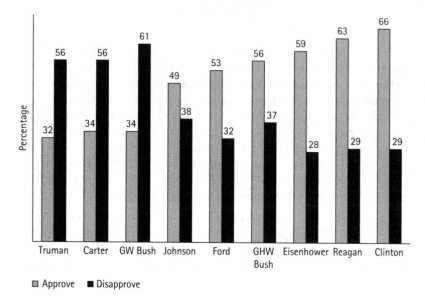

Source: Gallup polls.

spin and, ultimately, corrosive to Bush's standing with the American public. Bush finished his presidency with the second-lowest approval rating and the highest disapproval rating of any full-term president since the advent of modern polling (Figure 11.1).[14] Ironically, the highest end-term rating belongs to Bill Clinton, defiler, in Bush's 2000 campaign speeches, of the "honor and dignity" of the presidency. Asked by Gallup in January 2009 how the seven presidents from Nixon onward would be regarded by history, respondents rated Bush lowest. Even among Republicans, only 38 percent believed he would go down in history as "outstanding" or "above average," with 24 percent saying "below average" or "poor." The respective figures for Democrats were 3 percent and

---

[14] Only Richard Nixon, resigning under threat of impeachment because of Watergate, left under an appreciably darker cloud, with 22 percent approval and 66 percent disapproval.

84 percent; for independents, 13 percent and 63 percent.[15] Responses to a similar question posed by a Pew survey at the end of each of the last four presidencies also found Bush at the bottom by a wide margin. Nearly two-thirds thought that in the long run, his failures would outweigh his accomplishments.[16] Only 18 percent said that they would miss him when he left office.[17]

Considering the state of the country when Bush left office, the public's evaluation is not surprising. Americans celebrate presidents who bring peace and prosperity; Bush left office with two wars ongoing and the economy heading into the worst recession since the Great Depression. Although Bush's advisors and loyalists used the interregnum between the election and Obama's inauguration for a concerted campaign to remind Americans of the good things Bush had accomplished—the program to fight HIV/AIDS in Africa, the prescription drug program for seniors, avoiding any further terrorist attacks on United States soil—its effect on evaluations of his presidency, if any, was confined to Republicans (see Figure 1.2). It was also a curious exercise on behalf of a president who claimed to care not a whit about public approval, only about doing what he thought was right, and who expected historical vindication only after he and his current critics were dead.

THE POLITICAL LEGACY

In the short run at least, Bush's political legacy was the precise opposite of what he intended, for he neither united the country nor built a durable Republican majority. The trend toward increasing polarization among politicians and citizens alike that preceded his election (see the figures in

---

[15] Bush's net rating—the percentage "outstanding" or "average" minus the percentage "below average" or "poor"—was −42, even worse than Nixon's −33; Reagan was at the top (+55), with Clinton second (+30); see Lydia Saad, "Americans Expect History to Judge Bush Worse Than Nixon," Gallup report, January 16, 2009, at http://www.gallup.com/poll/113806/Americans-Expect-History-Judge-Bush-Worse-Than-Nixon.aspx (accessed September 12, 2009).

[16] Bush's net historical rating in the Pew poll was −47, compared with +45 for Reagan, +24 for the elder Bush, and +23 for Clinton; belief that G. W. Bush's failures would outweigh his accomplishments was at 33 percent among Republicans, 68 percent among independents, and 83 percent among Democrats. See "Reviewing the Bush Years and the Public's Final Version," press release, Pew Research Center for the People and the Press, December 18, 2008.

[17] Republicans were split 49 percent to 48 percent on this question; independents, 15 percent to 81 percent; and Democrats, 5 percent to 94 percent; NBC News/Wall Street Journal Poll, December 4–8, 2008, available through the Roper Center.

Chapter 2) continued unabated during his presidency. Partisan divisions widened on a variety of issues, not just on his job performance and the Iraq War. Some have been documented in this book. Others include attitudes toward gay rights, abortion, stem cell research, immigrants, torture of suspected terrorists, and global warming.[18] That final item represents an interesting case. Both manifestations of climate change and the scientific consensus that human activities are heating up the planet increased during the Bush years. Although Bush himself did not deny the reality of global warming, his administration did nothing to address the problem and censored or watered down reports from government scientists that treated it as a serious threat.[19] Meanwhile, Al Gore won an Academy Award and the Nobel Prize for a movie and campaign highlighting the danger, while the Republican senator chairing the Environment and Public Works Committee declared it "the greatest hoax ever perpetrated on the American people."[20] Figure 11.2 displays the public's response: Belief in and worry about global warming increased among Democrats but decreased among Republicans. Similarly, between 2003 and 2008, belief that human activity was its main cause declined from 52 percent to 42 percent among Republicans while rising from 68 percent to 73 percent among Democrats.[21] Americans thus grew ever further from consensus on the need to address what the vast majority of qualified climate scientists viewed as a real and potentially calamitous alteration of the earth's atmosphere.

Bush also failed to achieve his other political objective, a durable Republican majority. Well before Bush became president, his political guru, Karl Rove, had envisioned establishing a generation of Republican ascendancy of the sort that followed William McKinley's election in

---

[18] Lydia Saad, "Republicans Move to the Right on Several Moral Issues," Gallup report, May 20, 2009, at http://www.gallup.com/poll/118546/Republicans-Veer-Right-Several-Moral-Issues.aspx (accessed September 11, 2009); Carroll Doherty, "The Immigration Divide: Reform Is a Potential Wedge Issue for Both Republicans and Democrats," Pew Research Center for the People and the Press, April 12, 2007, at http://pewresearch.org/pubs/450/immigration-wedge-issue (accessed September 11, 2009); CBS News/*New York Times* Poll, April 22–26, 2009; "A Deeper Partisan Divide over Global Warming," press release, Pew Research Center for the People and the Press, May 8, 2008.

[19] Tim Dickinson, "The Secret Campaign of President Bush's Administration to Deny Global Warming," *Rolling Stone*, June 28, 2007, at http://www.rollingstone.com/politics/story/15148655/the_secret_campaign_of_president_bushs_administration_to_deny_global_warming (accessed September 11, 2009).

[20] Michael Barone and Richard E. Cohen, *The Almanac of American Politics 2008* (Washington, DC: National Journal, 2007), 1330.

[21] Riley E. Dunlap, "Climate-Change Views: Republican-Democratic Gaps Expand," Gallup report, May 29, 2008, at http://www.gallup.com/poll/107569/ClimateChange-Views-RepublicanDemocratic-Gaps-Expand.aspx (accessed September 11, 2009).

FIGURE 11.2
Opinions on Global Warming

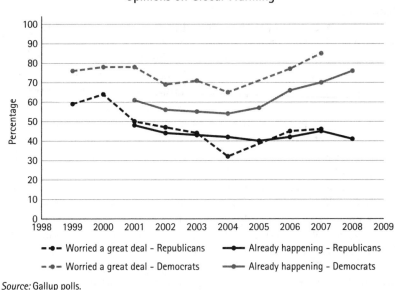

Source: Gallup polls.

1896. Bush evidently shared the vision and worked harder at party building than had any other modern president.[22] The "compassionate conservatism" of Bush's initial campaign for the White House aimed to expand the party's appeal to moderates, as did his promise to be a uniter. After 9/11, however, Rove and Bush made it clear that unity was dispensable, that only winning mattered, when they moved to exploit the terrorism issue for electoral advantage (see Chapter 4). In the 2002 and 2004 election campaigns, they sought to build majorities by mobilizing the party's conservative base and picking up swing voters who could be persuaded that the Democrats could not be trusted to keep them safe. Victory would then be followed by popular policy achievements that would solidify Republican majorities for the long run. As Rove told Fox News shortly after the 2004 election, "The victory in 1896 was similarly narrow,

---

[22] Sidney M. Milkis and Jesse H. Rhodes, "George W. Bush, the Republican Party, and the 'New American Party System,'" *Perspectives on Politics* 5 (September 2007): 467–471.

and . . . it was an election that realigned American politics years afterwards. And I think the same thing will be here. It depends on how Republicans act in office."[23]

It did indeed depend on how Republicans—most notably the president—acted in office, but popular reaction to the Iraq War, Hurricane Katrina, and the economic meltdown put the dream of a durable Republican majority on indefinite hold (see Chapter 10). The party's problems were not all the president's fault, to be sure. Important segments of his own coalition resisted his efforts to broaden the party's appeal through initiatives on education and health. Bush's considerable work to attract Latinos, the fastest-growing segment of the electorate, was undone when a majority of congressional Republicans rejected his immigration reforms, finding it more expedient to exploit public hostility to illegal immigrants for near-term electoral advantage. Bush met the financial crisis with a hugely expensive and interventionist bank rescue package that arguably prevented a much worse catastrophe, but it was nonetheless broadly unpopular and especially objectionable to Republican small-government conservatives (see Chapter 9). Nonetheless, the Iraq War, for which Bush bore undiluted responsibility, did the most to kill any prospect that his presidency would launch an era of Republican hegemony.

As the Republican Party shrank during Bush's second term, it became more conservative both in Congress and in the electorate. Republican House incumbents who retired or lost in 2006 and 2008 were significantly more moderate than those who remained, shifting the congressional party's ideological center of gravity further rightward.[24] The share of the Republican delegation composed of white southerners grew steadily, from 37 percent after the 2000 election to 45 percent after the 2008 election; meanwhile, the share from the Northeast and mid-Atlantic fell from 18 percent to 10 percent. After 2008, Democrats held every House seat in New England, once the Republicans' strongest region. Democrats, meanwhile, edged toward the center. Most of their House pickups from 2006 through 2008 occurred in Republican-leaning districts (thirty-four of fifty-five were in districts where Bush had

---

[23]"Transcript: Karl Rove on 'Fox News Sunday' for November 7, 2004," at http://www.foxnews.com/story/0,2933,137853,00.html (accessed September 14, 2009).
[24]Based on analysis of their Poole-Rosenthal DW- Nominate scores.

won more than 53 percent of the vote in 2004), and the newly elected members were on average significantly more conservative than the Democratic holdovers. The diminished Republican electoral base also became more uniformly conservative. Although Bush's ratings among Republicans generally fell during his second term, the drop was much smaller among the party's conservatives, and he remained popular with a large majority of them to the end. According to Gallup data, between January 2005 and December 2008, his ratings dropped by 40 points (from 84 percent to 44 percent) among moderate or liberal Republicans but by only 20 points (from 92 percent to 72 percent) among conservatives.[25] Not coincidentally, the erosion of Republican identification was also less severe among conservatives, leaving that faction increasingly dominant. The party's most conservative religious factions, traditionalist evangelical Protestants and Mormons, remained about as Republican in 2008 as they as they had been in 2004, while most other groups shifted toward the Democratic Party (Figure 11.3). A Gallup study based on January–May 2009 surveys found 69 percent of Republicans (including leaners) calling themselves conservatives; 26 percent, moderates; and only 4 percent, liberals. Democratic identifiers were considerably more heterogeneous: 36 percent liberals, 43 percent moderates, and 21 percent conservatives.[26]

Viewing the data from the perspective of ideological categories, Republicans had an advantage among conservatives, 67 percent to 27 percent, but Democrats had almost as wide a lead among moderates (60 percent to 28 percent) and were favored overwhelmingly by liberals (86 percent to 7 percent). To a considerable extent, then, at the end of Bush's presidency, the Democratic Party formed an evenly balanced center-left coalition, while the Republican Party was dominated by its

---

[25] Jeffrey Jones, "Liberal, Moderate Republicans Show Large Drop in Support for Bush," Gallup report, May 26, 2006, at http://www.gallup.com/poll/22954/liberal-moderate-republicans-show-large-drop-support-bush.aspx (accessed September 15, 2009); Jeffrey Jones, "Conservative Republicans Still Widely Support Bush," Gallup report, December 11, 2008, at http://www.gallup.com/poll/113083/conservative-republicans-still-widely-support-bush.aspx (accessed September 15, 2009).

[26] Lydia Saad, "'Conservatives' Are the Single-Largest Ideological Group," Gallup report, June 15, 2009, at http://www.gallup.com/poll/120857/Conservatives-Single-Largest-Ideological-Group.aspx (accessed September 15, 2009); excluding leaners, 73 percent of Republicans labeled themselves conservatives, 24 percent moderates, and 3 percent liberals; among Democrats, the figures were 38 percent liberals, 40 percent moderates, and 22 percent conservatives.

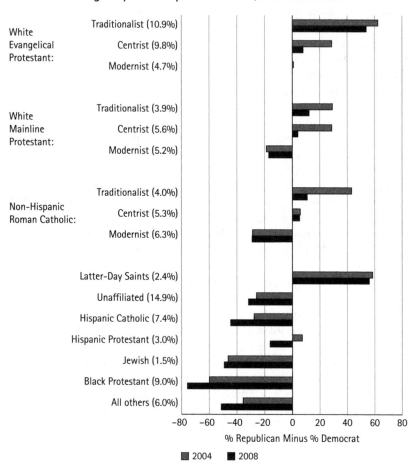

FIGURE 11.3
Religiosity and Party Identification, 2004 and 2008

Note: The percentage in the category in 2008 is in parentheses.
Source: National Survey of Religion and Politics, 2004 and 2008, courtesy of John C. Green.

conservative faction. Figure 11.4, which displays the percentage of Americans in each of the partisan and ideological categories, illustrates the configuration in place when Barack Obama entered the White House.

FIGURE 11.4
Partisanship and Ideology, 2009 (Percentages)

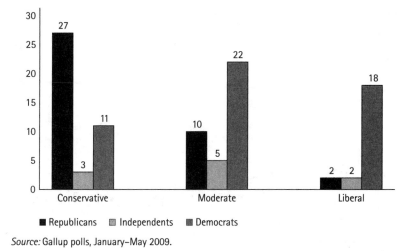

■ Republicans ▨ Independents ■ Democrats

Source: Gallup polls, January–May 2009.

OBAMA'S INHERITANCE

On January 20, 2009, the troubles that had done so much to undermine George W. Bush's standing with the public became Barack Obama's responsibility. Obama inherited two wars, bin Laden still on the loose, a deep recession, a swelling budget deficit, and a backlog of difficult issues—health care, climate change, renewable energy, financial regulation, immigration, and entitlements—crowding the national agenda. He also inherited leadership of a nation beset by wide partisan divisions that his campaign and victory had done little to bridge. With party line voting near record highs (see Chapter 10), Obama's electoral coalition contained the smallest proportion of opposite-party identifiers of any president elected since the advent of the ANES surveys in 1952, only 4.4 percent.[27] By his inauguration in January 2009, the honeymoon was over; partisans were nearly as divided about his job performance during his first quarter

---

[27] If leaners were treated as partisans, the figure was 8.0 percent, second to that for John Kennedy in 1960 (7.1 percent).

FIGURE 11.5
Approval of Barack Obama's Performance

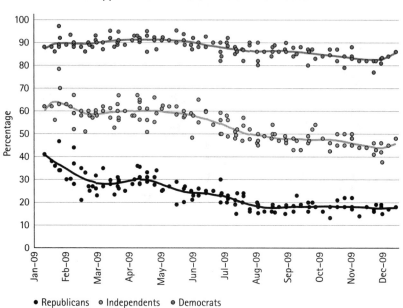

• Republicans   • Independents   • Democrats

Source: ABC News/*Washington Post*, CBS News/*New York Times*, CNN, Gallup, IPSOS, NBC News/
Wall Street Journal, *Newsweek*, and Pew Research Center for the People and the Press polls.

in office as they had been about Bush's performance during the comparable period in 2001 (see Figure 3.4), and the party divide widened
steadily through the first year of Obama's presidency (Figure 11.5).[28]
Although the vote count was not disputed, some of the loonier denizens
of the far right challenged Obama's legitimacy by claiming he was not
born a citizen. Displays of Obama's Hawaiian birth certificate and a local
newspaper's timely birth announcement notwithstanding, a remarkable
proportion of ordinary Republicans also doubted he was a true American.
In two surveys taken in the summer of 2009, less than half of the Republican respondents said they thought that Obama was born in America

---

[28] The gap displayed in Figure 3.4 for Bush was 57 points (Republicans 89 percent, Democrats 32 percent);
for Obama it was 55 points (Democrats 90 percent, Republicans 35 percent).

(36 percent in the first, 42 percent in the second); the rest said he was not (42 percent and 28 percent) or they were unsure (20 percent and 30 percent).[29]

Although most Republican leaders distanced themselves from the "birthers," as the disbelievers were called, their sentiments pointed up the dilemmas facing the party. Heightened economic anxiety, the massive spending programs adopted to keep the economy afloat by propping up the very institutions that had produced the financial crisis, and the social changes signaled by the election of an African American president had sparked fear and anger among many conservative whites. Railing against Obama as a "socialist," "communist," "facist," and "racist,"[30] conservative cable news and radio talk-show demagogues found a ready audience among the disaffected. Rallies and demonstrations in the summer of 2009 targeting Obama's health care initiative expanded to include other hot button issues such as guns and abortion. The display of anger and energy coming from the heart of their party's diminished base could hardly be ignored, and it killed any incentive for congressional Republicans to work with the Obama administration on reforming the health care system. Postelection discussions about how to reverse the party's decline by widening its appeal beyond its core of older conservative whites became moot, at least for the time being. Republican leaders instead took the cue from the party's populist right (sometimes gingerly, to avoid association with its more unhinged elements), adopting a strategy of reflexive opposition to Obama's domestic agenda in hopes of replicating their 1994 victories in 2010.

Partisan polarization thus returned with a vengeance. It was exemplified when an obscure South Carolina congressman, Joe Wilson, violated congressional rules and common courtesy by shouting, "You lie!" when Obama, in a September address to Congress making a pitch for his health care overhaul, said federal funds would not subsidize insurance for illegal immigrants. Although he apologized to the president, Wilson

---

[29] The first figure in each pair is from the Research 2000/Daily Kos survey taken July 27–30, 2009, reported at http://www.dailykos.com/storyonly/2009/7/31/760087/-Birthers-are-mostly-Republican-and-Southern (accessed September 11, 2009); the second is from Public Policy Polling, survey of August 14–17, 2009, reported at http://www.publicpolicypolling.com/pdf/surveys/2009_Archives/PPP_Release_National_9231210.pdf (accessed March 25, 2010).

[30] For example, Fox News commentator Glenn Beck's notorious allegation that Obama held "a deep-seated hatred for white people," *Fox & Friends*, July 28, 2009, displayed at http://mediamatters.org/mmtv/200907280008 (accessed September 17, 2009).

refused to apologize to the House and was voted a formal reprimand on a near party line vote. The incident made him a hero among conservative Republicans and a villain to Obama supporters, who smelled racism behind Wilson's outburst. Within a week, he and his Democratic opponent had both picked up more than $1.5 million for their 2010 campaigns.[31] One reason polarizing behavior is unlikely to fade any time soon is that, as the talk-radio ranters have long known, it so often pays.

Like Bush, Obama aspired to "change the tone" and to work across party lines in pursuing an ambitious national agenda. By the evidence of the vote on his economic stimulus package—opposed by every House Republican and all but three Republican Senators—and the unanimous opposition of Republicans to his health care package, he made no progress during his year in office. Public opinion on the proposals also divided in the familiar way along party lines; ordinary Democrats and Republicans were more than 40 points apart in their evaluations of the stimulus package.[32] And although partisan disagreements were relatively small on many individual elements of Obama's health care proposals, a CNN survey taken shortly after Wilson's outburst found 80 percent of Democrats but only 13 percent of Republicans favoring "Barack Obama's plan to reform health care."[33]

Ironically, it was Obama's policies for the Iraq and Afghan wars that attracted the most bipartisan support. Of the two wars he inherited from Bush, the Iraq War had been showing unmistakable signs of progress, while the situation in Afghanistan had been deteriorating rapidly. Obama's plan for Afghanistan involved sending an additional 17,000 troops to add to the 36,000 American and 32,000 allied NATO forces already there, with more to be added later.[34] His plan for Iraq was to withdraw most American troops by the summer of 2010, leaving 35,000 to 50,000 to train Iraqi security forces, protect United States personnel,

---

[31] Richard Simon, "House Votes to Chastise Rep. Wilson over Outburst," *Los Angeles Times,* September 16, 2009, at http://www.latimes.com/news/nationworld/nation/healthcare/la-na-wilson16-2009sep 16,0,7678149.story (accessed September 17, 2009).

[32] In the Pew survey taken February 3–8, 2009, 70 percent of Democrats but only 24 percent of Republicans thought the bill was a good idea; in the February 7–8 CNN survey, 75 percent of Democrats but only 32 percent of Republicans said they supported the bill (from my analysis of the surveys provided by the Roper Center).

[33] CNN Poll, September 11–13, 2009, reported at http://www.pollingreport.com/health.htm (accessed September 17, 2009).

[34] Ross Colvin, "Obama Sets Qaeda Defeat as Top Goal in Afghanistan," *Reuters,* March 27, 2009, at http://www.reuters.com/article/topNews/idUSTRE52P7CO20090327 (accessed June 12, 2009).

FIGURE 11.6

Support for Bush's Iraq Surge (2007) and Obama's Iraq Withdrawal and Afghan Buildup Plans (2009)

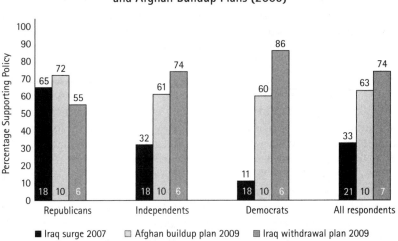

■ Iraq surge 2007   □ Afghan buildup plan 2009   ■ Iraq withdrawal plan 2009

Note: Number of polls averaged is shown at the bottom of each column.

Source: NBC News/*Wall Street Journal*, *Newsweek*, Pew, CNN, Gallup, ABC News/*Washington Post*, CBS News/*New York Times*, *Los Angeles Times*, Fox News, Marist, Democracy Corps, and Quinnipiac polls.

and hunt down terrorists. Those units would exit by December 2011 in accordance with the Status of Forces agreement.[35]

Majorities in both parties supported both moves. Republicans had no reflexive reason to object to the drawdown in Iraq because it followed the path laid out in the agreement signed by Bush with the Iraqi government in December 2008 and fit their assessment of the surge as a great success. Democrats and independents were happy to see a trajectory that would finally extract the United States from a misconceived venture, though many of them would have preferred an accelerated timetable. The contrast with the situation in early 2007, when Bush ordered the Iraq surge, is striking (Figure 11.6). Although Republicans were less enthusiastic than Democrats about the Iraq drawdown, a majority still supported it,[36]

[35] Peter Baker, "With Pledges to Troops and Iraqis, Obama Details Pullout," *Washington Post*, February 27, 2009, at http://www.nytimes.com/2009/02/28/washington/28troops.html (accessed June 12, 2009).
[36] This was true in all six polls from which the averages in Figure 22 were calculated; the data in the figure are from the NBC News/*Wall Street Journal*, *Newsweek*, Pew, CNN, Gallup, ABC News/*Washington Post*, CBS News/*New York Times*, *Los Angeles Times*, Fox News, Marist, Democracy Corps, and Quinnipiac polls.

whereas only 11 percent of Democrats had backed the surge. The buildup in Afghanistan fulfilled Obama's campaign promise but was even more popular among Republicans than among Democrats (or independents).

The challenge for Obama will come if either of these moves fails to achieve its purpose. Nearly two-thirds in a June 2009 CNN poll said the United States should not send the troops back in even if violence increases significantly.[37] If Iraq slides back toward civil war and terrorist violence, Obama will have to choose between reengaging American forces and thus angering his Democratic base, and holding to the timetable for withdrawal and risking Republican blame for "losing" Iraq.[38] And patience with his escalation in Afghanistan is not unlimited, especially within his own party; some House Democrats were already refusing to vote for funds for the increasingly unpopular war until he produced an exit strategy.[39]

Opinions of George W. Bush did not soften during the first year of Obama's presidency, perhaps because Bush was still accorded primary blame for the dismal economy as well as the wars. Responding to a retrospective question on his job performance asked in late April 2009, only 23 percent approved.[40] His favorability ratings rose a few points among Republicans after he was gone from the scene, but he remained as polarizing as ever; in a May 2009 survey, for example, 85 percent of Republicans rated him favorably, and 86 percent of Democrats rated him unfavorably.[41] Despite Bush's belief that history can judge his presidency only after he and his contemporary critics are dead, at least one verdict is already in the books: George W. Bush will go down as a consummate divider, not a uniter, of the American people.

---

[37] Democrats were against sending troops back, 74 percent to 25 percent; independents broke 64 percent to 34 percent against; Republicans were almost evenly divided, with 51 percent favoring going back in and 48 percent opposing it. Data are from the CNN Poll taken June 26–28, 2009, available through the Roper Center.

[38] Dick Cheney was busy laying the groundwork for just such an eventuality: "One might speculate that insurgents are waiting as soon as they get an opportunity to launch more attacks. I hope the Iraqis can deal with it. At some point they have to stand on their own, but I would not want to see the United States waste all the tremendous sacrifice that has gotten us to this point." Quoted from a radio interview, June 30, 2009, at http://blogs.abcnews.com/theworldnewser/2009/06/dick-cheney-worried-by-americas-pull-back-in-iraq.html (accessed July 8, 2009).

[39] Josh Rogin, "Disputes in House Delay War Funds," *CQ Weekly*, June 8, 2009, 1318–1319.

[40] "The Threat of Terrorism and the Treatment of Detainees," CBS News/*New York Times* Poll report, April 22–26, 2009, at http://www.cbsnews.com/htdocs/pdf/poll_042709_waterboarding.pdf (accessed July 7, 2009); 60 percent of Republicans, 20 percent of independents, and 6 percent of Democrats said they approved.

[41] CNN Poll, May 14–17, 2009, available through the Roper Center. See also the tables at http://www.pollingreport.com/BushFav.htm (accessed September 21, 2009).

Data Sources and Question Wordings

The survey data reported in this book were culled from a wide variety of sources; many of them are cited where appropriate, but some figures are based on data from so many sources that it was infeasible to list them all. Except for certain questions regarding the Iraq War, I used only surveys that sampled the adult population rather than registered or likely voters. My initial source for data on the distribution of responses for entire samples was PollingReport.com, an indispensable archive, updated daily, of survey results from all of the major commercial polling organizations. PollingReport.com reports findings from, among others, the ABC News/*Washington Post*, CBS/*New York Times*, Gallup (sometimes reported as Gallup/CNN/*USA Today*), NBC News/*Wall Street Journal*, Pew Research Center for the People and the Press, *Newsweek, Los Angeles Times, Time,* CNN/*Time*, Associated Press/IPSOS, Harris, Fox News, Democracy Corps, Quinnipiac College, *Investor's Business Daily,* and Zogby polls. Data from all of these polls were represented in one or more of the figures displayed in this book.

PollingReport.com does not routinely report results broken down by party identification, although it occasionally supplies these figures. For such information, I relied regularly on the CBS News/*New York Times* poll reports that are linked to the news stories of their polls (click on the "learn more" icon), ABC News/*Washington Post*'s Poll Vault, the Pew Research Center for the People and the Press news releases, and more irregularly on other surveys reported in news stories or made available online by the poll's sponsoring organization. I also subscribed to a Gallup service that provides demographic breakdowns on the presidential approval question (these are now available at the Gallup website). Some of the partisan breakdowns (and other findings) came from my own secondary analyses of surveys from CBS/*New York Times,* ABC News/*Washington Post,* the Pew Research Center for the People and the Press, Gallup, NBC News/*Wall Street Journal,* CNN, *Time, Los Angeles Times,* and *Newsweek.* The first two are archived at the Interuniversity Consortium for Political and Social Research (ICPSR); the third can be downloaded from the Pew Center's website. All of them are available to members from the Roper Center, University of Connecticut. I also analyzed data from the American National Election Studies and the Cooperative Congressional Election Surveys for 2006, 2007, and 2008 and got additional figures from the National Annenberg Election Survey, the PIPA/Knowledge Networks Poll, the 2000 and 2004 exit polls, and other published sources cited in the text.

THE IRAQ WAR QUESTIONS

It is infeasible to present the actual wording of every question asked in the thousands of surveys I used to create the figures, but I have included such information when I thought it necessary. The widest assortment of questions sought to tap support for the Iraq War, and I list them here. For analyses reported in Figure 6.3, I combined responses of closely related questions into a smaller number of categories. Here is the full range of questions (sources in parentheses):

I. Before the War

Do you approve or disapprove of the United States taking military
    action against Iraq to try to remove Saddam Hussein from power?
    (CBS News/*New York Times*)
Do you support or oppose U.S. military action to remove Iraqi President
    Saddam Hussein? (Fox News)
Would you favor or oppose having U.S. forces take military action
    against Iraq to force Saddam Hussein from power?
    (ABC News/*Washington Post*)
Would you favor or oppose invading Iraq with U.S. ground troops in an
    attempt to remove Saddam Hussein from power? (Gallup)

Would you favor or oppose taking military action in Iraq to end Saddam
Hussein's rule? (Pew Research Center for the People and the Press)

Would you favor or oppose sending American troops back to the Persian
Gulf in order to remove Saddam Hussein from power in Iraq? (Gallup)

Do you think that the United States should or should not take military
action to remove Saddam Hussein from power in Iraq?
(ABC News/*Washington Post*)

Do you think that the United States should or should not take military
action against Iraq and Saddam Hussein? (NBC News/*Wall
Street Journal*)

Do you think the United States should take military action in order to
remove Saddam Hussein from power in Iraq, or not?
(*Los Angeles Times*)

Do you think removing Saddam Hussein from power is worth the
potential loss of American life and the other costs of attacking Iraq,
or not? (CBS News/*New York Times*)

Would you support or oppose the United States going to war with Iraq?
(ABC News/*Washington Post*)

Would you support or oppose a U.S. invasion of Iraq with ground
troops? (ABC News/*Washington Post*)

Would you support using military force against Iraq, or not? (*Newsweek*)

Currently, would you strongly support, somewhat support, somewhat
oppose, or strongly oppose a war against Iraq? (Zogby)

Do you favor or oppose taking U.S. military action against Iraq?
(*Chicago Tribune*)

II. After the War Began

Do you support or oppose the Bush administration's decision to take
military action against Iraq at this time? (*Los Angeles Times*)

Do you support or oppose the United States having gone to war with
Iraq? (ABC News/*Washington Post*)

Do you approve or disapprove of the United States' decision to go to
war with Iraq in March 2003? (CNN/Gallup)

Looking back, do you think the United States did the right thing in taking military action against Iraq, or should the U.S. have stayed out?
(CBS News/*New York Times*)

Considering everything, do you think the United States did the right
thing in going to war with Iraq or do you think it was a mistake?
(ABC News/*Washington Post*)

Do you think the U.S. made the right decision or the wrong decision in using military force against Iraq? (Pew Research Center for the People and the Press)

Do you think going to war with Iraq was the right thing for the United States to do or the wrong thing? (Fox News, Quinnipiac College)

From what you know now, do you think the United States did the right thing in taking military action against Iraq last year, or not? (*Newsweek*)

Do you think the United States was right or wrong in going to war with Iraq? (*Time*)

Do you think the U.S. made the right decision or the wrong decision in going to war against Iraq? (PIPA/Knowledge Networks)

All in all, considering the costs to the United States versus the benefits to the United States, do you think the war in Iraq was worth fighting or not? (ABC News/*Washington Post*)

All in all, do you think it was worth going to war in Iraq, or not? (Gallup)

All in all, do you think the situation in Iraq was worth going to war over, or not? (National Annenberg Election Survey, *Los Angeles Times*)

All things considered, do you think the United States going to war with Iraq has been worth it or not? (Fox News)

Generally speaking, do you think the outcome of the war in Iraq has been worth the cost in U.S. military lives, or not? (*Los Angeles Times*)

Do you think the result of the war was worth the loss of American life and other costs of attacking Iraq, or not? (CBS News/*New York Times*)

In your view, is the war against Iraq worth the toll it has taken in American lives and other kinds of costs, or isn't the war worth these costs? (*Time*)

When it comes to the war in Iraq, do you think that removing Saddam Hussein from power was or was not worth the number of U.S. military casualties and the financial cost of the war? (NBC News/*Wall Street Journal*)

Do you think removing Saddam Hussein from power was worth the loss of American life and other costs of attacking Iraq, or not? (CBS News/*New York Times*)

Generally speaking, do you think the outcome of the war in Iraq has been worth the financial cost to the U.S., or not? (*Los Angeles Times*)

In view of the developments since we first sent our troops to Iraq, do you think the United States made a mistake in sending troops to Iraq, or not? (Gallup)

Generally speaking, do you support or oppose the U.S. military action
in Iraq? (*Investor's Business Daily*)

Do you favor or oppose the U.S. war with Iraq? (Gallup, CNN)

Do you support or oppose the United States taking military action
to disarm Iraq and remove Iraqi President Saddam Hussein?
(Fox News)

Do you think that the United States should or should not have taken
military action to remove Saddam Hussein from power in Iraq?
(NBC News/*Wall Street Journal*)

In general, do you approve or disapprove of current military policy in
Iraq? (*Time*)

Do you approve or disapprove of the United States' current occupation
of Iraq? (CBS News/*New York Times*)

Do you support or oppose the current U.S. military presence in Iraq?
(ABC News/*Washington Post*)

Index

Numbers preceded by an n indicate footnote number.

Schiavo, Terri, 164–165
Schickler, E., 237
Schimtt, E., 81
Schoomaker, Peter J., 200
Schweizer, P., 73
Schweizer, R., 73
Sears, D. O., 33
Selective exposure, 219
Senate Armed Service Committee, 95
Senate Intelligence Committee, 95
Shani, D., 216
Shanks, J. M., 3, 34
Shapiro, R. Y., 26
Shaw, D. R., 72
Shea, D. M., 19
Simon, R., 282
Smidt, C. E., 34
Smith, C. E., 243
Smith, S. S., 17
Snow, Tony, 200
Snyder, J. M. Jr., 17
Social Security
    approval by George W. Bush, 159
    bipartisan public consensus on, 162
    Bush's national campaign and, 157
    contributions in stock market, 161
    public backing for privatizing, 160–161
    taxes, 158
        on wages, 162
Southern Republicanism rise, 21–22
"Southern strategy," 29
Spiegel, P., 200
Stanley, H. W., 21
Stem-cell research, 72, 274
Stevenson, R. W., 162
Stewart, Jon, 250
Stimson, J. A., 228, 237
Stolberg, S. G., 193
Stonecash, J. M., 21
Straw man tactic, 190
Sunni tribal leaders, brutality and
        fanaticism, 210
Suskind, R., 271
Sussman, D., 126
"Swift Boat Veterans for Truth", 147

T

Taber, C. S., 215
Taliban government, 66
Tau-b statistic, 25n
Taylor, A., 48
Television news sources
    and opinions, 220
    party, ideology and choice, 221
Tenet, George, 82
Tenpas, K. D., 267

Terri Schiavo case, 164–165
Terrorist attacks of 9/11/01
    before
        Bush administration, 75
        religious conservatives, 72
    after
        Afghanistan war support, 66
        airline relief bill, 63
        invading Iraq, 78
        joint resolution, 63
        political fallout, 69
        revival of partisan acrimony, 71
        tectonic shift in national politics, 73
    evidence
        of Iraqi involvement in, 96
        linking, Iraqi government with, 81
        Saddam Hussein involvement in, 80, 82
Time/CNN Poll, 76n
Time Magazine/SRBI Poll, on mandates, 154
Toft, M. D., 201
Tomz, M., 223
Tort reform, 40, 152
Truman, Harry, 3, 177

U

United States
    and allies, win in Iraq, 93–94
    treasury and Iraq war, 94

V

Valentino, N. A., 33
Vietnam war, 103
    partisan differences in support for, 104
Vigna, S. D., 222
Voters
    ideological divergence in, 25
    new
        approval of Bush's job performance, 247
        Gallup polls, 249
        and Iraq War, 246–248
        party favorability among, 248
        party identification, 245–246
        Pew data, 244–245
        problem with Bush, 246
Voting
    Bush voters and Gore voters, 44
    defection rates, 44
    economic issues, 46
    exit polling, 44
    income category in, 46
    partisan opinions on legitimacy of 2000
        election, 52
    party-line, 44
    presidential vote
        demographic characteristics and,
            45–46
        issue positions, 47